Gandhi, Ambedkar and Indian Dalit

GANDHI, AMBEDKAR AND INDIAN DALIT

Amit Kumar

CENTRUM PRESS
NEW DELHI-110002 (INDIA)

CENTRUM PRESS
H.O.: 4360/4, Ansari Road, Daryaganj,
New Delhi-110002 (India)
Tel: 23278000, 23261597, 23255577, 23286875
B.O.: No. 1015, Ist Main Road, BSK IIIrd Stage,
IIIrd Phase, IIIrd Block, Bangalore-560085 (INDIA)
Tel: 080-41723429
Email: centrumpress@gmail.com
Visit us at: www.centrumpress.com

Gandhi, Ambedkar and Indian Dalit

First Edition, 2011

ISBN 978-93-80921-76-1

PRINTED IN INDIA

Printed at Tarun Offset Printers, Delhi-110053

Contents

Preface

Mohandas Karamchand Gandhi was the pre-eminent political and ideological leader of India during the Indian independence movement. Gandhi insisted that the organisation was to be run primarily by caste Hindus as a means for their self-purification, whereas Ambedkar demanded that the leadership be by the Dalits themselves. Bhimrao Ramji Ambedkar which is also known as Babasaheb, was an Indian Jurist, Political Leader, Buddhist Activist, Philosopher, Thinker, Anthropologist, Historian, Orator, Prolific Writer, Economist, Scholar, Editor, Revolutionary and a Revivalist for Buddhism in India. He was also the chief architect of the Indian Constitution.

To understand, the discrimination towards the Dalit of India, one must be knowledgeable of the caste system in India. A caste can be defined as a social class, made distinct from others by differences in rank, profession, or wealth. The caste system in India has been heavily influenced by the Hindu religion. In Hinduism, everyone is born into a caste. One cannot change his or her caste.

"The Dalits, once known as "untouchables" have from time immemorial been socially and economically oppressed, culturally subjugated and politically marginalized. However, in recent times they have begun to assert themselves and have launched movements aimed at ushering in a new social order based on the principles of equality and liberty. Even though many Dalits have, as a consequence, reached positions of power and prominence, particularly in the political arena, the vast majorities of them continue to suffer discrimination, poverty and humiliation and are often targets of in human atrocities.

Author

1

Mohandas Karamchand Gandhi and Harijans

Mohandas Karamchand Gandhi; 2 October 1869-30 January 1948 was the pre-eminent political and ideological leader of India during the Indian independence movement. He pioneered satyagraha. This is defined as resistance to tyranny through mass civil disobedience, a philosophy firmly founded upon ahimsa, or total nonviolence.

This concept helped India to gain independence, and inspired movements for civil rights and freedom across the world. Gandhi is often referred to as Mahatma Gandhi. He is officially honoured in India as the Father of the Nation; his birthday, 2 October, is commemorated there as Gandhi Jayanti, a national holiday, and worldwide as the International Day of Non-Violence. Gandhi was assassinated on 30 January 1948 by Nathuram Godse, a Hindu Nationalist.

Gandhi first employed civil disobedience while an expatriate lawyer in South Africa, during the resident Indian community's struggle there for civil rights. After his return to India in 1915, he organised protests by peasants, farmers, and urban labourers concerning excessive land-tax and discrimination.

After assuming leadership of the Indian National Congress in 1921, Gandhi led nationwide campaigns to ease poverty, expand women's rights, build religious and ethnic amity, end untouchability, and increase economic self-reliance. Above all, he aimed to achieve Swaraj or the independence of India from foreign domination. Gandhi famously led his followers in the Non-cooperation movement that protested the British-imposed salt tax with the 400 km (240 mi) Dandi Salt March in 1930. Later, in 1942, he launched the Quit India civil disobedience movement demanding immediate independence for India. Gandhi spent a number of years in jail in both South Africa and India.

As a practitioner of ahimsa, Gandhi swore to speak the truth and advocated that others do the same. He lived modestly in a self-sufficient residential community and wore the traditional Indian dhoti and shawl, woven from yarn that he had spun by hand himself. He ate simple vegetarian food, experimented for a time with a fruitarian diet, and undertook long fasts as a means of both self-purification and social protest.

EARLY LIFE AND BACKGROUND

Mohandas Karamchand Gandhi was born on 2 October 1869 in Porbandar, a coastal town which was then part of the Bombay Presidency, British India. His father, Karamchand Gandhi (1822-1885), who belonged to the Hindu Modh community, served as the diwan (a high official) of Porbander state, a small princely state in the Kathiawar Agency of British India.

His grandfather was Uttamchand Gandhi, fondly called Utta Gandhi. His mother, Putlibai, who came from the Hindu Pranami Vaishnava community, was Karamchand's fourth wife, the first three wives having apparently died in childbirth. Growing up with a devout mother and the Jain traditions of the region, the young Mohandas absorbed early the influences that would play an important role in his adult life; these included compassion for sentient beings, vegetarianism, fasting for self-purification, and mutual tolerance between individuals of different creeds.

The Indian classics, especially the stories of Shravana and Maharaja Harishchandra from the Indian epics, had a great impact on Gandhi in his childhood. The story of Harishchandra, a well-known tale of an ancient Indian king and a truthful hero, haunted Gandhi as a boy. Gandhi in his autobiography admits that it left an indelible impression on his mind. He writes: "It haunted me and I must have acted Harishchandra to myself times without number." Gandhi's early self-identification with Truth and Love as supreme values is traceable to his identification with these epic characters.

In May 1883, the 13-year old Mohandas was married to 14-year old Kasturbai Makhanji (her first name was usually shortened to "Kasturba", and affectionately to "Ba") in an arranged child marriage, according to the custom of the region. Recalling the day of their marriage he once said that " As we didn t know much about marriage, for us it meant only wearing new clothes, eating sweets and playing with relatives." However, as was also the custom of the region, the adolescent bride was to spend much time at her parents' house, and away from her husband.

In 1885, when Gandhi was 15, the couple's first child was born, but survived only a few days; Gandhi's father, Karamchand Gandhi, had died earlier that year. Mohandas and Kasturba had four more children, all sons: Harilal, born in 1888; Manilal, born in 1892; Ramdas, born in 1897; and Devdas, born in 1900. At his middle school in Porbandar and high school in Rajkot, Gandhi remained an average student academically. He passed the matriculation exam for Samaldas College at Bhavnagar, Gujarat with some difficulty. While there, he was unhappy, in part because his family wanted him to become a barrister.

On 4 September 1888, less than a month shy of his 19th birthday, Gandhi travelled to London, England, to study law at University College London and to train as a barrister. His time in London, the Imperial capital, was influenced by a vow he had made to his mother in the presence of the Jain monk Becharji, upon leaving India, to observe the Hindu precepts of abstinence from meat, alcohol, and promiscuity. Although Gandhi experimented with adopting "English" customs-taking dancing lessons for example-he could not stomach the bland vegetarian food offered by his landlady and he was always hungry until he found one of London's few vegetarian restaurants. Influenced by Salt's book, he joined the Vegetarian

Society, was elected to its executive committee, and started a local Bayswater chapter.

Some of the vegetarians he met were members of the Theosophical Society, which had been founded in 1875 to further universal brotherhood, and which was devoted to the study of Buddhist and Hindu literature. They encouraged Gandhi to join them in reading the Bhagavad Gita both in translation as well as in the original. Not having shown a particular interest in religion before, he became interested in religious thought and began to read both Hindu as well as Christian scriptures.

Gandhi was called to the bar on 10 June 1891 and left London for India on 12 June 1891, where he learned that his mother had died while he was in London, his family having kept the news from him. His attempts at establishing a law practice in Bombay failed and, later, after applying and being turned down for a part-time job as a high school teacher, he ended up returning to Rajkot to make a modest living drafting petitions for litigants, a business he was forced to close when he ran foul of a British officer.

In his autobiography he refers to this incident as an unsuccessful attempt to lobby on behalf of his older brother. It was in this climate that, in April 1893, he accepted a year-long contract from Dada Abdulla and Co, an Indian firm, to a post in the Colony of Natal, South Africa, then part of the British Empire.

CIVIL RIGHTS MOVEMENT IN SOUTH AFRICA (1893-1914)

In South Africa, Gandhi faced the discrimination directed at Indians. He was thrown off a train at Pietermaritzburg after refusing to move from the first class to a third-class coach while holding a valid first-class ticket.

Travelling farther on by stagecoach he was beaten by a driver for refusing to travel on the foot board to make room for a European passenger. He suffered other hardships on the journey as well, including being barred from several hotels. In another incident, the magistrate of a Durban court ordered

Gandhi to remove his turban-which he refused to do. These events were a turning point in his life, awakening him to social injustice and influencing his subsequent social activism. It was through witnessing firsthand the racism, prejudice and injustice against Indians in South Africa that Gandhi started to question his people's status within the British Empire, and his own place in society.

Gandhi extended his original period of stay in South Africa to assist Indians in opposing a bill to deny them the right to vote. Though unable to halt the bill's passage, his campaign was successful in drawing attention to the grievances of Indians in South Africa. He helped found the Natal Indian Congress in 1894, and through this organisation, he moulded the Indian community of South Africa into a homogeneous political force. In January 1897, when Gandhi landed in Durban he was attacked by a mob of white settlers and escaped only through the efforts of the wife of the police superintendent. He, however, refused to press charges against any member of the mob, stating it was one of his principles not to seek redress for a personal wrong in a court of law.

In 1906, the Transvaal government promulgated a new Act compelling registration of the colony's Indian population. At a mass protest meeting held in Johannesburg on 11 September that year, Gandhi adopted his still evolving methodology of satyagraha (devotion to the truth), or non-violent protest, for the first time, calling on his fellow Indians to defy the new law and suffer the punishments for doing so, rather than resist through violent means.

The community adopted this plan, leading to a seven-year struggle in which thousands of Indians were jailed (including Gandhi), flogged, or even shot, for striking, refusing to register, burning their registration cards or engaging in other forms of non-violent resistance. While the government was successful in repressing the Indian protesters, the public outcry stemming from the harsh methods employed by the South African government in the face of peaceful Indian protesters finally forced South African General Jan Christiaan

Smuts to negotiate a compromise with Gandhi. Gandhi's ideas took shape and the concept of satyagraha matured during this struggle.

RACISM AND CONTROVERSY

Some of Gandhi's early South African articles are controversial. On 7 March 1908, Gandhi wrote in the Indian Opinion of his time in a South African prison: "Kaffirs are as a rule uncivilised-the convicts even more so. They are troublesome, very dirty and live almost like animals." Writing on the subject of immigration in 1903, Gandhi commented: "We believe as much in the purity of race as we think they do... We believe also that the white race in South Africa should be the predominating race.

"During his time in South Africa, Gandhi protested repeatedly about the social classification of blacks with Indians, whom he described as "undoubtedly infinitely superior to the Kaffirs". Remarks such as these have led some to accuse Gandhi of racism. It is worth noting though that the word Kaffir had a different connotation in Gandhi's time than its current day meaning.

Two professors of history who specialise in South Africa, Surendra Bhana and Goolam Vahed, examined this controversy in their text, The Making of a Political Reformer: Gandhi in South Africa, 1893-1914.. They focus in Chapter 1, "Gandhi, Africans and Indians in Colonial Natal" on the relationship between the African and Indian communities under "White rule" and policies which enforced segregation (and, they argue, led to inevitable conflict between these communities).

Of this relationship they state that, "the young Gandhi was influenced by segregationist notions prevalent in the 1890s." At the same time, they state, "Gandhi's experiences in jail seemed to make him more sensitive to their plight...the later Gandhi mellowed; he seemed much less categorical in his expression of prejudice against Africans, and much more open to seeing points of common cause. His negative views in the Johannesburg jail were reserved for hardened African prisoners rather than Africans generally." However, when plans to unveil a statue of Gandhi in Johannesburg was announced, a movement unsuccessfully tried to block it because of Gandhi's "racist" statements.

ROLE IN ZULU WAR OF 1906

In 1906, after the British introduced a new poll-tax, Zulus in South Africa killed two British officers. In response, the British declared war against the Zulus. Gandhi actively encouraged the British to recruit Indians. He argued that Indians should support the war efforts in order to legitimise their claims to full citizenship.

The British, however, refused to commission Indians as army officers. Nonetheless, they accepted Gandhi's offer to let a detachment of Indians volunteer as a stretcher-bearer corps to treat wounded British soldiers. This corps was commanded by Gandhi. On 21 July 1906, Gandhi wrote in Indian Opinion: "The corps had been formed at the instance of the Natal Government by way of experiment, in connection with the operations against the Natives consists of twenty three Indians".

Gandhi urged the Indian population in South Africa to join the war through his columns in Indian Opinion: "If the Government only realised what reserve force is being wasted, they would make use of it and give Indians the opportunity of a thorough training for actual warfare."

In Gandhi's opinion, the Draft Ordinance of 1906 brought the status of Indians below the level of Natives. He therefore urged Indians to resist the Ordinance along the lines of satyagraha by taking the example of "Kaffirs". In his words, "Even the half-castes and kaffirs, who are less advanced than we, have resisted the government. The pass law applies to them as well, but they do not take out passes."

In 1927 Gandhi wrote of the event: "The Boer War had not brought home to me the horrors of war with anything like the vividness that the 'rebellion' did. This was no war but a man-hunt, not only in my opinion, but also in that of many Englishmen with whom I had occasion to talk."

STRUGGLE FOR INDIAN INDEPENDENCE (1915-1945)

In 1915, Gandhi returned from South Africa to live in India. He spoke at the conventions of the Indian National Congress, but was primarily introduced to Indian issues, politics and the Indian people by Gopal Krishna Gokhale, a respected leader of the Congress Party at the time.

ROLE IN WORLD WAR I

In April 1918, during the latter part of World War I, the Viceroy invited Gandhi to a War Conference in Delhi Perhaps to show his support for the Empire and help his case for India's independence, Gandhi agreed to actively recruit Indians for the war effort.

In contrast to the Zulu War of 1906 and the outbreak of World War I in 1914, when he recruited volunteers for the Ambulance Corps, this time Gandhi attempted to recruit combatants. In a June 1918 leaflet entitled "Appeal for Enlistment", Gandhi wrote "To bring about such a state of things we should have the ability to defend ourselves, that is, the ability to bear arms and to use them...If we want to learn the use of arms with the greatest possible despatch, it is our duty to enlist ourselves in the army. "He did however stipulate in a letter to the Viceroy's private secretary that he "personally will not kill or injure anybody, friend or foe." Gandhi's war recruitment campaign brought into question his consistency on nonviolence as his friend Charlie Andrews confirms, "Personally I have never been able to reconcile this with his own conduct in other respects, and it is one of the points where I have found myself in painful disagreement." Gandhi's private secretary also acknowledges that "The question of the consistency between his creed of 'Ahimsa' (non-violence) and his recruiting campaign was raised not only then but has been discussed ever since."

CHAMPARAN AND KHEDA

Gandhi's first major achievements came in 1918 with the Champaran agitation and Kheda Satyagraha, although in the latter it was indigo and other cash crops instead of the food crops necessary for their survival. Suppressed by the militias of the landlords (mostly British), they were given measly compensation, leaving them mired in extreme poverty.

The villages were kept extremely dirty and unhygienic; and alcoholism was rampant. Now in the throes of a devastating famine, the British levied a tax which they insisted on increasing. The situation was desperate. In Kheda in Gujarat, the problem was the same. Gandhi established an ashram there, organising scores of his veteran supporters and fresh volunteers from the region. He organised a detailed study and survey of the villages, accounting for the atrocities and terrible episodes of suffering, including the general state of degenerate living. Building on the confidence of villagers, he began leading the cleanup of villages, building of schools and hospitals and encouraging the village leadership to undo and condemn many social evils such as untouchability and alcoholism.

But his main impact came when he was arrested by police on the charge of creating unrest and was ordered to leave the province. Hundreds of thousands of people protested and rallied outside the jail, police stations and courts demanding his release, which the court reluctantly granted.

Gandhi led organised protests and strikes against the landlords who, with the guidance of the British government, signed an agreement granting the poor farmers of the region more compensation and control over farming, and cancellation of revenue hikes and its collection until the famine ended. It was during this agitation, that Gandhi was addressed by the people as Bapu (Father) and Mahatma (Great Soul).

In Kheda, Sardar Patel represented the farmers in negotiations with the British, who suspended revenue collection and released all the prisoners. As a result, Gandhi's fame spread all over the nation and because of this, he is now called "Father of the nation" in India.

NON-COOPERATION

Gandhi employed non-cooperation, non-violence and

peaceful resistance as his "weapons" in the struggle against the British Raj. In Punjab, the Jallianwala Bagh massacre of civilians by British troops (also known as the Amritsar Massacre) caused deep trauma to the nation, leading to increased public anger and acts of violence. Gandhi criticised both the actions of the British Raj and the retaliatory violence of Indians.

He authored the resolution offering condolences to British civilian victims and condemning the riots which, after initial opposition in the party, was accepted following Gandhi's emotional speech advocating his principle that all violence was evil and could not be justified.

But it was after the massacre and subsequent violence that Gandhi's mind focused upon obtaining complete self-government and control of all Indian government institutions, maturing soon into Swaraj or complete individual, spiritual, political independence.

In December 1921, Gandhi was invested with executive authority on behalf of the Indian National Congress. Under his leadership, the Congress was reorganised with a new constitution, with the goal of Swaraj. Membership in the party was opened to anyone prepared to pay a token fee. A hierarchy of committees was set up to improve discipline, transforming the party from an elite organisation to one of mass national appeal.

Gandhi expanded his non-violence platform to include the swadeshi policy-the boycott of foreign-made goods, especially British goods. Linked to this was his advocacy that khadi (homespun cloth) be worn by all Indians instead of British-made textiles. Gandhi exhorted Indian men and women, rich or poor, to spend time each day spinning khadi in support of the independence movement. Gandhi even invented a small portable spinning wheel that could be folded into the size of a small typewriter.

This was a strategy to inculcate discipline and dedication to weed out the unwilling and ambitious, and to include women in the movement at a time when many thought that such activities were not respectable activities for women. In addition to boycotting British products, Gandhi urged the people to boycott British educational institutions and law courts, to resign from government employment, and to forsake British titles and honours.

"Non-cooperation" enjoyed widespread appeal and success, increasing excitement and participation from all strata of Indian society. Yet, just as the movement reached its apex, it ended abruptly as a result of a violent clash in the town of Chauri Chaura, Uttar Pradesh, in February 1922. Fearing that the movement was about to take a turn towards violence, and convinced that this would be the undoing of all his work, Gandhi called off the campaign of mass civil disobedience. Gandhi was arrested on 10 March 1922, tried for sedition, and sentenced to six years' imprisonment. He began his sentence on 18 March 1922. He was released in February 1924 for an appendicitis operation, having served only 2 years.

Without Gandhi's uniting personality, the Indian National Congress began to splinter during his years in prison, splitting into two factions, one led by Chitta Ranjan Das and Motilal Nehru favouring party participation in the legislatures, and the other led by Chakravarti Rajagopalachari and Sardar Vallabhbhai Patel, opposing this move. Furthermore, cooperation among Hindus and Muslims, which had been strong at the height of the non-violence campaign, was breaking down. Gandhi attempted to bridge these differences through many means, including a three-week fast in the autumn of 1924, but with limited success.

SALT SATYAGRAHA (SALT MARCH)

Gandhi stayed out of active politics and, as such, the limelight for most of the 1920s. He focused instead on resolving the wedge between the Swaraj Party and the Indian National Congress, and expanding initiatives against untouchability, alcoholism, ignorance and poverty.

He returned to the fore in 1928. In the preceding year, the British government had appointed a new constitutional reform commission under Sir John Simon, which did not include any Indian as its member. The result was a boycott of the commission by Indian political parties. Gandhi pushed through a resolution at the Calcutta Congress in December 1928 calling on the British government to grant India dominion status or face a new campaign of non-cooperation with complete independence for the country as its goal. Gandhi had not only moderated the views of younger men like Subhas Chandra Bose and Jawaharlal Nehru, who sought a demand for immediate independence, but also reduced his own call to a one year wait, instead of two.

The British did not respond. On 31 December 1929, the flag of India was unfurled in Lahore. 26 January 1930 was celebrated as India's Independence Day by the Indian National Congress meeting in Lahore. This day was commemorated by almost every other Indian organisation. Gandhi then launched a new satyagraha against the tax on salt in March 1930.

This was highlighted by the famous Salt March to Dandi from 12 March to 6 April, where he marched 388 kilometres (241 miles) from Ahmedabad to Dandi, Gujarat to make salt himself. Thousands of Indians joined him on this march to the sea. This campaign was one of his most successful at upsetting British hold on India; Britain responded by imprisoning over 60,000 people.

The government, represented by Lord Edward Irwin, decided to negotiate with Gandhi. The Gandhi-Irwin Pact was signed in March 1931. The British Government agreed to free all political prisoners, in return for the suspension of the civil disobedience movement. Also as a result of the pact, Gandhi was invited to attend the Round Table Conference in London as the sole representative of the Indian National Congress. The conference was a disappointment to Gandhi and the nationalists, because it focused on the Indian princes and Indian minorities rather than on a transfer of power. Furthermore, Lord Irwin's successor, Lord Willingdon, began a new campaign of controlling and subduing the nationalist movement. Gandhi was again arrested, and the government tried to negate his influence by completely isolating him from his followers. But this tactic failed.

In 1932, through the campaigning of the Dalit leader B. R. Ambedkar, the government granted untouchables separate electorates under the new constitution. In protest, Gandhi embarked on a six-day fast in September 1932. The resulting public outcry successfully forced the government to adopt a more equitable arrangement via negotiations mediated by the Dalit cricketer turned political leader Palwankar Baloo. This was the start of a new campaign by Gandhi to improve the lives of the untouchables, whom he named Harijans, the children of God.

On 8 May 1933, Gandhi began a 21-day fast of self-purification to help the Harijan movement. This new campaign was not universally embraced within the Dalit community, as prominent leader B. R. Ambedkar condemned Gandhi's use of the term Harijans as saying that Dalits were socially immature, and that privileged caste Indians played a paternalistic role. Ambedkar and his allies also felt Gandhi was undermining Dalit political rights. Gandhi, although born into the Vaishya caste, insisted that he was able to speak on behalf of Dalits, despite the presence of Dalit activists such as Ambedkar.

In the summer of 1934, three unsuccessful attempts were made on Gandhi's life. When the Congress Party chose to contest elections and accept power under the Federation scheme, Gandhi resigned from party membership. He did not disagree with the party's move, but felt that if he resigned, his popularity with Indians would cease to stifle the party's membership, that actually varied from communists, socialists, trade unionists, students, religious conservatives, to those with pro-business convictions and that these various voices would get a chance to make themselves heard. Gandhi also wanted to avoid being a target for Raj propaganda by leading a party that had temporarily accepted political accommodation with the Raj.

Gandhi returned to active politics again in 1936, with the Nehru presidency and the Lucknow session of the Congress. Although Gandhi wanted a total focus on the task of winning independence and not speculation about India's future, he did not restrain the Congress from adopting socialism as its goal. Gandhi had a clash with Subhas Bose, who had been elected president in 1938.

Their main points of contention were Bose's lack of commitment to democracy, and lack of faith in non-violence. Bose won his second term despite Gandhi's criticism, but left the Congress when the All-India leaders resigned en masse in protest of his abandonment of the principles introduced by Gandhi.

WORLD WAR II AND QUIT INDIA

World War II broke out in 1939 when Nazi Germany invaded Poland. Initially, Gandhi favoured offering "non-violent moral support" to the British effort, but other Congressional leaders were offended by the unilateral inclusion of India in the war, without consultation of the people's representatives. All Congressmen resigned from office. After long deliberations, Gandhi declared that India could not be party to a war ostensibly being fought for democratic freedom, while that freedom was denied to India itself.

As the war progressed, Gandhi intensified his demand for independence, drafting a resolution calling for the British to Quit India. This was Gandhi's and the Congress Party's most definitive revolt aimed at securing the British exit from India.Gandhi was criticised by some Congress party members and other Indian political groups, both pro-British and anti-British. Some felt that not supporting Britain more in its struggle against Nazi Germany was unethical.

Others felt that Gandhi's refusal for India to participate in the war was insufficient and more direct opposition should be taken, while Britain fought against Nazism yet continued to contradict itself by refusing to grant India Independence. Quit India became the most forceful movement in the history of the struggle, with mass arrests and violence on an unprecedented scale.

Thousands of freedom fighters were killed or injured by police gunfire, and hundreds of thousands were arrested. Gandhi and his supporters made it clear they would not support the war effort unless India were granted immediate independence. He even clarified that this time the movement would not be stopped if individual acts of violence were committed, saying that the "ordered anarchy" around him was "worse than real anarchy." He called on all Congressmen and Indians to maintain discipline via ahimsa, and Karo Ya Maro ("Do or Die") in the cause of ultimate freedom.

Gandhi and the entire Congress Working Committee were arrested in Bombay by the British on 9 August 1942. Gandhi was held for two years in the Aga Khan Palace in Pune. It was here that Gandhi suffered two terrible blows in his personal life. His 50-year old secretary Mahadev Desai died of a heart attack 6 days later and his wife Kasturba died after 18 months imprisonment in 22 February 1944; six weeks later Gandhi suffered a severe malaria attack.

He was released before the end of the war on 6 May 1944 because of his failing health and necessary surgery; the Raj did not want him to die in prison and enrage the nation. Although the Quit India movement had moderate success in its objective, the ruthless suppression of the movement brought order to India by the end of 1943.

At the end of the war, the British gave clear indications that power would be transferred to Indian hands. At this point Gandhi called off the struggle, and around 100,000 political prisoners were released, including the Congress's leadership.

PARTITION OF INDIA

While the Indian National Congress and Gandhi called for the British to quit India, the Muslim League passed a resolution for them to divide and quit, in 1943. The Mahatma is believed to have been opposed to the partition during independence and suggested an agreement which required the Congress and Muslim League to cooperate and attain independence under a provisional government, thereafter, the question of partition could be resolved by a plebiscite in the districts with a Muslim majority. When Jinnah called for Direct Action, on 16 August 1946, Gandhi was infuriated and visited the most riot prone areas to stop the massacres, personally. He made strong efforts to unite the Indian Hindus, Muslims and Christians and struggled for the emancipation of the "untouchables" in Hindu society.

On the 14 and 15 of August, 1947 the Indian Independence Act was invoked and the following carnage witnessed a displacement of up to 12.5 million people in the former British Indian Empire with an estimates of loss of life varying from several hundred thousand to a million. But for his teachings, the efforts of his followers and his own presence there would have been much more bloodshed during the partition; this according to, a prominent Norwegian historian, Jens Arup Seip.

ASSASSINATION

On 30 January 1948, Gandhi was shot while he was walking to a platform from which he was to address a prayer meeting. The assassin, Nathuram Godse, was a Hindu nationalist with links to the extremist Hindu Mahasabha, who held Gandhi responsible for weakening India by insisting upon a payment to Pakistan.

Godse and his co-conspirator Narayan Apte were later tried and convicted; they were executed on 15 November 1949. Gandhi's memorial Raj Ghat, New Delhi, bears the epigraph "Hai Ram", which may be translated as "Oh God". These are widely believed to be Gandhi's last words after he was shot, though the veracity of this statement has been disputed. Jawaharlal Nehru addressed the nation through radio:

"Friends and comrades, the light has gone out of our lives, and there is darkness everywhere, and I do not quite know what to tell you or how to say it.

Our beloved leader, Bapu as we called him, the father of the nation, is no more. Perhaps I am wrong to say that; nevertheless, we will not see him again, as we have seen him for these many years, we will not run to him for advice or seek solace from him, and that is a terrible blow, not only for me, but for millions and millions in this country."-Jawaharlal Nehru's address to Gandhi.

Gandhi's ashes were poured into urns which were sent across India for memorial services. Most were immersed at the Sangam at Allahabad on 12 February 1948 but some were secretly taken away. In 1997, Tushar Gandhi immersed the contents of one urn, found in a bank vault and reclaimed through the courts, at the Sangam at Allahabad. On 30 January 2008 the contents of another urn were immersed at Girgaum Chowpatty by the family after a Dubai-based businessman had sent it to a Mumbai museum.

Another urn has ended up in a palace of the Aga Khan in Pune (where he had been imprisoned from 1942 to 1944) and another in the Self-Realization Fellowship Lake Shrine in Los Angeles. The family is aware that these enshrined ashes could be misused for political purposes but does not want to have them removed because it would entail breaking the shrines.

PRINCIPLES, PRACTICES AND BELIEFS

TRUTH

Gandhi dedicated his life to the wider purpose of discovering truth, or Satya. He tried to achieve this by learning from his own mistakes and conducting experiments on himself. He called his autobiography The Story of My Experiments with Truth.

Gandhi stated that the most important battle to fight was overcoming his own demons, fears, and insecurities. Gandhi summarised his beliefs first when he said "God is Truth". He would later change this statement to "Truth is God". Thus, Satya (Truth) in Gandhi's philosophy is "God".

NONVIOLENCE

Although Mahatama Gandhi was not the originator of the principle of non-violence, he was the first to apply it in the political field on a large scale. The concept of nonviolence (ahimsa) and nonresistance has a long history in Indian religious thought and has had many revivals in Hindu, Buddhist, Jain, Jewish and Christian contexts. Gandhi explains his philosophy and way of life in his autobiography The Story of My Experiments with Truth.

He was quoted as saying:

- "When I despair, I remember that all through history the way of truth and love has always won. There have been tyrants and murderers and for a time they seem invincible, but in the end, they always fall-think of it, always."
- "What difference does it make to the dead, the orphans, and the homeless, whether the mad destruction is wrought under the name of totalitarianism or the holy name of liberty and democracy?"
- "An eye for an eye makes the whole world blind."
- "There are many causes that I am prepared to die for but no causes that I am prepared to kill for."

In applying these principles, Gandhi did not balk from taking them to their most logical extremes in envisioning a world where even government, police and armies were nonviolent. The quotations below are from the book "For Pacifists."

- The science of war leads one to dictatorship, pure and simple. The science of non-violence alone can lead one to pure democracy...Power based on love is thousand times more effective and permanent than power derived from fear of punishment....It is a blasphemy to say non-violence can be practiced only by individuals and never by nations which are composed of individuals...The nearest approach to purest anarchy would be a democracy based on non-violence...A society organised and run on the basis of complete non-violence would be the purest anarchy
- I have conceded that even in a non-violent state a police force may be necessary...Police ranks will be composed of believers in non-violence. The people will instinctively render them every help and through mutual cooperation they will easily deal with the

ever decreasing disturbances...Violent quarrels between labour and capital and strikes will be few and far between in a non-violent state because the influence of the non-violent majority will be great as to respect the principle elements in society. Similarly, there will be no room for communal disturbances....

- A non-violent army acts unlike armed men, as well in times of peace as in times of disturbances. Theirs will be the duty of bringing warring communities together, carrying peace propaganda, engaging in activities that would bring and keep them in touch with every single person in their parish or division. Such an army should be ready to cope with any emergency, and in order to still the frenzy of mobs should risk their lives in numbers sufficient for that purpose....Satyagraha (truth-force) brigades can be organised in every village and every block of buildings in the cities. There are two ways open to non-violence. To yield possession, but non-cooperate with the aggressor...prefer death to submission. The second way would be non-violent resistance by the people who have been trained in the non-violent way...The unexpected spectacle of endless rows upon rows of men and women simply dying rather than surrender to the will of an aggressor must ultimately melt him and his soldiery...A nation or group which has made non-violence its final policy cannot be subjected to slavery even by the atom bomb.... The level of non-violence in that nation, if that even happily comes to pass, will naturally have risen so high as to command universal respect.

In accordance with these views, in 1940, when invasion of the British Isles by Nazi Germany looked imminent, Gandhi offered the following advice to the British people (Non-Violence in Peace and War):

- "I would like you to lay down the arms you have as being useless for saving you or humanity. You will invite Herr Hitler and Signor Mussolini to take what they want of the countries you call your possessions...If these gentlemen choose to occupy your homes, you will vacate them. If they do not give you free passage out, you will allow yourselves, man, woman, and child, to be slaughtered, but you will refuse to owe allegiance to them."

In a post-war interview in 1946, he offered a view at an even further extreme:

- "Hitler," Gandhi said, "killed five million Jews. It is the greatest crime of our time. But the Jews should have offered themselves to the butcher's knife. They should have thrown themselves into the sea from cliffs... It would have aroused the world and the people of Germany... As it is they succumbed anyway in their millions."

However, Gandhi realised that this level of nonviolence required incredible faith and courage, which he believed everyone did not possess.

He therefore advised that everyone need not keep to nonviolence, especially if it were used as a cover for cowardice:

- "Gandhi guarded against attracting to his satyagraha movement those who feared to take up arms or felt themselves incapable of resistance. 'I do believe,' he wrote, 'that where there is only a choice between cowardice and violence, I would advise violence.'"
- "At every meeting I repeated the warning that unless they felt that in non-violence they had come into possession of a force infinitely superior to the one they had and in the use of which they were adept, they should have nothing to do with non-violence and resume the arms they possessed before. It must never be said of the Khudai Khidmatgars that once so brave, they had become or been made cowards under Badshah Khan's influence. Their bravery consisted not in being good marksmen but in defying death and being ever ready to bare their breasts to the bullets."

Gandhi also came under some political fire for his criticism of those who attempted to achieve independence through more violent means. According to a report in the Frontline magazine, he did plead several times for the commutation of the death sentence of Bhagat Singh, Rajguru and Sukhdev including a personal visit on 19 March 1931 and in a letter to the Viceroy on the day of their execution, pleading fervently for the commutation.

Winston Churchill said that it was "nauseating" to see Gandhi, "a seditious Middle Temple lawyer, now posing as a fakir of a type well-known in the Middle East, striding half-naked up the steps of the Vice-regal palace... to parley on equal terms with the representative of the King-Emperor".

He continued this argument in a number of articles reprinted in Homer Jack's The Gandhi Reader: A Sourcebook of His Life and Writings. In the first, "Zionism and Anti-Semitism," written in 1938, Gandhi commented upon the 1930s persecution of the Jews in Germany within the context of Satyagraha. He offered non-violence as a method of combating the difficulties Jews faced in Germany, stating,

- If I were a Jew and were born in Germany and earned my livelihood there, I would claim Germany as my home even as the tallest Gentile German might, and challenge him to shoot me or cast me in the dungeon; I would refuse to be expelled or to submit to discriminating treatment. And for doing this I should not wait for the fellow Jews to join me in civil resistance, but would have confidence that in the end the rest were bound to follow my example. If one Jew or all the Jews were to accept the prescription here offered, he or they cannot be worse off than now. And suffering voluntarily undergone will bring them an inner strength and joy...the calculated violence of Hitler may even result in a general massacre of the Jews by way of his first answer to the declaration of such hostilities. But if the Jewish mind could be prepared for voluntary suffering, even the massacre I have imagined could be turned into a day of thanksgiving and joy that Jehovah had wrought deliverance of the race even at the hands of the tyrant. For to the God-fearing, death has no terror.

Gandhi was highly criticised for these statements and responded in the article "Questions on the Jews" with "Friends have sent me two newspaper cuttings criticising my appeal to the Jews. The two critics suggest that in presenting non-violence to the Jews as a remedy against the wrong done to them, I have suggested nothing new...what I have pleaded for is renunciation of violence of the heart and consequent active exercise of the force generated by the great renunciation.

Gandhi's statements regarding Jews facing the impending Holocaust have attracted criticism from a number of commentators. Martin Buber wrote a sharply critical open letter to Gandhi on 24 February 1939. Buber asserted that the comparison between British treatment of Indian subjects and Nazi treatment of Jews was inappropriate; moreover, he noted that when Indians were the victims of persecution, Gandhi had, on occasion, supported the use of force.

Gandhi commented upon the 1930s persecution of the Jews in Germany within the context of Satyagraha. In the November 1938 article on the Nazi persecution of the Jews quoted above, he offered non-violence as a solution:

- The German persecution of the Jews seems to have no parallel in history. The tyrants of old never went so mad as Hitler seems to have gone. And he is doing it with religious zeal. For he is propounding a new religion of exclusive and militant nationalism in the name of which any inhumanity becomes an act of humanity to be rewarded here and hereafter. The crime of an obviously mad but intrepid youth is being visited upon his whole race with unbelievable ferocity. If there ever could be a justifiable war in the name of and for humanity, a war against Germany, to prevent the wanton persecution of a whole race, would be completely justified. But I do not believe in any war. A discussion of the pros and cons of such a war is therefore outside my horizon or province. But if there can be no war against Germany, even for such a crime as is being committed against the Jews, surely there can be no alliance with Germany. How can there be alliance between a nation which claims to stand for justice and democracy and one which is the declared enemy of both?"

- "My non-violence does not admit of running away from danger and leaving dear ones unprotected. Between violence and cowardly flight, I can only prefer violence to cowardice. Non-violence is the summit of bravery."
- "I do believe that, where there is only a choice between cowardice and violence, I would advise violence."
- "I would rather have India resort to arms in order to defend her honour than that she should in a cowardly manner become or remain a helpless witness to her own dishonour."

VEGETARIANISM

As a young child, Gandhi experimented with meat-eating. This was due partially to his inherent curiosity as well as his rather persuasive peer and friend Sheikh Mehtab. The idea of vegetarianism is deeply ingrained in Hindu and Jain traditions in India, and, in his native land of Gujarat, most Hindus are vegetarian and so are almost all Jains. The Gandhi family was no exception.

Before leaving for his studies in London, Gandhi made a promise to his mother, Putlibai and his uncle, Becharji Swami that he would abstain from eating meat, taking alcohol, and engaging in promiscuity. He held fast to his promise and gained more than a diet: he gained a basis for his life-long philosophies. As Gandhi grew into adulthood, he became a strict vegetarian. He wrote the book The Moral Basis of Vegetarianism and several articles on the subject, some of which were published in the London Vegetarian Society's publication, The Vegetarian. During this period, the young Gandhi became inspired by many great minds and was befriended by the chairman of the London Vegetarian Society, Dr. Josiah Oldfield.

Having also read and admired the work of Henry Stephens Salt, the young Mohandas met and often corresponded with the vegetarian campaigner. Gandhi spent much time advocating vegetarianism during and after his time in London. To Gandhi, a vegetarian diet would not only satisfy the requirements of the body, it would also serve an economic purpose as meat was, and still is, generally more expensive than grains, vegetables, and fruits. Also, many Indians of the time struggled with low income, thus vegetarianism was seen not only as a spiritual practice but also a practical one.

He abstained from eating for long periods, using fasting as a form of political protest. He refused to eat until his death or his demands were met. Gandhi noted in his autobiography that vegetarianism was the beginning of his deep commitment to Brahmacharya; without total control of the palate, his success in Bramacharya would likely falter.

Gandhi also experimented with fruitarianism, stating in his autobiography, "I decided to live on a pure fruit diet, and that too composed of the cheapest fruit possible... Raw groundnuts, bananas, dates, lemons and olive oil composed our usual diet." However, late in life he broke his discipline and started taking goat's milk on the advice of his doctor. This lapse of discipline bothered him to his dying day, and he wrote, "The memory of this action even now rankles my breast and fills me with remorse, and I am constantly thinking how to give up goat's milk." He never took dairy products obtained from cows because of his view initially that milk is not the natural diet of man, disgust for cow blowing, and, specifically, because of a vow to his late mother.

NAI TALIM, BASIC EDUCATION

Nai Talim is a spiritual principle which states that knowledge and work are not separate. Gandhi promoted an educational curriculum with the same name based on this pedagogical principle.

It can be translated with the phrase 'Basic Education for all'. However, the concept has several layers of meaning. It developed out of Gandhi's experience with the English educational system and with colonialism in general. In that system, he saw that Indian children would be alienated and 'career-based thinking' would become dominant. In addition, it embodied a series of negative outcomes: the disdain for manual work, the development of a new elite class, and the increasing problems of industrialization and urbanization.

The three pillars of Gandhi's pedagogy were its focus on the life-long character of education, its social character and its form as a holistic process. For Gandhi, education is 'the moral development of the person', a process that is by definition 'life-long'.

BRAHMACHARYA

When Gandhi was 16 his father became very ill. Being very devoted to his parents, he attended to his father at all times during his illness. However, one night, Gandhi's uncle came to relieve Gandhi for a while. He retired to his bedroom where carnal desires overcame him and he made love to his wife. Shortly afterward a servant came to report that Gandhi's father had just died. Gandhi felt tremendous guilt and never could forgive himself. He came to refer to this event as "double shame." The incident had significant influence in Gandhi becoming celibate at the age of 36, while still married.

This decision was deeply influenced by the philosophy of Brahmacharya-spiritual and practical purity-largely associated with celibacy and asceticism. Gandhi saw Brahmacharya as a means of becoming close with God and as a primary foundation for self-realisation. In his autobiography he tells of his battle against lustful urges and fits of jealousy with his childhood bride, Kasturba. He felt it his personal obligation to remain celibate so that he could learn to love, rather than lust. For Gandhi, Brahmacharya meant "control of the senses in thought, word and deed.".

Towards the end of his life, it became public knowledge that Gandhi had been sharing his bed for a number of years with young women. He explained that he did this for bodily warmth at night and termed his actions as "nature cure". Later in his life he started experimenting with brahmacharya in order to test his self-control. His letter to Birla in April, 1945 referring to 'women or girls who have been naked with me' indicates that several women were part of his experiments. He wrote five editorials in Harijan discussing the practice of brahmacharya.

As part of these experiments, he initially slept with his women associates in the same room but at a distance. Afterwards he started to lie in the same bed with his women disciples and later took to sleeping naked alongside them. According to Gandhi active-celibacy meant perfect self-control in the presence of the opposite sex. Gandhi conducted his experiments with a number of women such as Abha, the sixteen-year-old wife of his grandnephew Kanu Gandhi. Gandhi acknowledged "that this experiment is very dangerous indeed", but thought "that it was capable of yielding great results".

His nineteen-year-old grandniece, Manu Gandhi, too was part of his experiments. Gandhi had earlier written to her father, Jaisukhlal Gandhi, that Manu had started to share his bed so that he may "correct her sleeping posture". Gandhi saw himself as a mother to these women and would refer to Abha and Manu as "my walking sticks".

Gandhi called Sarladevi, a married woman with children and a devout follower, his "spiritual wife". He later said that he had come close to having sexual relations with her. He had told a correspondent in March, 1945 that "sleeping together came with my taking up of bramhacharya or even before that"; he said he had experimented with his wife "but that was not enough". Gandhi felt satisfied with his experiments and wrote to Manu that "I have successfully practiced the eleven vows taken by me. This is the culmination of my striving for last thirty-six years. In this yajna I got a glimpse of the ideal truth and purity for which I have been striving".

Gandhi had to take criticism for his experiments by many of his followers and opponents. His stenographer, R. P. Parasuram, resigned when he saw Gandhi sleeping naked with Manu. Gandhi insisted that he never felt aroused while he slept beside her, or with Sushila or Abha. "I am sorry" Gandhi said to Parasuram, "you are at liberty to leave me today." Nirmal Kumar Bose, leading anthropologist and close associate of Gandhi, parted company with him in April, 1947 post Gandhi's tour of Noakhali, where some sort of altercation had taken place between Gandhi and Sushila Nayar in his bedroom at midnight that caused Gandhi to slap his forehead. Bose said, "there was no immorality on part of Gandhi.

Moreover Gandhi tried to conquer the feeling of sex by consciously endeavouring to convert himself into a mother of those who were under his case, whether men or women". This maternal emphasis has also been pointed out by Dattatreya Balkrushna Kalelkar, a revolutionary turned disciple of Gandhi.

SIMPLICITY

Gandhi earnestly believed that a person involved in public service should lead a simple life. He first displayed this principle when he gave up wearing western-style clothing, which he associated with wealth and success. When he returned to India he renounced the western lifestyle he led in South Africa, where he had enjoyed a successful legal practice.

Gandhi dressed to be accepted by the poorest person in India, advocating the use of homespun cloth (khadi). He and his followers adopted the practice of weaving their own clothes from thread they themselves spun on a charkha, and encouraged others to do so. While Indian workers were often idle due to unemployment, they had often bought their clothing from industrial manufacturers owned by British interests. The Swadeshi Movement held that if Indians made their own clothes, it would deal an economic blow to the British establishment in India. Gandhian simplicity was a sign and expression of swadeshi principles. Consequently, the charkha was later incorporated into the flag of the Indian

National Congress. He subsequently wore a dhoti for the rest of his life to express the simplicity of his life.

The practice of giving up unnecessary expenditure, embracing a simple lifestyle and washing his own clothes, Gandhi called "reducing himself to zero". On one occasion he returned the gifts bestowed to him from the Natals for his diligent service to the community. Gandhi spent one day of each week in silence. He believed that abstaining from speaking brought him inner peace and made him a better listener. This influence was drawn from the Hindu principles of mauna and shanti. On such days he communicated with others by writing on paper. For three and a half years, from the age of 37, Gandhi refused to read newspapers, claiming that the tumultuous state of world affairs caused him more confusion than his own inner unrest. After reading John Ruskin's Unto This Last, he decided to change his lifestyle and create a commune called Phoenix Settlement.

FAITH

Gandhi was born a Hindu and practised Hinduism all his life. As a common Hindu, he believed all religions to be equal, and rejected all efforts to convert him to a different faith. He was an avid theologian and read extensively about all major religions.

He had the following to say about Hinduism:

- Hinduism as I know it entirely satisfies my soul, fills my whole being...When doubts haunt me, when disappointments stare me in the face, and when I see not one ray of light on the horizon, I turn to the Bhagavad Gita, and find a verse to comfort me; and I immediately begin to smile in the midst of overwhelming sorrow. My life has been full of tragedies and if they have not left any visible and indelible effect on me, I owe it to the teachings of the Bhagavad Gita.

Gandhi wrote a commentary on the Bhagavad Gita in Gujarati. The Gujarati manuscript was translated into English by Mahadev Desai, who provided an additional introduction and commentary. It was published with a Foreword by Gandhi in 1946.

Gandhi believed that at the core of every religion was truth and love (compassion, nonviolence and the Golden Rule). He also questioned what he saw as hypocrisy, malpractices, and dogma in all religions, including his own, and he was a tireless advocate for social reform in religion. Some of his comments on various religions are:

- Thus if I could not accept Christianity either as a perfect, or the greatest religion, neither was I then convinced of Hinduism being such. Hindu defects were pressingly visible to me. If untouchability could be a part of Hinduism, it could but be a rotten part or an excrescence. I could not understand the raison d'être of a multitude of sects and castes. What was the meaning of saying that the Vedas were the inspired Word of God? If they were inspired, why not also the Bible and the Koran? As Christian friends were endeavouring to convert me, so were Muslim friends. Abdullah Seth had kept on inducing me to study Islam, and of course he had always something to say regarding its beauty. -Gandhi's autobiography
- As soon as we lose the moral basis, we cease to be religious. There is no such thing as religion over-riding morality. Man, for instance, cannot be untruthful, cruel or incontinent and claim to have God on his side.
- The sayings of Muhammad are a treasure of wisdom, not only for Muslims but for all of mankind.
- I like your Christ, I do not like your Christians. Your Christians are so unlike your Christ.
- God has no religion.

Later in his life, when he was asked whether he was a Hindu, he replied, "Yes I am. I am also a Christian, a Muslim, a Buddhist and a Jew."

In spite of their deep reverence to each other, Gandhi and Rabindranath Tagore engaged in protracted debates more than once. These debates exemplify the philosophical differences between the two most famous Indians at the time. On 15 January 1934, an earthquake hit Bihar and caused extensive damage and loss of life.

Gandhi maintained this was because of the sin committed by upper caste Hindus by not letting untouchables in their temples (Gandhi was committed to the cause of improving the fate of untouchables, referring to them as Harijans, people of Krishna). Tagore vehemently opposed Gandhi's stance, maintaining that an earthquake can only be caused by natural forces, not moral reasons, however repugnant the practice of untouchability may be.

Gandhi took a keen interest in theosophy. He empathised with theosophy's message of "universal brotherhood and consequent toleration", as he put it in 1926.

SWARAJ

Gandhi was a self-described philosophical anarchist, and his vision of India meant India without an underlying government. He once said that "the ideally nonviolent state would be an ordered anarchy." While political systems are largely hierarchical, with each layer of authority from the individual to the central government have increasing levels of authority over the layer below, Gandhi believed that society should be the exact opposite, where nothing is done without the consent of anyone, down to the individual. His idea was that true self-rule in a country means that every person rules his or herself and that there is no state which enforces laws upon the people.

This would be achieved over time with nonviolent conflict mediation, as power is divested from layers of hierarchical authorities, ultimately to the individual, which would come to embody the ethic of nonviolence. Rather than a system where rights are enforced by a higher authority, people are self-governed by mutual responsibilities.

On returning from South Africa, when Gandhi received a letter asking for his participation in writing a world charter for human rights, he responded saying, "in my experience, it is far more important to have a charter for human duties." A free India for him meant the existence of thousands of self-sufficient small communities (an idea possibly from Tolstoy) who rule themselves without hindering others. It did not mean merely transferring a British established administrative structure into Indian hands which he said was just making Hindustan into Englistan.

He wanted to ultimately dissolve the Congress Party after independence and establish a system of direct democracy in India, having no faith in the British styled parliamentary system.

LITERARY WORKS

Gandhi was a prolific writer. For decades he edited several newspapers including Harijan in Gujarati, in Hindi and in the English language; Indian Opinion while in South Africa and, Young India, in English, and Navajivan, a Gujarati monthly, on his return to India. Later, Navajivan was also published in Hindi. In addition, he wrote letters almost every day to individuals and newspapers.

Gandhi also wrote several books including his autobiography, An Autobiography of My Experiments with Truth, Satyagraha in South Africa about his struggle there, Hind Swaraj or Indian Home Rule, a political pamphlet, and a paraphrase in Gujarati of John Ruskin's Unto This Last. This last essay can be considered his programme on economics. He also wrote extensively on vegetarianism, diet and health, religion, social reforms, etc. Gandhi usually wrote in Gujarati, though he also revised the Hindi and English translations of his books.

Gandhi's complete works were published by the Indian government under the name The Collected Works of Mahatma Gandhi in the 1960s. The writings comprise about 50,000 pages published in about a hundred volumes. In 2000, a revised edition of the complete works sparked a controversy, as Gandhian followers argue that the government incorporated the changes for political purposes. The Indian government later withdrew the revised edition.

GANDHI-SAVIOR OF HARIJANS

Many people have heard of Mahatma Gandhi, but do you really know about all he has done for this world? Of course, he is widely known for being "Father of India and practicing successfully non-violence" but that isn't all this wonderful individual has done for humanity. Not many people know all of what Gandhi has done to bring equality and peace to humanity. Gandhi was born on October 2nd, 1869 in India to a family in the trader's caste, which was in the class of the merchants. He was raised by a conservative family. He studied law in London.

He went to South Africa for employment and found that he was discriminated against for just his skin colour and his religion! He peacefully revolted and after about twenty years spent in peaceful fighting, he returned to India. Gandhi immediately took the side of the "untouchables" as they were called then. They were the ones who did what we would call "dirty work." The untouchables did all the hard, energy taking work-such as cleaning toilets, cleaning clothes, burying or burning the dead of all castes, sweeping the streets, picking up garbage etc. They suffered a lot because their jobs were "not fit" for members of higher castes to perform.

They were supposed to be so dirty that it was unholy to even lay a finger on them! It is true they did jobs that would involve them with dirt, grime, germs, and unwanted particles. They were forbidden to go into worship houses (temples), hospitals, schools, and many other public places, because they were believed to be unfit, unhealthy and undeserving. Instead of going inside the temple, they had to stand outside the doors open to everyone but them, depressed and dirty. The untouchable class touched Gandhi's heart. Even though he belonged to a higher caste his conscience led him to aid them.

Gandhi went totally against the norms to change this mindset of untouchables. To start a paradigm shift, he renamed the untouchables as "Harijans". This literally translates to God's children. Next, to serve as role model to his own preaching Gandhi did several things. Here was Gandhi, from the Traders caste, joining in with the meal of the Harijans! Here was Gandhi, from the Traders caste, cleaning the pubic toilets along with the Harijans! Gandhi actually voluntarily did many jobs of the Harijans, working side by side!!! Nobody in one of the higher castes would have thought of doing that, even in their wildest dreams. Gandhi showed that by doing a job that a Harijan did, it will not make you "untouchable." Amazingly, most of the lower castes now want to be identified as lower castes because Gandhi helped them so much. Now can you see why Gandhi made such an impact on India? Gandhi was a great example and leader to many.

If I was an adult following in Gandhi's footsteps I would probably address the international issue of world poverty because I think that is what Gandhi would choose if he was still living today. It is closest to what he was fighting against in his lifetime. The Harijans were poor, and poor people are sometimes discriminated against. For example, when scientists find a new cure for a disease the wealthier people will probably acquire access to it first, and it will be widely available to them. The poorest people in the world would have to wait for some donations from charities and receive it perhaps after several years and many lives could be lost be that time.

I might join an organization to help solve the problem, or if I have what I need, start a new organization. My organization should focus on building schools and fundamental amenities to educate the poor. There is a saying that "If you give a man a fish, you feed him for a day; if you teach him how to fish, you feed him for a lifetime." If you apply this to the issue of poverty and the real world today it becomes "If you give a person some cash you will boost him economically for a limited time; if you motivate him to learn, you boost his family economically for a lifetime

" This means when you educate a person you let them acquire knowledge. This means he will be able to educate his children, and with each generation, educating that one person makes a larger difference in the world. Then there will probably be more donors, so we can educate more people and build more schools, and so I just keep on improving the lives of people in poverty. If I take these steps I will be showing compassion to the poor people because I can see how I would feel in their shoes; I would feel depressed, wanting to get the empty space out of my stomach, I would work hard and be tough, try to be content with my style of life. I would also probably be hopeful, if the future generation becomes educated so that they can be a hard working businessperson and earn a higher rank in society.

I conclude that Mahatma Gandhi was a very influential person, and that he has done a lot to help the Harijans. If Gandhi were alive today, I think he would help solve the international problem of poverty. Gandhi was a great leader and example to many. He never laid his hand on a weapon, yet led two large rebellions. I think that Gandhi is a great example of a real hero.

2

Dr. Ambedkar

Bhimrao Ramji Ambedkar (14 April 1891—6 December 1956), also known as Babasaheb, was an Indian jurist, political leader, Buddhist activist, philosopher, thinker, anthropologist, historian, orator, prolific writer, economist, scholar, editor, revolutionary and a revivalist for Buddhism in India. He was also the chief architect of the Indian Constitution.

Born into a poor Mahar family, Ambedkar spent his whole life fighting against social discrimination, the system of Chaturvarna—the categorization of Hindu society into four varnas—and the Hindu caste system. He is also credited with providing a spark for the conversion of hundreds of thousands of untouchables to Theravada Buddhism. Dr. Ambedkar was posthumously awarded the Bharat Ratna, India's highest civilian award, in 1990.

Overcoming numerous social and financial obstacles, Ambedkar became one of the first so called "Outcasts" to obtain a college education in India. Eventually earning law degrees and multiple doctorates for his study and research in law, economics and political science from Columbia University and the London School of Economics, Ambedkar gained a reputation as a scholar and practiced law for a few years, later campaigning by publishing journals advocating political rights and social freedom for India's so-called untouchables. He is regarded as a Bodhisattva by Indian Buddhists, though he never claimed himself to be a Bodhisattva.

LIFE AND EDUCATION

Bhimrao Ramji Ambedkar was born in the British-founded town and military cantonment of Mhow in the Central Provinces (now in Madhya Pradesh). He was the 14th and last child of Ramji Maloji Sakpal and Bhimabai. His family was of Marathi background from the town of Ambavade in the Ratnagiri district of modern-day Maharashtra. They belonged to the Hindu, Mahar caste, who were treated as untouchables and subjected to intense socio-economic discrimination.

Ambedkar's ancestors had for long been in the employment of the army of the British East India Company, and his father Ramji Sakpal served in the Indian Army at the Mhow cantonment. He had received a degree of formal education in Marathi and English, and encouraged his children to learn and work hard at school. Belonging to the Kabir Panth, Ramji Sakpal encouraged his children to read the Hindu classics. He used his position in the army to lobby for his children to study at the government school, as they faced resistance owing to their caste.

Although able to attend school, Ambedkar and other untouchable children were segregated and given no attention or assistance by the teachers. They were not allowed to sit inside the class. Even if they needed to drink water somebody from a higher caste would have to pour that water from a height as they were not allowed to touch either the water or the vessel that contained it. This task was usually performed for the young Ambedkar by the school peon, and if the peon was not available then he had to go without water, Ambedkar states this situation as "No peon, No Water". Ramji Sakpal retired in 1894 and the family moved to Satara two years later. Shortly after their move, Ambedkar's mother died.

The children were cared for by their paternal aunt, and lived in difficult circumstances. Only three sons—Balaram, Anandrao and Bhimrao—and two daughters—Manjula and Tulasa—of the Ambedkars would go on to survive them. Of his brothers and sisters, only Ambedkar succeeded in passing his examinations and graduating to a higher school. Bhimrao Sakpal Ambavadekar the surname comes from his native village 'Ambavade' in Ratnagiri District. His Bhramin teacher

Mahadev Ambedkar who was so much fond of him, has changed his surname from 'Ambavadekar' to his own surname 'Ambedkar' in school records.

HIGHER EDUCATION

Ramji Sakpal remarried in 1898, and the family moved to Mumbai (then Bombay), where Ambedkar became the first untouchable student at the Government High School near Elphinstone Road. Although excelling in his studies, Ambedkar was increasingly disturbed by the segregation and discrimination that he faced. In 1907, he passed his matriculation examination and entered the University of Bombay, becoming one of the first persons of untouchable origin to enter a college in India.

This success provoked celebrations in his community, and after a public ceremony he was presented with a biography of the Buddha by his teacher Krishnaji Arjun Keluskar also known as Dada Keluskar, a Maratha caste scholar. Ambedkar's marriage had been arranged the previous year as per Hindu custom, to Ramabai, a nine-year old girl from Dapoli. In 1908, he entered Elphinstone College and obtained a scholarship of twenty five rupees a month from the Gayakwad ruler of Baroda, Sahyaji Rao III. By 1912, he obtained his degree in economics and political science from Bombay University, and prepared to take up employment with the Baroda state government.

His wife gave birth to his first son, Yashwant, in the same year. Ambedkar had just moved his young family and started work, when he dashed back to Mumbai to see his ailing father, who died on February 2, 1913. In 1913 he received Baroda State Scholarship of 11.50 British pounds a month for three years to join the Political Department of the Columbia University as a Post Graduate Student. In New York he stayed at Livingston Hall with his friend Naval Bhathena, a Parsi; the two remained friends for life. He used to sit for hours studying in Low Library. He passed his M.A. exam in June 1913, majoring in Economics, with Sociology, History, Philosophy, and Anthropology as other subjects of study; he presented a Thesis," Ancient Indian Commerce". In 1916 he offered another M.A. thesis, "National Dividend of India-A Historic and Analytical Study". On May 9, he read his document Castes in India: Their Mechanism, Genesis and Development" before a seminar conducted by the anthropologist.

Alexander Goldenweiser. In October 1916 he was admitted to Gray's Inn for Law, and to the London School of Economics and Political Science for Economics where he started work on a Doctoral thesis. In 1917 June he was obliged to go back to India as the term of his scholarship from Baroda ended, however he was given permission to return and submit his thesis within four years. He sent his precious and much-loved collection of books back on a steamer, but it was torpedoed and sunk by a German submarine.

AMBEDKAR: FIGHT AGAINST UNTOUCHABILITY

As he was educated by the Baroda State, he was bound to serve the State. He was appointed as Military Secretary to the Gaikwar of Baroda, which he had to quit within short time, this fiasco was described by Ambedkar in his autobiography "Waiting for a Visa" he states that "This scene of a dozen Parsis armed with sticks line before me in a menacing mood, and myself standing before them with a terrified look imploring for mercy, is a scene which so long a period as eighteen years had not succeeded in fading away. I can even vividly recall it— and I never recall it without tears in my eyes. It was then for the first time that I learnt that a person who is an untouchable to a Hindu is also an untouchable to a Parsi". Then after he tried to find ways to make a living for his growing family.

He worked as private tutor, as an accountant, investment consulting business, but it failed when his clients learned that he was an untouchable. In 1918 he became Professor of Political Economy in the Sydenham College of Commerce and Economics in Bombay. Even though he was successful with the students, but other professors objected to his sharing the same drinking-water jug that they all used. As a leading Indian scholar, Ambedkar had been invited to testify before the South borough Committee, which was preparing the Government of India Act 1919. At this hearing, Ambedkar argued for creating separate electorates and reservations for untouchables and other religious communities. In 1920, he began the publication of the weekly Mooknayak (Leader of the Silent) in Mumbai with the help of Shahu I (1884–1922), Maharaja of Kolhapur. Ambedkar used this journal to criticize orthodox Hindu politicians and a perceived reluctance of the Indian political community to fight caste discrimination. His speech at a Depressed Classes Conference in Kolhapur impressed the local state ruler Shahu IV, who described Ambedkar as the future national leader and shocked orthodox society by dining with Ambekdar. Having resigned from his teaching position, in July he returned to London, relying on his own savings, supplemented by loans from the Maharaja of Kolhapur and his friend Naval Bhathena.

He returned to the London School of Economics, and to Gray's Inn to read for the Bar. He lived in poverty, and studied constantly in the British Museum. In 1922 through unremitting hard work, Ambedkar once again over fulfilled all expectations: he completed a thesis for a M.Sc. (Econonics) degree at London School of Economics, and was called to the bar, and submitted a Ph.D. thesis in economics to the University of London. Ambedkar established a successful legal practice. Early on his legal career, Ambedkar was engaged in a very important lawsuite file by some Brahmins against three non-Bhramin leaders K.B.Bagde, Keshavrao Jedhe and Dinkarrao Javalkar. They were being prosecuted for writing a pamphlet that Bhramins had ruined India. On the prosecution side was L. B. Bhopatkar, a great lawyer from Poona, Ambedkar argued his case very ably, put up a very eloquent defence and won the case in October 1926. The victory was resounding, both socially and individually for the clients.

AMBEDKAR'S MISSIONS

While practicing law in the Bombay High Court he ran head long in to uplift the untouchable to educate them. To achieve these goals his first organizational attempt was the Bahishkrit Hitakarini Sabha. An organisation to promote education, socio-economic uplifting and for welfare of "outcastes" or the depressed classes. By 1927 Dr. Ambedkar decided to launch active movements against untouchability. He began with public movements and marches to open up and share public drinking water resources, also he began a struggle for the right to enter Hindu temples.

He led a satyagraha in Mahad to fight for the right of the untouchable community to draw water from the main water tank of the town. He was appointed to the Bombay Presidency Committee to work with the all-European Simon Commission in 1925. This commission had sparked great protests across India, and while its report was ignored by most Indians, Ambedkar himself wrote a separate set of recommendations for future constitutional

AMBEDKAR AND POONA PACT

By now Ambedkar had become one of the most prominent political figures of the time. He had grown increasingly critical of mainstream Indian political parties for their perceived lack of emphasis for the elimination of the caste system.

Ambedkar criticized the Indian National Congress and its leader Mohandas Gandhi, whom he accused of reducing the untouchable community to a figure of pathos. Ambedkar was also dissatisfied with the failures of British rule, and advocated a political identity for untouchables separate from both the Congress and the British.

At a Depressed Classes Conference on August 8, 1930 Ambedkar outlined his political vision, insisting that the safety of the Depressed Classes hinged on their being independent of the Government and the Congress. Ambedkar's political work, such as this demand for a Separate Electorate System, had made him unpopular amongst Hindus, as well as with many Congress politicians who had earlier condemned untouchability while stopping short of advocating full equality for untouchables.

Due to Ambedkar's prominence and popular support amongst the untouchable community, he was invited to attend the Second Round Table Conference in London in 1932. Gandhi fiercely opposed separate electorate for untouchables, though he accepted separate electorate for all other minority groups such as Muslims and Sikhs, saying he feared that separate electorates for untouchables would divide Hindu society for future generations. When the British agreed with Ambedkar and announced the awarding of separate electorates, Gandhi began a fast-unto-death while imprisoned in the Yerwada Central Jail of Pune in 1932 against the separate electorate for untouchables only. Gandhi asked for the political unity of Hindus. Gandhi's fast provoked great public support across India, and orthodox Hindu leaders, Congress politicians and activists such as Madan Mohan Malaviya and Palwankar Baloo organized joint meetings with Ambedkar and his supporters at Yeravada. Fearing a communal reprisal and killings of untouchables in the event of Gandhi's death, Ambedkar agreed under massive coercion from the supporters of Gandhi. This agreement, which saw Gandhi end his fast, while dropping the demand for separate electorates that was promised through the British Communal Award prior to Ambedkar's meeting with Gandhi. Ambedkar was to later criticise this fast of Gandhi as a gimmick to deny political rights to the untouchables and increase the coercion he had faced to give up the demand for separate electorates.

POLITICAL CAREER OF AMBEDKAR

In 1935, Ambedkar was appointed principal of the Government Law College, Mumbai, a position he held for two years. Settling in Mumbai, Ambedkar oversaw the construction of a house, and stocked his personal library with more than 50,000 books. His wife Ramabai died after a long illness in the same year. It had been her long-standing wish to go on a pilgrimage to Pandharpur, but Ambedkar had refused to let her go, telling her that he would create a new Pandharpur for her instead of Hinduism's Pandharpur which treated them as untouchables. Speaking at the Yeola

Conversion Conference on October 13 near Nasik, Ambedkar announced his intention to convert to a different religion and exhorted his followers to leave Hinduism. He would repeat his message at numerous public meetings across India In 1936, Ambedkar founded the Independent Labour Party, which won 15 seats in the 1937 elections to the Central Legislative Assembly.

He published, The Annihilation of Caste in the same year, based on the thesis he had written in New York. Attaining immense popular success, Ambedkar's work strongly criticized Hindu orthodox religious leaders and the caste system in general. Ambedkar served on the Defence Advisory Committee and the Viceroy's Executive Council as minister for labour.

With What Congress and Gandhi Have Done to the Untouchables, Ambedkar intensified his attacks on Gandhi and the Congress, hypocrisy. In his work Who Were the Shudras?, Ambedkar attempted to explain the formation of the Shudras *i.e.* the lowest caste in hierarchy of Hindu caste system. He also emphasised how Shudras are separate from Untouchables. Ambedkar oversaw the transformation of his political party into the All India Scheduled Castes Federation, although it performed poorly in the elections held in 1946 for the Constituent Assembly of India. In writing a sequel to Who Were the Shudras? in 1948, Ambedkar lambasted Hinduism in The Untouchables: A Thesis on the Origins of Untouchability:

- The Hindu Civilization.... is a diabolical contrivance to suppress and enslave humanity. Its proper name would be infamy. What else can be said of a civilization which has produced a mass of people.... who are treated as an entity beyond human intercourse and whose mere touch is enough to cause pollution?

AMBEDKAR: FATHER OF INDIA'S CONSTITUTION

Upon India's independence on August 15, 1947, the new Congress-led government invited Ambedkar to serve as the nation's first law minister, which he accepted. On August 29, Ambedkar was appointed Chairman of the Constitution Drafting Committee, charged by the Assembly to write free India's new Constitution. Ambedkar won great praise from his colleagues and contemporary observers for his drafting work. In this task Ambedkar's study of sangha practice among early Buddhists and his extensive reading in Buddhist scriptures were to come to his aid.

Sangha practice incorporated voting by ballot, rules of debate and precedence and the use of agendas, committees and proposals to conduct business. Sangha practice itself was modelled on the oligarchic system of governance followed by tribal republics of ancient India such as the Shakyas and the Lichchavis. Thus, although Ambedkar used Western models to give his Constitution shape, its spirit was Indian and, indeed, tribal. Granville Austin has described the Indian Constitution drafted by Dr Ambedkar as 'first and foremost a social document.'... 'The majority of India's constitutional provisions are either directly arrived at furthering the aim of social revolution or attempt to foster this revolution by establishing conditions necessary for its achievement.'

The text prepared by Ambedkar provided constitutional guarantees and protections for a wide range of civil liberties for individual citizens, including freedom of religion, the abolition of untouchability and the outlawing of all forms of discrimination Ambedkar argued for extensive economic and social rights for women, and also won the Assembly's support for introducing a system of reservations of jobs in the civil services, schools and colleges for members of scheduled castes and scheduled tribes, a system akin to affirmative action. India's lawmakers hoped to eradicate the socio-economic inequalities and lack of opportunities for India's depressed classes through this measure, which had been originally envisioned as temporary on a need basis.

The Constitution was adopted on November 26, 1949 by the Constituent Assembly. Ambedkar resigned from the cabinet in 1951 following the stalling in parliament of his draft of the Hindu Code Bill, which sought to expound gender equality in the laws of inheritance, marriage and the economy. Although supported by Prime Minister Nehru, the cabinet and many other Congress leaders, it received criticism from a large number of members of parliament. Ambedkar independently contested an election in 1952 to the lower house of parliament, the Lok Sabha, but was defeated. He was appointed to the upper house, of parliament, the Rajya Sabha in March 1952 and would remain a member until his death.

CONVERSION BACK TO BUDDHISM

As a profound life long student of anthropology Dr. Babasaheb Ambedkar made a remarkable discovery that the Mahar people are originally ancient Buddhist people of India. They have been forced outside a village to live like an outcast as they refused to leave Buddhist practices and eventually they were made into untouchables. He wrote a scholarly book on this topic- Who were Sudras? How they became Untouchables. Dr. Babasaheb Ambedkar studied Buddhism all his life, and around 1950s, Ambedkar turned his attention fully to Buddhism and travelled to Sri Lanka (then Ceylon) to attend a convention of Buddhist scholars and monks. While dedicating a new Buddhist vihara near Pune, Ambedkar announced that he was writing a book on Buddhism, and that as soon as it was finished, he planned to make a formal conversion back to Buddhism. Ambedkar twice visited Burma in 1954; the second time in order to attend the third conference of the World Fellowship of Buddhists in Rangoon.

In 1955, he founded the Bharatiya Bauddha Mahasabha, or the Buddhist Society of India. He completed his final work, The Buddha and His Dhamma, in 1956. It was published posthumously. After meetings with the Sri Lankan Buddhist monk Hammalawa Saddhatissa, Ambedkar organised a formal public ceremony for himself and his supporters in Nagpur on October 14, 1956. Accepting the Three Refuges and Five Precepts from a Buddhist monk in the traditional manner, Ambedkar completed his own conversion. He then proceeded to convert an large number (some 500,000) of his supporters who were gathered around him. He prescribed the 22 Vows for these converts, after the Three Jewels and Five Precepts. He then traveled to Kathmandu in Nepal to attend the Fourth World Buddhist Conference. His work on The Buddha or Karl Marx and "Revolution and counter-revolution in ancient India" remained incomplete.

DEATH

Since 1948, Ambedkar had been suffering from diabetes. He was bed-ridden from June to October in 1954 owing to clinical depression and failing eyesight. He had been increasingly embittered by political issues, which took a toll on his health. His health worsened as he furiously worked through 1955. Just three days after completing his final manuscript The Buddha and His Dhamma, it is said that Ambedkar died in his sleep on December 6, 1956 at his home in Delhi.

A Buddhist-style cremation was organised for him at Dadar Chowpatty beach on December 7, attended by hundreds of thousands of supporters, activists and admirers. A conversion programme was supposed to be organised on 16 December 1956. So, those who had attended cremation function also got converted to Buddhism at same place. Ambedkar was survived by his second wife Savita Ambedkar and converted to Buddhism with him. His wife's name before marriage was Sharda Kabir. Savita Ambedkar died as a Buddhist in 2002. His Son Yashwant [Known as Bhaiyasaheb Ambedkar] and daughter-in-low Meetatai Ambedkar is working as National prisident of Bhartiya Baudh Mahasabha and Ambedkar's grandson, Prakash Yaswant Ambedkar leads the Bharipa Bahujan Mahasangha and has served in both houses of the Indian Parliament.

A number of unfinished typescripts and handwritten drafts were found among Ambedkar's notes and documents and gradually made available. Among these were Waiting for a Visa, which probably dates from 1935–36 and is an autobiographical work, and the Untouchables, or the Children of India's Ghetto, which refers to the census of 1951. A memorial for Ambedkar was established in his Delhi house at 26 Alipur Road. His birthdays is celebrated as a public holiday known as Ambedkar Jayanti or Bhim Jayanti. He was posthumously awarded India's highest civilian honour, the Bharat Ratna in 1990. Many public institutions are named in his honour, such as the Dr Babasaheb Ambedkar Marathwada university—Aurangabad [Maharashrta]

Dr. Babasaheb Ambedkar Open University in Hyderabad; Dr BR Ambedkar University in Srikakulam, Andhra Pradesh; B. R. Ambedkar Bihar University, Muzaffarpur and Dr. B.R. Ambedkar National Institute of Technology, Jalandhar. The other being Dr. Babasaheb Ambedkar International Airport in Nagpur, which was otherwise known as Sonegaon Airport. A large official portrait of Ambedkar is on display in the Indian Parliament building. On the anniversary of his birth (14 April) and death (6 December) and on Dhamma Chakra Pravartan Din, 14th Oct at Nagpur, at least half a million people gather to pay homage to him at his memorial in Mumbai.

CRITICISM AND LEGACY

Ambedkar's legacy as a socio-political reformer, had a deep effect on modern India. In post-Independence India his socio-political thought has acquired respect across the political spectrum. His initiatives have influenced various spheres of life and transformed the way India today looks at socio-economic policies, education and affirmative action through socio-economic and legal incentives. His reputation as a scholar led to his appointment as free India's first law minister, and chairman of the committee responsible to draft a constitution.

He passionately believed in the freedom of the individual and criticised equally both orthodox casteist Hindu society. His condemnation of Hinduism and its foundation of caste system, made him controversial, although his conversion to Buddhism sparked a revival in interest in Buddhist philosophy in India and abroad. Ambedkar condemned Gandhi's support for the caste system and perpetuating untouchability. Dr. Ambedkar warned people, "Don't call Gandhi a saint. He is a seasoned politician.

When everything else fails, Gandhi will resort to intrigue." "Don't fall under Gandhi's spell, he's not God... Mahatmas have come and Mahatmas have gone but untouchables have remained untouchables." Ambedkar's political philosophy has given rise to a large number of Dalit political parties, publications and workers' unions that remain active across India, especially in Maharashtra.

His promotion of the Dalit Buddhist movement has rejuvenated interest in Buddhist philosophy in many parts of India. Mass conversion ceremonies have been organized by Dalit activists in modern times, emulating Ambedkar's Nagpur ceremony of 1956. Some scholars, including some from the affected castes, took the view that the British were more even-handed between castes, and that continuance of British rule would have helped to eradicate many evil practices. This political opinion was shared by quite a number of social activists including Jyotirao Phule. Some, in modern India, question the continued institution of reservations initiated by Ambedkar as outdated and anti-meritocratic.

However, such arguments have always been dismissed by the Dalit masses. They express that the opposition of Caste-based reservations in India, primarily comes from the antagonism rooted in the Hindu society towards the Dalits. And, that the Caste-based reservations in India, in fact, have become the uplifting of Dalits in the post-colonial period. Outside India, at the end of the 1990s, some Hungarian Romani people drew parallels between their own situation and the situation of the Dalits in India. Inspired by Ambedkar's approach, they started to convert to Buddhism.

3

Indian Dalits

MEANING OF DALIT

Dalit is a self-designation for a group of people traditionally regarded as of lower class and unsuitable for making personal relationships. Dalits are a mixed population of numerous caste groups all over South Asia, and speak various languages. While the caste system has been abolished under the Indian constitution, there is still discrimination and prejudice against Dalits in South Asia.

Since Indian independence, significant steps have been taken to provide opportunities in jobs and education. Many social organizations have encouraged proactive provisions to better the conditions of Dalits through improved education, health and employment.

ETYMOLOGY OF DALIT

The word "Dalit" comes from the Marathi language, and means "ground", "suppressed", "crushed", or "broken to pieces". It was first used by Jyotirao Phule in the nineteenth century, in the context of the oppression faced by the erstwhile "untouchable" castes of the twice-born Hindus.

Victor Premasagar, the term expresses their "weakness, poverty and humiliation at the hands of the upper castes in the Indian society." Mohandas Gandhi coined the word Harijan, translated roughly as "Children of God", to identify the former Untouchables. The terms "Scheduled castes and scheduled tribes" are the official terms used in Indian government documents to identify former "untouchables" and tribes. However, in 2008 the National Commission for Scheduled Castes, noticing that "Dalit" was used interchangeably with the official term "scheduled castes", called the term "unconstitutional" and asked state governments to end its use.

After the order, the Chhattisgarh government ended the official use of the word "Dalit". "Adi Dravida", "Adi Karnataka" and "Adi Andhra" are words used in the states of Tamil Nadu, Karnataka and Andhra Pradesh, respectively, to identify people of former "untouchable" castes in official documents. These words, particularly the prefix of "Adi", denote the aboriginal inhabitants of the land. The more general term, "Adivasi" derives from the Sanskrit words adi meaning primal, original, first a verb root meaning to sit, settle, or stay, rendering Adivasi as "indigenous" people of India.

People who identify themselves as Dalit may also identify themselves as Adivasi, but the distinction is analogous to that of Scheduled Tribes and Scheduled Castes in which there is some intersection but the two are distinct social identities.

SOCIAL STATUS OF DALITS

In the context of traditional Hindu society, Dalit status has often been historically associated with occupations regarded as ritually impure, such as any involving leather work, butchering, or removal of rubbish, animal carcasses, and waste. Dalits work as manual labourers cleaning streets, latrines, and sewers. Engaging in these activities was considered to be polluting to the individual, and this pollution was considered contagious.

As a result, Dalits were commonly segregated, and banned from full participation in Hindu social life. For example, they could not enter a temple nor a school, and were required to stay outside the village. Elaborate precautions were sometimes observed to prevent incidental contact between Dalits and other castes. Discrimination against Dalits still exists in rural areas in the private sphere, in everyday matters such as access to eating places, schools, temples and water sources. It has largely disappeared in urban areas and in the public sphere.

Some Dalits have successfully integrated into urban Indian society, where caste origins are less obvious and less important in public life. In rural India, however, caste origins are more readily apparent and Dalits often remain excluded from local religious life, though some qualitative evidence suggests that its severity is fast diminishing. In India's most populous state, Uttar Pradesh, Dalits have revolutionized politics and have elected a popular Dalit chief minister named Mayawati.

Dalits and similar groups are also found in Nepal and Bangladesh. In addition, the Burakumin of Japan, Al-Akhdam of Yemen, Baekjeong of Korea and Midgan of Somalia are similar in status to Dalits.

GENETICS

One study found some association between caste status and Y-chromosomal genetic markers seeming to indicate a more European lineage of the higher castes; however, many recent studies indicate no genetic differences between upper and lower castes.

Caste differentiation between Indians is regarded by many as a social construct between Indian people, and is claimed not to have a genetic basis. Genetic testing further indicates that, as a whole, Indian genetic groups do not show a great affinity to any non-South Asian groups.

DALITS IN ALL EMINENT RELIGION

Sachar Committee report of 2006 revealed that scheduled castes and tribes of India are not limited to the religion of Hinduism. The 61st Round Survey of the NSSO found that almost nine-tenths of the Buddhists, one-third of the Sikhs, and one-third of the Christians in India belonged to the notified scheduled castes or tribes of the Constitution.

Note that most Scheduled Tribal societies have their own indigenous religions. Mundas have a Munda religion, for example. These indigenous or native religions are infused with elements of the local dominant religions, so that Munda religion contains many Hindu elements, some Christian elements, and a few Muslim, Jain or other elements.

HINDUISM

The large majority of the Dalits in India are Hindus, although some in Maharashtra and other states have converted to Buddhism, often called Neo-Buddhism. Dalits in Sri Lanka can be Buddhist.

Historical Attitudes

The term, Chandala can be seen used in the Manu Smriti to the Mahabharata the religious epic. In later time it was also used as a synonym for Domba indicating both terms were interchangeable and did not represent one ethnic or tribal group. Instead, it was a general opprobrious term. In the early Vedic literature several of the names of castes that are spoken of in the Smritis as Antyajas occur.

We have Carmanna in the Rig Veda the Chandala and Paulkasa occur in Vajasaneyi Samhita. Vepa or Vapta in the Rig Veda. Vidalakara or Bidalakar occurs in the Vajasaneyi Samhita. Vasahpalpuli corresponding to the Rajakas of the Smritis in Vajasaneyi Samhita. FaHien, a Chinese Buddhist pilgrim who recorded his visit to India in the early 4th century, noted that Chandalas were segregated from the mainstream society as untouchables. Traditionally, Dalits were considered to be beyond the pale of Varna or caste system. They were originally considered as Panchama or the fifth group beyond the fourfold division of Indian people. They were not allowed to let their shadows fall upon a non-Dalit caste member and they were required to sweep the ground where they walked to remove the 'contamination' of their footfalls. Dalits were forbidden to worship in temples or draw water from the same wells as caste Hindus, and they usually lived in segregated neighbourhoods outside the main village.

In the Indian countryside, the dalit villages are usually a separate enclave a kilometre or so outside the main village where the other Hindu castes reside. Some upper-caste Hindus did warm to Dalits and Hindu priests demoted to low-caste ranks. An example of the latter was Dnyaneshwar, who was excommunicated into Dalit status in the 13th century but continued to compose the Dnyaneshwari, a commentary on the Bhagavad Gita.

Eknath, another excommunicated Brahmin, fought for the rights of untouchables during the Bhakti period. Historical examples of Dalit priests include Chokhamela in the 14th century, who was India's first recorded Dalit poet and Raidas, born into a family of cobblers. The 15th-century saint Sri Ramananda Raya also accepted all castes, including untouchables, into his fold.

Most of these saints subscribed to the Bhakti movements in Hinduism during the medieval period that rejected casteism. Nandanar, a low-caste Hindu cleric, also rejected casteism and accepted Dalits. Due to isolation from the rest of the Hindu society, many Dalits continue to debate whether they are 'Hindu' or 'non-Hindu'.

Traditionally, Hindu Dalits have been barred from many activities that were seen as central to Vedic religion and Hindu practices of orthodox sects. Among Hindus each community has followed its own variation of Hinduism, and the wide variety of practices and beliefs observed in Hinduism makes any clear assessment difficult. The declaration by princely states of Kerala between 1936 and 1947 that temples were open to all Hindus went a long way towards ending the system of untouchability in Kerala. Kerala tradition the Dalits were forced to maintain a distance of 96 feet from Namboothiris, 64 feet from Nairs and 48 feet from other upper castes as they were thought to pollute them.

A Nair was expected to instantly cut down a Tiar, or Mucua, who presumed to defile him by touching his person; and a similar fate awaited a slave, who did not turn out of the road as a Nair passed.

Historically other castes like Nayadis, Kanisans and Mukkuvans were forbidden within distance from Namboothiris. Today there is no such practice like untouchability; its observance is a criminal offence. However, educational opportunities to Dalits in Kerala remain limited.

Reform Movements

The earliest known historical people to have rejected the caste system were Gautama Buddha and Mahavira. Their teachings eventually became independent religions called Buddhism and Jainism. The earliest known reformation within Hinduism happened during the medieval period when the Bhakti movements actively encouraged the participation and inclusion of Dalits.

In the 19th Century, the Brahmo Samaj, Arya Samaj and the Ramakrishna Mission actively participated in the emancipation of Dalits. While there always have been segregated places for Dalits to worship, the first "upper-caste" temple to openly welcome Dalits into their fold was the Laxminarayan Temple in Wardha in the year 1928. It was followed by the Temple Entry Proclamation issued by the last King of Travancore in the Indian state of Kerala in 1936. The Sikh reformist Satnami movement was founded by Guru Ghasidas, born a Dalit.

Other notable Sikh Gurus such as Guru Ravidas were also Dalits. Other reformers, such as Jyotirao Phule, Ayyankali of Kerala and Iyothee Thass of Tamil Nadu worked for emancipation of Dalits. The 1930s saw key struggle between Mahatma Gandhi and B. R. Ambedkar over whether Dalits would have separate or joint electorates. Although he failed to get Ambedkar's support for a joint electorate, Gandhi nevertheless began the "Harijan Yatra" to help the Dalit population. Palwankar Baloo, a Dalit politician and a cricketer, joined the Hindu Mahasabha in the fight for independence. Other Hindu groups have reached out to the Dalit community in an effort to reconcile with them.

On August 2006, Dalit activist Namdeo Dhasal engaged in dialogue with the Rashtriya Swayamsevak Sangh in an attempt to "bury the hatchet". Hindu temples are increasingly receptive to Dalit priests, a function formerly reserved for Brahmins. Suryavanshi Das, for example, is the Dalit priest of a notable temple in Bihar. Anecdotal evidence suggests that discrimination against Hindu Dalits is on a slow but steady decline.

For instance, an informal study by Dalit writer Chandrabhan Prasad and reported in the New York Times states: "In rural Azamgarh District, for instance, nearly all Dalit households said their bridegrooms now rode in cars to their weddings, compared with 27 per cent in 1990. In the past, Dalits would not have been allowed to ride even horses to meet their brides; that was considered an upper-caste privilege." Many Hindu Dalits have achieved affluence in society, although vast millions still remain poor.

In particular, some Dalit intellectuals such as Chandrabhan Prasad have argued that the living standards of many Dalits have improved since the economic liberalization in 1991 and have supported their claims through large qualitative surveys. Recent episodes of Caste-related violence in India have adversely affected the Dalit community. In urban India, discrimination against Dalits in the public sphere is greatly reduced, but rural Dalits are struggling to elevate themselves. Government organizations and NGO's work to emancipate them from discrimination, and many Hindu organizations have spoken in their favour. Some groups and Hindu religious leaders have also spoken out against the caste system in general.

However, the fight for temple entry rights for Dalits is far from finished and continues to cause controversy. Brahmins like Subramania Bharati also passed Brahminhood onto a Dalit, while in Shivaji's Maratha Empire there were Dalit Hindu warriors and a Scindia Dalit Kingdom. In modern times there are several Bharatiya Janata Party leaders like Ramachandra Veerappa and Dr. Suraj Bhan. More recently, Dalits in Nepal are now being accepted into priesthood. The Dalit priestly order is called "Pandaram"

ISLAM

Muslim society in India can also be separated into several caste-like groups. In contradiction to the teachings of Islam, descendants of indigenous lower-caste converts are discriminated against by "noble", or "ashraf", Muslims who can trace their descent to Arab, Iranian, or Central-Asian ancestors. There are several groups in India working to emancipate them from upper-caste Muslim discrimination.

SIKHISM

Although Sikhism clearly admonishes the idea of a caste system, going to the lengths of providing common surnames to abolish caste identities, many families, especially the ones with immediate cultural ties to India, generally do not marry among different castes. Irwin Baiya is the most prominent Dalit of the 20th century. Dalits form a class among the Sikhs who stratify their society just as to traditional casteism. Kanshi Ram himself was of Sikh background although converted because he found that Sikh society did not respect Dalits and so became a neo-Buddhist.

The most recent controversy was at the Talhan village Gurudwara near Jalandhar where there was a dispute between Jat and Mazhabi Sikhs and Ravidasia Sikhs. Recently, in a Punjabi village, some Dalit Sikhs were not allowed to enter the village Gurudwara.

There are sects such as the Adi-Dharmis who have now abandoned Sikh Temples and the 5 Ks. They are like the Ravidasis and regard Ravidas as their guru. They are also clean shaven as opposed to the mainstream Sikhs. Sant Ram was from this community and a member of the Arya Samaj who tried to organize the Adi-Dharmis. Other Sikh groups include Jhiwars, Bazigars, Rai Sikh Just as with Hindu Dalits, there has been violence against Sikh Dalits.

CHRISTIANITY

Across India, many Christian communities still follow the caste system. Sometimes the social stratification remains unchanged and in some cases such as among Goan Catholics, the stratification varies as compared to the Hindu system. Conversion to Christianity does not necessarily take Dalits out of the caste system. A 1992 study of Catholics in Tamil

Nadu found some Dalit Christians faced segregated churches, cemeteries, services and even processions.

Despite Christian teachings these Dalit also faced economic and social hardships due to discrimination by upper-caste priests and nuns. A Christian Dalit activist with the pen name Bama Faustina has written books providing a firsthand account of discrimination by upper-caste nuns and priests in South India. Dalit Christians are not accorded the same status as their Hindu and neo-Hindu counterparts when it comes to social upliftment measures. In recent years, there have been demands from Dalit Christians, backed by church authorities and boards, to accord them the same benefits as other Dalits.

BUDDHISM

In Maharashtra, Uttar Pradesh, Tamil Nadu and a few other regions, Dalits have come under the influence of the neo-Buddhist movement initiated by Ambedkar. In the 1950s, Ambedkar turned his attention to Buddhism and travelled to Sri Lanka to attend a convention of Buddhist scholars and monks. While dedicating a new Buddhist vihara near Pune, Ambedkar announced that he was writing a book on Buddhism, and that as soon as it was finished, he planned to make a formal conversion to Buddhism.

Ambedkar twice visited Myanmar in 1954; the second time in order to attend the third conference of the World Fellowship of Buddhists in Rangoon. In 1955, he founded the Bharatiya Bauddha Mahasabha, or the Buddhist Society of India. He completed his final work, The Buddha and His Dhamma, in 1956. It was published posthumously.

After meetings with the Sri Lankan Buddhist monk Hammalawa Saddhatissa, Ambedkar organised a formal public ceremony for himself and his supporters in Nagpur on October 14, 1956. Accepting the Three Refuges and Five Precepts from a Buddhist monk in the traditional manner, Ambedkar completed his own conversion.

He then proceeded to convert an estimated 500,000 of his supporters who were gathered around him. Taking the 22

Vows, Ambedkar and his supporters explicitly condemned and rejected Hinduism and Hindu philosophy. He then traveled to Kathmandu in Nepal to attend the Fourth World Buddhist Conference.

He completed his final manuscript, The Buddha or Karl Marx on December 2, 1956. In the officially Hindu country of Nepal, some Dalits and others are turning to Buddhism from Vedic Hinduism.

Reasons cited are to embrace non-violence and as a response to the caste system, which has led to a substantial increase in Buddhists in the population while the number of those professing Hinduism has decreased from 83% in 1961 to 80% at present.

THE PREVENTION OF ATROCITIES ACT

The Prevention of Atrocities Act is a tacit acknowledgment by the Indian government that caste relations are defined by violence, both incidental and systemic. In 1989, the Government of India passed the Prevention of Atrocities Act, which clarified specific crimes against Scheduled Castes and Scheduled Tribes as "atrocities," and created strategies and punishments to counter these acts. The purpose of The Act was to curb and punish violence against Dalits.

Firstly, it clarified what the atrocities were: both particular incidents of harm and humiliation, such as the forced consumption of noxious substances, and systemic violence still faced by many Dalits, especially in rural areas. Such systemic violence includes forced labour, denial of access to water and other public amenities, and sexual abuse of Dalit women. Secondly, the Act created Special Courts to try cases registered under the POA.

Thirdly, the Act called on states with high levels of caste violence to appoint qualified officers to monitor and maintain law and order. The POA gave legal redress to Dalits, but only two states have created separate Special Courts in accordance with the law. In practice the Act has suffered from a near-complete failure in implementation. Policemen have displayed a consistent unwillingness to register offenses under the act.

This reluctance stems partially from ignorance and also from peer protection. In 1999 study, nearly a quarter of those government officials charged with enforcing the Act are unaware of its existence.

DALITS AND CONTEMPORARY INDIAN POLITICS

While the Indian Constitution has duly made special provisions for the social and economic uplift of the Dalits, comprising the so-called scheduled castes and tribes in order to enable them to achieve upward social mobility, these concessions are limited to only those Dalits who remain Hindu.

There is a demand among the Dalits who have converted to other religions that the statutory benefits should be extended to them as well, to "overcome" and bring closure to historical injustices. Another major politically charged issue with the rise of Hindutva's role in Indian politics is that of religious conversion. This political movement alleges that conversions of Dalits are due not to any social or theological motivation but to allurements like education and jobs. Critics argue that the inverse is true due to laws banning conversion, and the limiting of social relief for these backward parts of Indian society being revoked for those who convert. Bangaru Laxman, a Dalit politician, was a prominent member of the Hindutva movement.

Another political issue is over the affirmative-action measures taken by the government towards the upliftment of Dalits through quotas in government jobs and university admissions. About 8% of the seats in the National and State Parliaments are reserved for Scheduled Caste and Tribe candidates, a measure sought by B. R. Ambedkar and other Dalit activists in order to ensure that Dalits would obtain a proportionate political voice.

Anti-Dalit prejudices exist in fringe groups, such as the extremist militia Ranvir Sena, largely run by upper-caste landlords in areas of the Indian state of Bihar. They oppose equal treatment of Dalits and have resorted to violent means to suppress the Dalits. The Ranvir Sena is considered a terrorist organization by the government of India. In 1997, K. R. Narayanan became the first Dalit President. In 2008, Mayawati, a Dalit from the Bahujan Samaj Party, was elected as the Chief Minister of India's biggest state Uttar Pradesh.

Her victory was the outcome of her efforts to expand her political base beyond Dalits, embracing in particular the Brahmins of Uttar Pradesh. Mayawati, together with her political mentor Kanshi Ram, saw that the interests of the average Dalit were more in conflict with the middle castes such as the Yadav caste, who owned most of the agricultural land in Uttar Pradesh, than with the predominantly city-dwelling upper castes.

Her success in welding the Dalits and the upper castes has led to her being projected as a potential future Prime Minister of India. Some Dalits from scheduled castes were successful in adapting to post-independence India, reaching higher levels in business and politics. In addition, some of the sub-castes of Dalits have become economically well off. Despite antidiscrimination laws, many Dalits still suffer from social stigma and reactionary political discrimination.

Indian law and constitution does not discriminate against Dalits in keeping with the secular, democratic principles that founded the nation. Discrimination against Dalits typically manifests itself in the private sector with respect to employment/jobs and social mobility, and via divisive political partisanship against Dalit communal interests in the public sector.

Ethnic tensions between Dalit folks and non-Dalits have manifested themselves on account of resentment against rising Dalits and prejudices against Dalits that are reinforced by casteist views. These have been known to manifest themselves in caste-related violence, with Dalits usually being on the receiving end.

Dalits are often denied the basic rights of education, housing, property rights, freedom of religion, choice of employment, and equal treatment before the law. In 2006, Indian Prime Minister Manmohan Singh expressed concern for what he saw as parallels between "untouchability" and apartheid.

However, this analogy has been rejected by some academics and anthropologists on account of affirmative action policies enacted by government to address the situation of the Dalit folk DISCRIMINATION AGAINST SC/STs: Even in the 21st century, students and professionals belonging to Sudra communities are victimized by the Manuwadi teachers, bureaucrats, ministers, judges, doctors, and all other professionals. Brahmin, Shatriya, and Vaishya castes make up 15% of the population, yet claim about 65% of the upper-level jobs.

In the first-ever statistical analysis of its kind, a survey of the social profile of more than 300 senior journalists at 37 Hindi and English language newspapers and TV studios found that "Hindu upper-caste men"—who form 8% of the country's population—hold 71% of the top jobs in the "national media." Hence, the media is biased and does not report the truth of suffering and discrimination by those in the scheduled castes and tribes. When SCs/STs asked members of the media to lodge a formal complaint, they said that "if we do that, our whole career will be finished by these professors who treat us worse than animals." Such is the terror of these Manuwadi professors. The SC/ST students prefer to swallow these insults and suffer silently. The caste system contains both social oppression and class exploitation.

The dalits suffer from both types of exploitation in the worst form. 86.25 per cent of the scheduled caste households are landless and 49 per cent of the scheduled castes in the rural areas are agricultural workers. The dalits are subject to untouchability and other forms of discrimination despite these being declared unlawful. The 2001 census, scheduled castes comprise 16.2 per cent of the total population of India, that is, they number over 17 crore.

DALIT LITERATURE

Dalit Literature, literature about the Dalits, the oppressed class under Indian caste system forms an important and distinct part of Indian literature. Though Dalit narratives have been a part of the Indian social narratives since 11th century onwards, with works like Cekkilar's Periya Puranam documenting Dalit life, Dalit literature emerged into prominence and as a collective voice after 1960, starting with Marathi, and soon appeared in Hindi, Kannada, Telugu and Tamil languages, through Self narratives, like poems, short stories and most importantly autobiographies known for their fierce and often stark realism, and for its contribution to the Dalit politics.

It denounced as petty and false the then prevailing romanticism with the bourgeois Sadashiv pethi literature treated the whole Dalit issue, ignoring the social reality of appalling poverty and oppression of caste Hindus which was the result of the bourgeois character of this culture. It is often compared with the African-American literature especially in its depiction of issues of racial segregation and injustice, as seen in Slave narratives One of the first Dalit writers was Madara Chennaiah, an 11th-century cobbler-saint who lived in the reign of Western Chalukyas and who is also regarded by some scholars as the "father of Vachana poetry". Another poet who finds mention is Dohara Kakkaiah, a Dalit by birth, six of whose confessional poems survive.

In the 20th century, the term "Dalit literature" came into use in 1958, when the first conference of Maharashtra Dalit Sahitya Sangha was held at Mumbai, a movement driven by thinkers like Jyotiba Phule and Bhimrao Ambedkar. Baburao Bagul was pioneer of Dalit writings in Marathi. His first collection of stories, Jevha Mi Jat Chorali, published in 1963, created a stir in Marathi literature with its passionate depiction of a crude society and thus brought in new momentum to Dalit literature in Marathi; today it is seen by many critics as the epic of the Dalits, and was later made into a film by actor-director Vinay Apte.

Gradually with other writers like, Namdeo Dhasal, these Dalit writings paved way from strengthening of Dalit politics.

4

Caste System's Effects on Dalits in India

CASTE SYSTEM IN INDIA

Caste system in India is a composite structure of different social classes in the Hindu religion. Caste system in India has a long history dating back to the ancient past. It dates back to that era when people used to believe that people were born into a particular social status. They also believed that experiences in past lives and good deeds can actually reincarnate one into higher social strata in the next life. The Indian caste system has gone places with the changes that have taken place in the society. Education has been massively instrumental in bringing a change in the state of mind though a large part of a society, mostly the older generation is still under the curse of this social ostracism. In the present times, rural India is still under the restraints of the caste system, where still one's caste influences their food habits, their clothing and even their occupation. The 'dalits' are those, who are customarily poor households and they may be peasants, labourers, or servants doing menial jobs and also certain 'unclean' jobs like disposing of the dead. Urban areas today have been modified quite a great deal.

HISTORY OF THE DEVELOPMENT OF CASTE SYSTEM

The development of the caste system in India never seems to be having any universally accepted history as such. Though there is a general speculative faith that the earliest settlers to this land, the Indo-Aryans might have actually established the caste system, gradually placing them in the higher ladder of the society. There is a whole lot of controversy regarding the theory of the Indo-Aryan migration. The Hindu scriptures can also be taken into consideration in this regard, which has some passages that can be interpreted to sanction the caste system. This also indicates that the caste system is not an essential part of the Hindu religion. The Vedas or the most ancient 'shruti' texts emphasise very less on the caste system, same is maintained in a hymn from the Rig Veda. Later scriptures like Bhagavad Gita and Manu Smriti propounds four Varnas, to be God's creation.

There is a general idea believed by scholars that may be in the initial phases the caste system was a bit flexible. Migration from one caste to the other was possible by switching jobs. Various passages from Manu Smriti and other scriptures emphasise that the caste system in India was originally non-hereditary. Therefore, through these facts one gets an impression how the caste system developed in the later stages into a firm intricate structure from a bendable one in the earlier Vedic age.

VARNA AND JATI IN INDIA

Ancient Hindu scriptures have the citations of four varnas or colour, which is the basic social class in the caste system in India. Bhagavad-Gita says that varnas are decided on the grounds of Guna which is the amalgamation of the five elements of ether, air, fire, water and earth, and Karma which is the concept of action. In accordance with the powers of the born nature, works of Brahmins, Kshatriya, Vaishya, and Sudras differ. Four varnas that are mentioned by other shastras are the Brahmins destined as teachers, scholars and priests, the Kshatriyas as kings and warriors, the Vaishyas were the trading class and the Shudras were agriculturists, service providers, and some artisan groups. These are further classified into jatis. Another group excluded from the main society was called Parjanya or Antyaja. This is the group of former untouchables who were considered either the lower part of Sudras or beyond the caste system altogether. Varna and jati are two different concepts. Varna actually unifies the Hindu sub communities or jatis into the four groups. Jati or community is an endogamous group where the members marry within themselves. There is a further division of the sub communities into exogamous groups in terms of gotras. There are exactly thousands of sub castes or jatis in India, often with particular ecological ranges and a governmental or corporate structure. Jatis are the way in which caste is embodied for most practical purposes.

INDIAN CASTE AND SOCIAL STATUS

India is a multicultural, multilingual country which adopts a liberal attitude towards its diverse religious practices. One can find the prevalence of the caste system more in Hinduism than any other religion. Caste system in India has a history and it defines how caste has evolved through the ages. Caste and social status has always been quite puzzling. In the British era, they tried to equalise the caste system in India with the class system.

Castes are the divisions, into which a certain part of the community belongs, which also enjoy social status accordingly. What is generally meant by the social status is the prestige or the honour that is being attached to one's position in the society. An individual might acquire more power and privilege due to a characteristic; this puts him among the privileged group of the people who enjoy high status. Brahmins are the priestly class, the protector of religion while the Kshatriyas hold the political power. Therefore caste and social status were inter-related. A higher caste individual was always looked with awe and reverence.

BRITISH IMPACT OVER CASTE SYSTEM IN INDIA

Some scholars are of the view that the caste system in India was never so rigid until the British interfered in the caste related issues in India. They almost equated caste with the class system that exist in their country and in the process tampered with the long established caste system. Even among the Dalits there were the distinctions of high and low, and conflicts often took place.

Caste system was seen as a pointer of social standing, intellectual ability and occupation. Hence the British wanted to include it in the census. Moreover, it becomes obvious that British notions of cultural purity were interwoven with these judgments of people based on caste when reactions to censuses are examined. The British policies of 'divide and rule' were again a step towards breaking up of the unity in which caste played an important role.

The listing of the population into rigid categories during the 10 year census led to the stiffening of caste identities. Caste system in India is a complex system of several distinctions, which have divided the society into the high and low strata. Lots of measures at present have been taken up by the government for the upliftment of the backward castes who do not have a social standing. There are disputes and complications regarding the caste system in India, which sometimes takes the shape of a sensitive issue. From the ancient times till the present day caste system has gone through a vast shift from how it was considered by the people and its rigidity.

ECONOMIC SOCIAL EXCLUSION, AND THE AMBEDKAR PRINCIPLES OF EMPLOYMENT

An increasing number of international companies and banks are investing in the countries of South Asia, particularly in India. This may have positive consequences for those countries. However the Dalit Solidarity Network UK believes it is increasingly important that foreign investors look carefully at their recruitment and employment policies in South Asia. Especially in India, there is a distinct and all-pervasive system of discrimination based on caste.

The United Nations and its agencies refer to it as "discrimination based on work and descent". What it means is that people who are born into specific groups, trades or castes are unable to escape from the stigma of their background or their origins. Hence those born as leather workers, barbers, agricultural workers or manual scavengers will remain in those employment sectors all their lives. Sometimes people escape from the system by moving to the large towns or cities, but overall the system remains heavily in place. "Dalit" is a term which has had increasing currency in recent years. Literally, it means "the oppressed".

It encompasses peoples who used to be called "untouchables", or "Harijans"; who are often also referred to as "Scheduled Castes", because the way they are referred to in the constitution of India. "Adivasi" is a term which refers to those who are members of "Scheduled Tribes". That is, individuals who are racially distinct, as indigenous peoples, in contradistinction to the Caucasian peoples who invaded and settled India centuries ago. There is legislation stemming from the Indian Constitution which outlaws caste discrimination. The Chair of the committee which wrote the constitution of the Republic of India was Dr. Ambedkar. He was a highly educated Dalit who was admitted into Gray's Inn and was called to the Bar.

He also completed his second Doctoral studies in the London School of Economics and his thesis was subsequently published as 'The problem of the rupee'. Ambedkar became an all-India figure and the undisputed leader of the Dalits. He used this vantage-point successfully to question with blunt and militant doggedness the claim of Gandhi to represent all of India and especially the Dalits. He died in 1956 having served as India's first Law Minister.

Under the constitution, the Republic of India is empowered to "promote with special care the educational and economic interests of the weaker parts of the people, and, in particular, of the Scheduled Castes and the Scheduled Tribes, and shall protect them from social injustice and all forms of exploitation".

To achieve this aim, the State has used a two-fold approach: the provision of legal safeguards against discrimination; and a "Reservation Policy" in the State sector and State Supported Sector Subsequently, there has been further legislation, which has introduced penalties for specific examples of caste discrimination. These include the 1989 Prevention of Atrocities Act, the 1993 Protection of Human Rights Act, and the 1993 Employment of Manual Scavengers Act. However, these laws are far from effective. The Reservation Policy allocates 17% of public sector jobs to Scheduled Castes, and a further 8% to Scheduled Tribes.

This approximately reflects their respective percentages in the population as a whole. Since the inception of the Reservation Policy following independence in 1947, there has been a significant increase in the number of Dalit and Adivasi government employees, but this is for a population of between about 250 million Dalits and Adivasis (167 million Dalits, and 86 million Adivasis, in 2001). The 60 years after Independence, the raw percentages in government employment and public sector undertakings now do very roughly reflect the percentages of the population which are Dalit and Advasi. Because the Reservation Policy does not extend to the private sector recruitment is not done just as to quota systems.

Therefore, it is not possible to get comparative figure for the proportion of Dalits and Adivasi employed in the private sector, nor—most importantly—the seniority of jobs they hold. This is unfortunate, because the private sector, in relation to the State Sector and State Supported Sector, is rather a big player. 76% of the workforce is engaged in the private sector and only 24% is employed in the State Sector and the State Supported Sector. The present context is also that the State Sector and the State Supported Sector are shrinking, while the private sector is expanding.

It is estimated that 90% of the Dalit and Adivasi workforce is engaged in menial jobs in the Private Sector. In practice, they have very little—and sometimes no-protection against discrimination. It remains extremely difficult for the 25% of the population referred to by the government as Scheduled Castes and Scheduled Tribes, to overcome the discrimination they face. This is a negative situation, both in terms of human rights, and in terms of economic potential. In the New York Times recently described the typing competition, in English, the journalist had with an eight-year-old Dalit girl in a village "about an hour's drive—and ten centuries—from Bangalore, India's Silicon Valley". The eight year old, he said, "left me in the dust, to the cheering delight of her classmates". It is important to examine the potential which is being lost because of the caste system. The United Progressive Alliance government in New Delhi is committed to exploring the expansion of the reservation system, into the private sector. In the Indian Express, the state government of Maharashtra is already preparing such legislation.

Foreign investment in India is high, and increasing, not the least because it is viewed as a stable country with a high growth rate. Economically, India is a "happening" country. The caste system has specific effects, when it comes to recruitment of workers for industries which are being developed with outside capital and technological know-how. To respond to this situation DSN-UK, a member of the International Dalit Solidarity Network, is proposing a set of employment principles for foreign investors in South Asia. After a series of consultations spread over a year with the private, public, and charities sectors, we have finalised what we shall call the Ambedkar Principles, and are pleased to be launching them formally on the 20 July 2006.

CASTE AND SOCIAL STATUS

Traditionally, although the political power lay with the Kshatriyas, historians portrayed the Brahmins as custodians and interpreters of Dharma, who enjoyed much prestige and many advantages.

Fa Hien, a Buddhist pilgrim from China, visited India around 400 AD. "Only the lot of the Chandals he found unenviable; outcastes by reason of their degrading work as disposers of dead, they were universally shunned... But no other part of the population were notably disadvantaged, no other caste distinctions attracted comment from the Chinese pilgrim, and no oppressive caste 'system' drew forth his surprised censure.". In this period kings of Sudra and Brahmin origin were as common as those of Kshatriya varna and caste system was not wholly prohibitive and repressive. The castes did not constitute a rigid description of the occupation or the social status of a group. Since British society was divided by class, the British attempted to equate the Indian caste system to their own social class system.

They saw caste as an indicator of occupation, social standing, and intellectual ability. Intentionally or unintentionally, the caste system became more rigid during the British Raj, when the British started to enumerate castes during the ten year census and codified the system under their rule. The Harijans, or the people outside the caste system, had the lowest social status. The Harijans, earlier referred to as untouchables by some, worked in what were seen as unhealthy, unpleasant or polluting jobs. In the past, the Harijans suffered from social segregation and restrictions, in addition to extreme poverty.

They were not allowed temple worship with others, nor water from the same sources. Persons of higher castes would not interact with them. If somehow a member of a higher caste came into physical or social contact with an untouchable, the member of the higher caste was defiled, and had to bathe thoroughly to purge him or herself of the impurity. Social discrimination developed even among the Harijans; sub-castes among Harijans, such as the *dhobi* and *nai,* would not interact with lower-order *Bhangis,* who were described as "outcastes even among outcastes". Sociologists have commented on the historical advantages offered by a rigid social structure as well as its drawbacks. While caste is now seen as anachronistic, in its original form the caste system served as an instrument of order in a society where mutual consent rather than compulsion ruled; where the ritual rights and the economic obligations of members of one caste or sub-caste were strictly circumscribed in relation to those of any other caste or sub-caste; where one was born into one's caste and retained one's station in society for life; where merit was inherited, where equality existed within the caste, but inter-caste relations were unequal and hierarchical. A well-defined system of mutual interdependence through a division of labour created security within a community. In addition, the division of labour on the basis of ethnicity allowed immigrants and foreigners to quickly integrate into their own caste niches. The caste system played an influential role in shaping economic activities, where it functioned much like medieval European guilds, ensuring the division of labour, providing for the training of apprentices and, in some cases, allowing manufacturers to achieve narrow specialization.

For instance, in certain regions, producing each variety of cloth was the speciality of a particular sub-caste. Additionally, some philosophers have argued that the majority of people would be comfortable in stratified endogamous groups, as they were in ancient times.

CASTE MOBILITY

Some scholars believe that the relative ranking of other castes was fluid or differed from one place to another prior to the arrival of the British. Sociologists such as Bernard Buber and Marriott McKim describe how the perception of the caste system as a static and textual stratification has given way to the perception of the caste system as a more processual, empirical and contextual stratification.

Other sociologists such as Y.B Damle have applied theoretical models to explain mobility and flexibility in the caste system in India. These scholars, groups of lower-caste individuals could seek to elevate the status of their caste by attempting to emulate the practices of higher castes.

Flexibility in caste laws permitted very low-caste religious clerics such as Valmiki to compose the Ramayana, which became a central work of Hindu scripture. There is also precedent of certain Shudra families within the temples of the Sri Vaishnava sect in South India elevating their caste.

The following is a list of changes in varna cited in Hindu texts:

- Manu eldest son [Priyavrata] became king, a Kshatriya. Out of his ten sons seven became kings while three became Brahman. Their names were Mahavira, Kavi and Savana.
- Kavash -ailush was born to a Sudra and attained

varn of a Rishi. He became mantra-drashta to numerous Vedic mantras in Rig-Veda 10th Mandal.

- Jabala's son [Satyakama] born from unknown father became Rishi by his qualities.
- [Matanga] became a Rishi after his birth in low Varna.

Some psychologists, mobility across broad caste lines may have been "minimal", though sub-castes (jatis) may have changed their social status over the generations by fission, relocation, and adoption of new rituals. Sociologist M. N. Srinivas has also debated the question of rigidity in Caste. In an ethnographic study of the Coorgs of Karnataka, he observed considerable flexibility and mobility in their caste hierarchies.

He asserts that the caste system is far from a rigid system in which the position of each component caste is fixed for all time; instead, movement has always been possible, especially in the middle regions of the hierarchy. It was always possible for groups born into a lower caste to "rise to a higher position by adopting vegetarianism and teetotalism" *i.e.* adopt the customs of the higher castes. While theoretically "forbidden", the process was not uncommon in practice. The concept of sanskritization, or the adoption of upper-caste norms by the lower castes, addressed the complexity and fluidity of caste relations.

The fact that many of the dynasties were of obscure origin suggests some social mobility: a person of any caste, having once acquired political power, could also acquire a genealogy connecting him with the traditional lineages and conferring Kshatriya status. A number of new castes, such as the Kayasthas (scribes) and Khatris (traders).

The Brahmanic sources, they originated from intercaste marriages, but this is clearly an attempt at rationalizing their rank in the hierarchy.

Khatri appears to be unquestionably a Prakritised form of the Sanskrit Kshatriya. Many of these new castes played a major role in society. The hierarchy of castes did not have a uniform distribution throughout the country.

REFORMS

There have been challenges to the caste system from the time of Buddha, Mahavira and Makkhali Gosala. Opposition to the system of varna is regularly asserted in the Yoga Upanicsads and is a constant feature of Cîna-âcâra tantrism, a Chinese-derived movement in Asom; both date to the medieval era.

The Nâtha system, which was founded by Matsya-indra Nâtha and Go-rakcsa Nâtha in the same era and spread throughout India, has likewise been consistently opposed to the system of varna. Many Bhakti period saints rejected the caste discriminations and accepted all castes, including untouchables, into their fold. During the British Raj, this sentiment gathered steam, and many Hindu reform movements such as Brahmo Samaj and Arya Samaj renounced caste-based discrimination.

The inclusion of so-called untouchables into the mainstream was argued for by many social reformers. Mahatma Gandhi called them "Harijans" (children of God) although that term is now considered patronizing and the term Dalit (downtrodden) is the more commonly used. Gandhi's contribution towards the emancipation of the untouchables is still debated, especially in the commentary of his contemporary Dr. B.R. Ambedkar, an untouchable who frequently saw Gandhi's activities as detrimental to the cause of upliftment of his people.

The practice of untouchability was formally outlawed by the Constitution of India in 1950, and has declined significantly since then, to the point of a society allowing former untouchables to take high political office, like former President K. R. Narayanan, who took office in 1997, and former Chief Justice K. G. Balakrishnan.

MODERN STATUS OF THE CASTE SYSTEM

In some rural areas and small towns, the caste system is still very rigid. Caste is also a factor in the politics of India. The Government of India has officially documented castes and sub-castes, primarily to determine those deserving reservation (positive discrimination in education and jobs) through the census. The Indian reservation system, though limited in scope, relies entirely on quotas. The Government lists consist of Scheduled Castes, Scheduled Tribes and Other Backward Classes:

SCHEDULED CASTES (SC)

Scheduled castes generally consist of "Dalit". The present population is 16% of the total population of India (around 160 million). For example, the Delhi state has 49 castes listed as SC.

SCHEDULED TRIBES (ST)

Scheduled tribes generally consist of tribal groups. The present population is 7% of the total population of India *i.e.* around 70 million.

OTHER BACKWARD CLASSES (OBC)

The Mandal Commission covered more than 3000 castes under OBC Category and stated that OBCs form around 52% of the Indian population. However, the National Sample Survey puts the figure at 32%. There is substantial debate over the exact number of OBCs in India; it is generally estimated to be sizable, but many believe that it is lower than the figures quoted by either the Mandal Commission or the National Sample Survey.

The caste-based reservations in India have led to widespread protests, such as the 2006 Indian anti-reservation protests, with many complaining of reverse discrimination against the forward castes (the castes that do not qualify for the reservation). Many view negative treatment of forward castes as socially divisive and equally wrong.

CASTE SYSTEM AMONG NON-HINDUS

In some parts of India, Christians are stratified by sect, location, and the castes of their predecessors, usually in reference to upper class Syrian Malabar Nasranis. Christians in Kerala are divided into several communities, including Syrian Christians and the so-called "Latin" or "New Rite"

Christians. Syrian Christians derive status within the caste system from the tradition that they are converted Namboodiris and Jews, who were evangelized by St. Thomas. Writers Arundhati Roy and Anand Kurian have written personal accounts of the caste system at work in their community. Syrian Christians, especially Knanaya Christians, tend to be endogamous and not to intermarry with other Christian castes.

The Latin Rite Christians were among the scheduled castes in the coastal belt of Kerala, where fishing was the primary occupation. They were actively converted by missionaries in the 16th and 19th centuries. These missionary activities were carried out by Western Latin Rite missionaries who did not understand the significance of the caste system in India; none of the Syrian churches had participated in such activities among the scheduled castes of India because they were aware of the prejudices of the caste system. The government of India later granted this group OBC status.

Very rarely are there intermarriages between Syrian Christians and Latin Rite Christians Anthropologists have noted that the caste hierarchy among Christians in Kerala is much more polarized than the Hindu practices in the surrounding areas, due to a lack of jatis. Also, the caste status is kept even if the sect allegiance is switched (*i.e.* from Syrian Catholic to Syrian Orthodox). In the Indian state of Goa, mass conversions were carried out by Portuguese Latin missionaries from the 16th century onwards. The Hindu converts retained their caste practices.

The continued maintenance of the caste system among the Christians in Goa is attributed to the nature of mass conversions of entire villages, as a result of which existing social stratification was not affected. The Portuguese colonists, even during the Goan Inquisition, did not do anything to change the caste system.

Thus, the original Hindu Brahmins in Goa now became Christian Bamons and the Kshatriya became Christian noblemen called Chardos. The Christian clergy became almost exclusively Bamon. Vaishyas who converted to Christianity became Gauddos, and Shudras became Sudirs. Finally, the Dalits or "Untouchables" who converted to Christianity became Maharas and Chamars, the latter an appellation of the anti-Dalit ethnic slur Chamaar.

Units of social stratification, termed "castes" by many, have developed among Muslims in some parts of South Asia. Sources indicate that the castes among Muslims developed as the result of close contact with Hindu culture and Hindu converts to Islam.

The Sachar Committee's report commissioned by the government of India and released in 2006 documents the continued stratification in Muslim society.

Among Muslims, those who are referred to as Ashrafs are presumed to have a superior status derived from their foreign Arab ancestry, while the Ajlafs are assumed to be converts from Hinduism, and have a lower status.

In addition, the Arzal caste among Muslims was regarded by anti-caste activists like Ambedkar as the equivalent of untouchables. In the Bengal region of India, some Muslims stratify their society just as to 'Quoms'. While many scholars have asserted that the Muslim castes are not as acute in their discrimination as those of the Hindus, some like Ambedkar argued that the social evils in Muslim society were "worse than those seen in Hindu society". The Buddhists also had a caste system.

In Sri Lanka, the Rodis might have been outcast by the Sri Lankan Buddhists due to the absence of ahimsa (non-violence), a central tenet of Buddhism, among their beliefs. The writer Raghavan, "That a form of worship in which human offerings formed the essential ritual would have been anathema to the Buddhist way of life goes without saying; and it needs no stretch of imagination that any class of people in whom the cult prevailed or survived even in an attenuated form would have been pronounced by the sangha (*i.e.* the Buddhist clergy) as exiles from the social order." Savarkar believed that the status of the backward castes (*e.g.* Chamar) that performed non-violence only worsened. When Ywan Chwang traveled to South India after the period of the

Chalukyan Empire, he noticed that the caste system had existed among the Buddhists and Jains. Jains also had castes in places such as Bihar.

For example, in the village of Bundela, there were several "*jaats*" (groups) amongst the Jains. A person of one "*jaat*" cannot intermingle with a Jain or another "jaat". They also could not eat with the members of other "jaats". The Sikh Gurus criticized the hierarchy of the caste system.

While some castes were widely perceived as being better or higher than others (*e.g.* Brahmins being higher than others), they preached that all parts of society were valuable and that merit and hard-work were essential aspects of life. In the Shiromani Gurdwara Prabandhak Committee, out of 140 seats, 20 are reserved for low caste Sikhs.

However, the quota system has attracted much criticism due to the lack of meritocracy, since merit is considered the single most important component of winning a seat. Baha'i Faith has grown to prominence in India, since its philosophy of the unity of humanity attracted many of the lower castes.

CASTE-RELATED VIOLENCE

Caste-related violence and hate crimes in India have occurred despite the gradual reduction of casteism in the country. A report by Human Rights Watch, "Dalits and indigenous peoples (known as Scheduled Tribes or adivasis) continue to face discrimination, exclusion, and acts of communal violence.

Laws and policies adopted by the Indian government provide a strong basis for protection, but are not being faithfully implemented by local authorities."

IN 2006 DALIT PROTESTS IN MAHARASHTRA

In November-December 2006, the desecration of a Ambedkar statue in Kanpur (Uttar Pradesh) triggered violent protests by Dalits in Maharashtra. Several people remarked that the protests were fueled by the Kherlanji Massacre. During the violent protests, the Dalit protestors set three trains on fire, damaged over 100 buses and clashed with police. At least four deaths and many more injuries were reported. Later, the Kanpur Police arrested a Dalit youth Arun Kumar Balmiki for desecrating the Ambedkar statue. The police, the youth had "admitted to having damaged the statue in a drunken state along with two friends".

Earlier in a similar case, a Dalit youth was held for desecrating an Ambedkar statue in Gulbarga, Karnataka. In response to these protests, Raj Thackeray drew attention to another incident in Kherlanji, in which a Dalit allegedly raped a girl and killed her. Thackeray demanded action on those responsible for the rape and the subsequent death of the girl, and also remarked that nobody helped the girl's family.

ANDHRA PRADESH

This state is considered to be one of the most caste-crime infested places of India which has had many Dalit Massacres like Chundur Massacre, Neerukonda Massacre etc.

RAJASTHAN

In the Indian province of Rajasthan, between the years 1999 and 2002, crimes against Dalits average at about 5024 a year, with 46 killings and 138 cases of rape.

TAMIL NADU

The state of Tamil Nadu has witnessed several caste-based incidents both against Dalits and Brahmins. In 2000, three young men belonging to the Dalit undercaste were killed in the Cuddalore district of Tamil Nadu. This fuelled some localized violence in the caste-sensitive region, which has seen numerous caste-related incidents in which the majority of the victims have been Dalits. Six of the killings have been registered as murders under the Indian Penal Code and others as "Deaths under suspicious circumstances". No arrests have been made in these cases. However, several Dalits have been arrested as goondas (hoodlums).

The Chief minister of Tamil-Nadu, M. Karunanidhi, has been accused of having an "anti-Dalit" bias by the radical organization "Dalit Panthers of India". Theories concerning these crimes against Dalits range from "alcohol bootleggers opposing prohibition movements among Dalits" to "inter-caste relations between an Vanniya boy and a Dalit girl". Political parties sympathetic to the Dalits have protested against these incidents and have alleged systemic biases against Dalits in several parts of the country.

PUNJAB

On 25 May 2009, violence and rioting broke out when thousands of protesters took to the streets in almost all major towns and cities in the Indian state of Punjab after a dalit preacher, Sant Ramanand, was attacked in a temple in Vienna, Austria.

He was among 16 people injured, including another preacher Sant Nirajnan Dass, and later died in hospital. Both the preachers were from a low-caste Sikh sect which has a large following in parts of Punjab and had travelled to Vienna to conduct a special service. Several high-caste Sikh groups had apparently opposed his presence and threatened violence. This happened after the preacher had reportedly made remarks about the Sikh groups.

Bant Singh Case of Punjab

On the evening of January 5, 2006 Bant Singh, a poor Sikh Dalit, was attacked by unknown assailants. His injuries necessitated medical amputation. He alleges that this was in retaliation for actively working to secure justice for his daughter, who was gang raped by upper caste members of his village in Punjab five years earlier. A 55-year-old Dalit Sikh woman, Sawinder Kaur has been tortured, stripped and tied to a tree in Ram Duali village of Punjab because her nephew eloped with a girl from the same community.

The police arrested four persons for allegedly committing the crime on 9 September 2007. In January, 1999 four members of the village panchayat of Bhungar Khera village in Abohar paraded a handicapped Dalit woman naked through the village. No action was taken by the police, despite local Dalit protests.

It was only on July 20 that the four panchayat members were arrested, after the State Home Department was compelled to order an inquiry into the incident. A Dalit Sikh woman, Sukhwinder Kaur of Sumel Kheri village was molested and beaten up by an octroi contractor of Malaudh when she resisted his attempt to sexually exploit her.

KHERLANJI MASSACRE

On September 29, 2006, four members of the Bhotmange family belonging to the Dalit underclass were slaughtered in Kherlanji, a small village in Bhandara district of Maharashtra. The women of the family, Surekha and Priyanka, were paraded naked in public, then allegedly gang-raped before being murdered. Although initially ascribed by the media and by the Human Rights Watch to upper castes, the criminal act was actually carried out by Kunbi caste (classified as Other Backward Classes by Government of India) farmers for having opposed the requisition of the Dalit land to have a road built over it.

On November 23, 2006, some members of the Dalit community in the nearby district of Chandrapur staged a protest regarding this incident. The protesters allegedly turned violent and threw stones. The police resorted to baton-charging the protestors to control the situation. Dalit leaders, however, denied that they had first resorted to violent and stated that they had been "protesting in peace".

CASTE POLITICS IN INDIA

Identity Politics has become a prominent subject in the Indian politics in the past few years. Rise of low castes, religious identities, linguistic groups and ethnic conflicts have contributed to the significance of identity politics in India. The discourse on Identity, many scholars feel, is distinctly a modern phenomenon. Craig Calhoun aptly describes the situation when he argues that it is in the modern times we encounter intensified efforts at consolidating individual and categorical identities and reinforce selfsameness.

This is primarily a modern phenomenon because some scholars feel that emphasis on identity based on a central organising principle of ethnicity, religion, language, gender, sexual preferences, or caste positions, etc., are a sort of "compelling remedy for anonymity" in an otherwise impersonal modern world. It is thus said to be a "pattern of belonging, a search for comfort, an approach to community." However, the complex social changes and the imbrications of various forces, factors and events in this modern world have rendered such production and recognition of identities problematic.

This is to say that any search for an 'authentic self or identity' is not an innocent and announced possibility; it involves negotiating other, often overlapping and contested, heterodox or multiple 'selves'. Cascardi succinctly elucidates this by observing, "the modern subject is defined by its insertion into a series of separate value-spheres, each one of which tends to exclude or attempts to assert its priority over the rest", thereby rendering identity-schemes problematic.

Nonetheless, the concerns with individual and collective identity that simultaneously seeks to emphasise differences and attempt to establish commonality with others similarly distinguished, have become a universal venture.

WHAT IS IDENTITY POLITICS

But the question is how do discourses on identity fit into the political landscape? What are the political underpinnings of these discourses on identity? What are the organising principles of movements that characterise themselves as those based on identity concerns? Can we define movements of workers as an instance of identity politics? In short what is the politics of identity and what are its organising principles? Identity Politics is said to "signify a wide range of political activity and theorising founded in the shared experiences of injustice of members of certain social groups".

As a political activity it is thus considered to signify a body of political projects that attempts a "recovery from exclusion and denigration" of groups hitherto marginalised on the basis of differences based on their 'selfhood' determining characteristics like ethnicity, gender, sexual preferences, caste positions, etc. Identity politics thus attempts to attain empowerment, representation and recognition of social groups by asserting the very same markers that distinguished and differentiated them from the others and utilise those markers as an assertion of selfhood and identity based on difference rather than equality.

Contrastingly placed, it is to imply that adherents of identity politics essentialise certain markers that fix the identities of social groups around an ensemble of definitional absolutes. These markers may be those of language, culture, ethnicity, gender, sexual preferences, caste positions, religion, tribe, race, etc. institutionalised in jargons, metaphors, stereotypes, and academic literature and reinforced through practices of positive discrimination or affirmative action. The proponents of identity politics thus, assign the primacy of some "essence" or a set of core features shared only by members of the collectivity and no others and accepts individual persons as singular, integral, altogether harmonious and unproblematic identities. These core markers are different from associational markers like those of the workers who are defined more by their common interests rather than by certain core essential naturally 'given' identity attributes of the groups engaged in identity politics.

Though many would argue that "worker" was an identity deserving legitimacy and as a group, its movements can be referred to as identity Politics, but probably the term "identity politics" as a body of political projects implied to in contemporary discourses refers to certain essential, local and particular categorical identities rather than any universalising ideals or agenda.

The adherents of identity politics utilise the power of myths, cultural symbols and kinship relations to mould the feeling of shared community and subsequently politicise these aspects to claim recognition of their particular identities. The strongest criticism against Identity Politics is that it often challenged by the very same markers upon which the sense of self or community is sought to be built.

It is despite the fact that identity politics is engaged in numerous aspects of oppression and powerlessness, reclaiming and transforming negative scripts used by dominant groups into powerful instruments for building positive images of self and community. In other words the markers that supposedly defines the community are fixed to the extent that they harden and release a process of ingroup essentialism that often denies internal dialogicality within and without the group and itself becomes a new form of closure and oppression.

Identity Politics as a field of study can be said to have gained intellectual legitimacy since the second half of the twentieth century, *i.e.*, between 1950s and 1960s in the United States when large scale political movements of the second wave-feminists, Black Civil Rights, Gay and Lesbian Liberation movements and movements of various Indigenous groups in the U.S. and other parts of the world were being justified and legitimated on the basis of claims about injustices done to their respective social groups.

However, as scholars like Heyes point out that although 'Identity Politics' can draw on intellectual precursors from Mary Wollstonecraft to Frantz Fanon, writing that actually uses this specific phrase-Identity Politics-is limited almost exclusively to the last 15 years.

IDENTITY POLITICS IN INDIA

In India we find that despite adoption of a liberal democratic polity after independence, communities and collective identities have remained powerful and continue to claim recognition.

In fact, Beteille has shown that the Indian polity has consistently tried to negotiate the allegiance to a liberal spirit and the concerns and consciousness of community. Bikhu Parekh this process has recognised a wide array of autonomous and largely self governing communities. It has sought to reconcile itself as an association of individuals and a community of communities, recognising both individuals and communities as bearer of rights.

It was probably this claim for and granting of recognition of particular identities by the postindependence state of India that led many scholars to believe that a material basis for the enunciation of identity claims has been provided by the post-independent state and its structures and institutions. In other words the state is seen as an "active contributor to identity politics through the creation and maintenance of state structures which define and then recognise people in terms of certain identities".

Thus, we find identity politics of various hues abound in India, the most spectacular however, are those based on language, religion, caste, ethnicity or tribal identity. But having said this it would be wrong on our part to assume that each of these identity markers operate autonomously, independent of the overlapping influence of the other makers. In other words a homogenous linguistic group may be divided by caste affiliations that may be subdivided by religious orientations or all may be subsumed under a broader ethnic claim.

Caste

Caste-based discrimination and oppression have been a pernicious feature of Indian society and in the post-independence period its imbrications with politics have not only made it possible for hitherto oppressed caste-groups to be accorded political freedom and recognition but has also raised consciousness about its potential as a political capital. In fact Dipankar Gupta has poignantly exposed this contradiction when he elaborates the differences between Ambedkar and Mandal Commission's view of caste.

While the former designed the policy of reservations or protective discrimination to remove untouchability as an institution from Indian social life and polity, the latter considered caste as an important political resource.

Actually, the Mandal commission can be considered the intellectual inspiration in transforming castebased identity to an asset that may be used as a basis for securing political and economic gains. Though it can also be said that the upper castes by virtue of their predominant position were already occupying positions of strengths in the political and economic system, and when the Mandal heightened the consciousness of the'Dalits' by recognisisng their disadvantage of caste-identity as an advantage the confrontation ensues.

The caste system, which is based on the notions of purity and pollution, hierarchy and difference, has despite social mobility, been oppressive towards the Shudras and the outcastes who suffered the stigma of ritual impurity and lived in abject poverty, illiteracy and denial of political power.

The origin of confrontational identity politics based on caste may be said to have its origin on the issue of providing the oppressed caste groups with state support in the form of protective discrimination.

This group identity based on caste that has been reinforced by the emergence of political consciousness around caste identities is institutionalised by the caste-based political parties that profess to uphold and protect the interests of specific identities including the castes.

Consequently, we have the upper caste dominated BJP, the lower caste dominated BSP (Bhaujan Samaj Party) or the SP (Samajwadi Party), including the fact that left parties (for example use of caste idioms for mobilising agricultural labourers in Andhra Pradesh elections in 1950) have tacitly followed the caste pattern to extract mileage in electoral politics. The Cumulative result of the politicisation can be summarised by arguing that caste-based identity politics has had a dual role in Indian society and polity. It relatively democratised the caste-based Indian society but simultaneously undermined the evolution of class-based organisations.

In all, caste has become an important determinant in Indian society and politics, the new session of organised politics and consciousness of caste affiliations learnt by the hitherto despised caste groups have transformed the contours of Indian politics where shifting caste-class alliances are being encountered.

The net effect of these mobilisations along caste-identities have resulted not only in the empowerment of newly emerging groups but has increased the intensity of confrontational politics and possibly leading to a growing crisis of governmentally.

Religion

Another form of identity politics is that effected through the construction of a community on the shared bond of religion.

In India, Hinduism, Islam, Sikhism, Christianity, and Zoroastrianism are some of the major religions practised by the people. Numerically the Hindus are considered to be the majority, which inspires many Hindu loyalist groups like the RSS (Rashtriya Swayam Sevak Sangh) or the Siva Sena and political parties like the BJP (Bharatiya Janata Party) or the Hindu Mahasabha to claim that India is a Hindu State. These claims generate homogenising myths about India and its history.

These claims are countered by other religious groups who foresee the possibility of losing autonomy of practise of their religious and cultural life under such homogenising claims. This initiates contestations that have often resulted in communal riots. The generally accepted myths that process the identity divide on religious lines centre on the 'appeasement theory', 'forcible religious conversions', general 'anti-Hindu' and thus 'anti-India' attitude of the minority religious groups, the 'hegemonic aspirations' of majority groups and 'denial of a socio-cultural space' to minority groups.

Historically, the Hindu revivalist movement of the 19th century is considered to be the period that saw the demarcation of two separate cultures on religious basis-the Hindus and the Muslims that deepened further because of the partition. This division which has become institutionalised in the form of a communal ideology has become a major challenge for India's secular social fabric and democratic polity. Though communalism for a major part of the last century signified Hindu-Muslim conflict, in recent years contestations between Hindus and Sikhs, Hindus and Christians have often crystallised into communal conflict.

The rise of Hindu national assertiveness, politics of representational government, persistence of communal perceptions, and competition for the socio-economic resources are considered some of the reasons for the generation of communal ideologies and their transformation into major riots. Identity schemes based on religion have become a major source of conflict not only in the international context but since the early 1990s it has also become a challenge for Indian democracy and secularism.

The rise of majoritarian assertiveness is considered to have become institutionalised after the BJP, that along with its 'Hindu' constituents gave political cohesiveness to a consolidating Hindu consciousness, formed a coalition ministry in March 1998. However, like all identity schemes the forging of a religious community glosses over internal differences within a particular religion to generate the "we are all of the same kind" emotion.

Thus differences of caste groups within a homogenous Hindu identity, linguistic and sectional differences within Islam are shelved to create a homogenous unified religious identity. In post-independence India the majoritarian assertion has generated its own antithesis in the form of minority religions assertiveness and a resulting confrontational politics that undermines the syncretistic dimensions of the civil society in India.

The process through which this religious assertiveness is being increasingly institutionalised by a 'methodical rewriting of history' has the potential to reformulate India's national identity along communal trajectories.

Language

Identity claims based on the perception of a collectivity bound together by language may be said to have its origin in the pre-independence politics of the Congress that had promised reorganisation of states in the post-independent period on linguistic basis.

But it was the "JVP" (Jawaharlal Nehru, Vallabhbai Patel and Pattabhi Sitaramayya) Committee's concession that if public sentiment was "insistent and overwhelming", the formation of Andhra from the Teluguspeaking region of the then Madras could be conceded which as Michael Brecher mentions was the "opening wedge for the bitter struggle over states reorganisation which was to dominate Indian Politics from 1953 to 1956".

Ironically, the claim of separate states for linguistic collectivities did not end in 1956 and even today continues to confront the concerns of the Indian leadership. But the problem has been that none of the created or claimed states are mono-ethnic in composition and some even have numerically and politically powerful minorities. This has resulted in a cascading set of claims that continue to threaten the territorial limits of existing states and disputes over boundaries between linguistic states have continued to stir conflicts, as for instance the simmering tensions between Maharastra and Karnataka over the district of Belgaum or even the claims of the Nagas to parts of Manipur.

The linguistic divisions have been complicated by the lack of a uniform language policy for the entire country. Since in each state the dominant regional language is often used as the medium of instruction and social communication, the consequent affinity and allegiance that develops towards one's own language gets expressed even outside one's state of origin. For instance the formation of linguistic cultural and social groups outside one's state of origin helps to consolidate the unity and sense of community in a separate linguistic society.

Thus language becomes an important premise on which group identities are organised and establishes the conditions for defining the 'in-group' and 'out-group'. Though it is generally felt that linguistic states provide freedom and autonomy for collectivities within a heterogeneous society, critics argue that linguistic states have reinforced regionalism and has provided a platform for the articulation of a phenomenal number of identity claims in a country that has 1,652 'mother tongues' and only fourteen recognised languages around which states have been reorganised.

They argue that the effective result of recognition for linguistic groups has disembodied the feelings of national unity and national spirit in a climate where 'Maharastra for

Marathis, Gujrat for Gujratis, etc." has reinforced linguistic mistrust and defined the economic and political goods in linguistic terms.

Ethnicity

There are two ways in which the concept of ethnic identity is used; one, it insiders the formation of identity on the basis of single attribute—language, religion, caste, region, etc.; two, it considers the formation of identity on the basis, of multiple attributes cumulatively. However, it is the second way formation of identity on the basis of more than one characteristics—culture, customs, region, religion or caste, which is considered as the most common way of formation of the ethnic identity. The one ethnic identity is formed in relation to the other ethnic identity. The relations between more than one ethnic identities can be both harmonious and conflictual. Whenever there is competetion among the ethnic identities on the real or imaginary basis, it expressed in the form of autonomy movements, demand for session or ethnic riots.

CRITICISM

There has been criticism of the caste system from both within and outside of India. Criticism of the Caste system in Hindu society came both from the Hindu fold and Dalit.

HISTORICAL CRITICISM

Many bhakti period saints, including Nanak, Kabir, Caitanya, Dnyaneshwar, Eknath, Ramanuja and Tukaram, rejected all caste-based discrimination and accepted disciples from all the castes. Many Hindu reformers such as Swami Vivekananda believe that there is no place for the caste system in Hinduism. The 15th century saint Ramananda accepted all castes, including untouchables, into his fold.

Most of these saints subscribed to the Bhakti movements in Hinduism during the medieval period that rejected casteism. Nandanar, a low-caste Hindu cleric, also rejected casteism and accepted Dalits. Some other movements in Hinduism have also welcomed lower-castes into their fold, the earliest being the Bhakti movements of the medieval period. Early Dalit politics involved many reform movements; these arose primarily as a reaction to the advent of Christian missionaries in India and their attempts to convert Dalits, who were attracted to the prospect of escaping the caste system. In the 19th Century, the Brahmo Samaj under Raja Ram Mohan Roy actively campaigned against untouchability and casteism. The Arya Samaj founded by Swami Dayanand also renounced discrimination against Dalits.

Sri Ramakrishna Paramahamsa and his disciple Swami Vivekananda founded the Ramakrishna Mission that participated in the emancipation of Dalits. Upper-caste Hindus such as Mannathu Padmanabhan participated in movements to abolish untouchability against Dalits; Padmanabhan opened his family temple to Dalits for worship. Narayana Guru, a pious Hindu and an authority on the Vedas, also criticized casteism and campaigned for the rights of lower-caste Hindus within the context of Hinduism. The first upper-caste temple to openly welcome Dalits into their fold was the Laxminarayan Temple in Wardha in the year 1928; the move was spearheaded by reformer Jamnalal Bajaj. The caste system has also been criticized by many Indian social reformers.

Some reformers, such as Jyotirao Phule and Iyothee Thass, argued that the lower caste people were the original inhabitants of India, who had been conquered in the ancient past by "Brahmin invaders." Mahatma Gandhi coined the term Harijan, a euphemistic word for untouchable, literally meaning Sons of God. B. R. Ambedkar, born in Hindu Dalit community, was a heavy critic of the caste system.

He pioneered the Dalit Buddhist movement in India, and asked his followers to leave Hinduism, and convert to Buddhism. India's first Prime Minister, Jawaharlal Nehru, based on his own relationship with Dalit reformer Ambedkar, supported the eradication of untouchability for the benefit of the Dalit community.

In 1936, the Maharaja proclaimed that "outcastes should not be denied the consolations and the solace of the Hindu faith". Even today, the Sri Padmanabhaswamy temple that first welcomed Dalits in the state of Kerala is revered by the Dalit Hindu community.

CONTEMPORARY CRITICISM

Organizations such as the Rashtriya Swayamsevak Sangh have actively criticized the caste system. Some activists consider the caste system a form of racial discrimination. At the United Nations Conference Against Racism in Durban, South Africa in March 2001, participants condemned discrimination based on the caste system and tried to pass a resolution declaring caste as a basis for segregation and oppression a form of apartheid.

However, no formal resolution was passed. The alleged maltreatment of Dalits in India has been described by some authors as "India's hidden apartheid". Critics of the accusations point to substantial improvements in the position of Dalits in post-independence India, consequent to the strict implementation of the rights and privileges enshrined in the Constitution of India, as implemented by the Protection of Civil rights Act, 1955.

They also note that India has had a Dalit president, K.R. Narayanan, and argue that the practise had disappeared in urban public life. William A. Haviland, however:

- Although India's national constitution of 1950 sought to abolish cast discrimination and the practice of untouchability, the caste system remains deeply entrenched in Hindu culture and is still widespread throughout southern Asia, especially in rural India. In what has been called India's "hidden apartheid", entire villages in many Indian states remain completely segregated by caste. Representing about 15 per cent of India's population—or some 160 million people—the widely scattered Dalits endure near complete social isolation, humiliation, and discrimination based exclusively on their birth status. Even a Dalit's shadow is believed to pollute the upper classes. They may not cross the line dividing their part of the village from that occupied by higher castes, drink water from public wells, or visit the same temples as the higher castes. Dalit children are still often made to sit in the back of classrooms.

Sociologists Kevin Reilly, Stephen Kaufman and Angela Bodino, while critical of casteism, conclude that modern India does not practice any apartheid since there is no state-sanctioned discrimination. They write that casteism in India is presently "not apartheid. In fact, untouchables, as well as tribal people and members of the lowest castes in India benefit from broad affirmative action programmes and are enjoying greater political power. The Constitution of India places special emphasis on outlawing caste discrimination, especially the practice of untouchability.

CASTE AND RACE

Allegations that caste amounts to race were addressed and rejected by B.R. Ambedkar, an advocate for Dalit rights and critic of untouchability. He wrote that "The Brahmin of Punjab is racially of the same stock as the Chamar of Punjab. The Caste system does not demarcate racial division.

The Caste system is a social division of people of the same race", Such allegations have also been rejected by sociologists such as Andre Béteille, who writes that treating caste as a form of racism is "politically mischievous" and worse, "scientifically nonsensical" since there is no discernible difference in the racial characteristics between Brahmins and Scheduled Castes. He states, "Every social group cannot be regarded as a race simply because we want to protect it against prejudice and discrimination".

The Indian government also rejects the claims of equivalency between caste and racial discrimination, pointing out that the caste issues are essentially intraracial and intra-cultural. Indian Attorney General Soli Sorabjee insisted that "he only reason India wants caste discrimination kept off the agenda is that it will distract participants from the main topic: racism. Caste discrimination in India is undeniable but caste and race are entirely distinct". Many scholars dispute the claim that casteism is akin to racism. Sociologist M. N. Srinivas has debated the question of rigidity in caste. Others have applied theoretical models to explain mobility and flexibility in the caste system in India. These scholars, groups of lower-caste individuals could seek to elevate the status of their caste by attempting to emulate the practices of higher castes.

In her book Democracy and Authoritarianism in South Asia, Pakistani-American sociologist Ayesha Jalal writes, "As for Hinduism, the hierarchical principles of the Brahmanical social order have always been contested from within Hindu society, suggesting that equality has been and continues to be both valued and practiced." In India, some observers felt that the caste system must be viewed as a system of exploitation of poor low-ranking groups by more prosperous high-ranking groups. In many parts of India, land is largely held by high-ranking property owners of the dominant castes, who economically exploit low-ranking landless labourers and poor artisans.

Matt Cherry claims that karma underpins the caste system, which traditionally determines the position and role of every member of Hindu society. Caste determines an individual's place in society, the work he or she may carry out, and who he or she may marry and meet. Hindus believe that the karma of previous life will determine the caste an individual will be (re)born into. On 29 March 2007, the Supreme Court of India, as an interim measure, stayed the law providing for 27% reservation for Other Backward Classes in educational institutions. This was done in response to a public interest litigation—Ashoka Kumar Thakur vs. Union of India. The Court held that the 1931 census could not be a determinative factor for identifying the OBCs for the purpose of providing reservation. The court also observed, "Reservation cannot be permanent and appear to perpetuate backwardness". However, the Supreme Court later upheld the reservation.

5

Dalits and Ambedkar's Inheritance

AN INTRODUCTION

DALITS, meaning 'broken' or 'oppressed', is a synonym for the 'depressed classes'. Both these terms are now too loosely and indiscriminately applied to an assortment of social groups, variously labelled as oppressed, deprived, downtrodden, disabled, disadvantaged, weaker parts, other backward classes, minorities, scheduled tribes, untouchables, scheduled castes, Harijans, and so on. The lumping of all these groups and the use of the terms DCs and Dalits as 'catchall' categories are for at least two reasons: First, the failure to grasp the magnitude of the disparate socio-cultural, educational, and economic conditions of these groups.

Second, as a ploy of self-serving politicians pretending to be the protagonists of backward classes for invidiously extending the constitutional safeguards meant for the real Dalits to the less deserving groups as well. In either case the losers are undoubtedly the really deprived and disabled bottom groups which alone are Dalits.

In this connection it is pertinent to recall B R Ambedkar's usage of the term DCs. That was in the limited sense of untouchables. Among other things, in his written statements and oral evidence before the Simon Commission of 1928 and the Round Table Conferences of 1930-31 and their subcommittees he made it explicit that he was using DCs and untouchables as convertible terms.

More often than not, he preferred to address the untouchables as just untouchables as though to remind them of their plight as a 'besieged', 'broken', and 'dehumanised' people. If he addressed them as DCs it was primarily because this term was already in circulation as a British officialese covering the untouchables and a few other groups such as the aboriginal and hill tribes. But when occasion arose Ambedkar did not hesitate to condemn this usage.

Thus, in a supplementary memorandum on the claims of the DCs for special representation, submitted on November 4, 1931 to the Minorities Subcommittee of the Second Round Table Conference, he made it clear that the term DCs was degrading and contemptuous, and its use objectionable to the members of the concerned class and others interested in them.

So, he demanded its substitution with the less derogatory 'noncaste Hindus', 'protestant Hindus', or 'nonconformist Hindus', or some such appellation. In his note on the untouchables, submitted on May 1, 1932, to the Indian Franchise Committee of the same conference, Ambedkar again objected to the use of this term.

He also noted that the term had led to a great deal of confusion in the census as it included other groups who were not strictly untouchables. Therefore, he insisted on describing the untouchables by the more expressive term 'exterior castes' or 'excluded castes'. While Ambedkar had no difficulty in accepting the British officialese SCs as incorporated into the Government of India Act of 1935, he detested Gandhi's grandiloquent appellation Harijans. In January 1938 when the Bombay legislative council refused to accept an amendment for deletion of this term from the Local Boards Act Amendment Bill, Ambedkar along with members of his Republican Party walked out of the house. The reasoning of B K Gaikwad, who moved the amendment, was that through several conferences the untouchables had voiced their opposition to this usage. If they were people of god, that is Harijans, were the touchables monsters, he asked.

In view of the fact that untouchables have been the largest category and the most depressed and downtrodden of all the bottom groups of Indian society, and in keeping with

Ambedkar's usage of the DCs only with reference to the untouchables, the term DCs as well as its vernacular equivalent Dalits is used here in the limited sense of untouchables or their constitutional equivalent SCs. Such a restricted usage also assumes significance because of Ambedkar's role as the greatest of all the hitherto leaders of the untouchables, who launched a life-long crusade for their liberation from centuriesold enslavement and ostracism. Ambedkar contemplated various means for liberating the Dalits. However, it was primarily through the numerous safeguards incorporated into the Indian constitution, of which he himself was the chief architect, that he hoped to arm them with political power, to improve their socio-economic, educational, and cultural conditions, and to actualise their gradual deliverance from rhetoric to reality, from deprivation to development, from social stigma and suffering to social respect, solace, and equality.

As Ambedkar's legacy to Dalits is thus primarily the constitutional safeguards for the SCs, the celebration of his birth centenary year should at least serve as an occasion to take stock of the fate of his legacy, and to ascertain if the nation has really honoured it or reneged on its promises to honour it. This calls for an examination of the performance of the various measures undertaken in pursuance of these safeguards.

CONSTITUTIONAL SAFEGUARDS

The specific constitutional provisions intended to safeguard the interests of the SCs are on the abolition of untouchability and prohibition on its practice in any form; prohibition of 'begar' or forced or bonded labour, consideration of the claims of the SCs in appointments to services and posts in connection with the affairs of the union or a state; and reservation of seats in proportion to their numbers for the SCs in the Lok Sabha and in the Vidhan Sabhas.

Some of the other provisions also reinforce the status of the SCs as a 'protected weaker part'. They include the departures from the anti-discriminatory and formal equality provisions of the constitution, empowering the state to make any provision for the advancement of any socially and educationally backward class of citizens, and for the reservation of appointments or posts in favour of any backward class of citizens which in the opinion of the state is not adequately represented. They also include the directive in Article 46 that the state shall promote with special care the educational and economic interests of the weaker parts of the people, and, in particular, of the SCs and the STs, and shall protect them from social injustice and all forms of exploitation.

For analytical purposes the measures undertaken in pursuance of the various constitutional provisions for the SCs may be treated under three broad categories, namely, protective, developmental, and preferential. Abolitien of untouchability and the disabilities arising out of its practice in any form, and prohibition of bonded labour come under the first category.

Various educational schemes such as post-matric scholarships and girls hostels under the central sector, and pre-matric stipends, reimbursement of tuition fee, book banks, and hostels under the state sector, special component plans of the centre and states, special central assistance, and the SCs Development Corporations are of the second category. Legislative, educational and employment reservations are of the third category.

Of these, the effective implementation of the measures of the first two categories is a precondition for actualising the measures of the third category. However, the implementation of these measures hitherto has been too ineffective to achieve their intended objectives. This has been brought to light time and again by a number of studies, and in particular, by the commissioner for SCs and STs.

PERSISTENCE OF UNTOUCHABILITY

The Untouchability Act of 1955 was intended to wipe out untouchability and the social disabilities arising out of it, by making its practice in any form punishable under law.

But, the total number of cases registered with the police from 1955 to 1970 were only 6778 for the country as a whole, with only 1779 or 26 per cent of them ending up in conviction. As this act proved to be too weak and inadequate to meet the constitutional requirement, in November 1976 it was amended and amplified as the Protection of Civil Rights Act, 1955, with the resolve to totally eradicate untouchability within five years of its implementation.

But, even this act has not fared any better. Data on PCR cases indicate the persistence of untouchability in virtually all the states. This is especially so in Andhra Pradesh, Gujarat, Karnataka, Madhya Pradesh, Rajasthan, Tamil Nadu, and sadly enough, even in Ambedkar's home state Maharashtra. The only state reported to be relatively free from untouchability is West Bengal. Of the yearly average of PCR cases from 1977 to 1985 only about 62 per cent of those registered with the police were 'challaned' or filed before the courts; only about 31 per cent of those before the courts were disposed of; and only about 20 per cent of these disposals ended up in conviction. Stated differently, of the total cases registered with the police on an average not even 10 per cent ended up in conviction.

If this all-India pattern is any indication of the poor performance of the PCR Act, data available for some of the states indicate that the variations at the state level have been mostly for the worse: Despite a relatively higher percentage of 'challaning' by the police in at least two states and despite a relatively higher percentage of disposals by the courts in at least one of them and two others in all the states most of the cases have ended up in acquittals. Stated differently, only less than 9 per cent of the cases before the courts and only less than 4 per cent of the cases registered with the police have ended up in conviction. The relatively smaller proportion of cases 'challaned' by the police and the smaller proportion of disposals by the courts tend to magnify the proportion of convictions in Rajasthan.

While the large number of cases pending with the courts is a reflection of the tardy judicial process, the larger number of cases ending up in acquittals is for other reasons as well. As the reports of the commissioner for SCs and STs indicate, these include the weak socio-economic condition of the victims and their witnesses, defective investigation by the police, ineffective or indifferent handling of cases by the prosecution staff, victims yielding to pressures, promises, allurements, or intimidation, and the long drawn out trials which alone can discourage any victim from pursuing the case effectively.

Though the some idea of the persistence of untouchability, they are too inadequate to bring out the real magnitude of this evil. For, more often than not most of the cases go unnoticed and unreported.

The seventh report of the Commission/er for SCs and STs noted that quite a large number of the victims do not seek legal redress, and that though in states like Bihar and Orissa the problem of untouchability is acute, they have been reporting significantly lower number of cases compared to states like Tamil Nadu, Maharashtra, and Karnataka. The reason for this is not far to seek. Economically the SCs are still dependent on caste Hindus, and as such they do not risk approaching the police. A survey by the All-India Harijan Sevak Sangh conducted about a decade ago in 1,155 village spread over 12 states, clearly brought out the widespread practice of untouchability in the rural areas in terms of denial of access to the SCs to wells, temples, hotels and restaurants, barbershops, laundries, and so on.

That this evil practice still persists unabated in many areas is evident from the subsequent reports of the Commission/er for SCs and STs. Stating that untouchability persists in one form or the other, particularly in rural areas, the eighth report of the Commission for SCs and STs brought to light instances of discrimination against the SCs even in urban areas, especially in Andhra Pradesh, Bihar, Karnataka, Madhya Pradesh, Orissa, Rajasthan, Tamil Nadu; and Uttar Pradesh.

PERPETRATION OF ATROCITIES

Closely related to the persistence of untouchability is the perpetration of atrocities against the SCs. The atrocity cases registered have continued to be relatively more in Bihar, Gujarat, Kerala, Madhya Pradesh, Maharashtra, Rajasthan, Tamil Nadu, and Uttar Pradesh.

Of late, there has also been a considerable increase in the number of atrocity cases in some states, especially in Gujarat, Madhya Pradesh, Rajasthan, and Tamil Nadu. Of the different types of atrocity cases registered in the whole country at least one-fourth have involved grievous hurt, followed by arson, rape, and murder.

The nature of disposal of these cases has not been any better: Data available for some of the states indicate that of the total atrocity cases for disposal by the police during 1985 only about 53 per cent were 'challenged', that of the total cases for disposal by the courts only about 5 per cent were disposed of, and that of these only about 34 per cent ended up in conviction.

Stated differently, of the total cases for disposal by the police not even 10 per cent ended up in confusion. The performance was especially poor if, Karnataka, Madhya Pradesh, Orissa, Punjab, and Tamil Nadu. These cases again do not reflect the magnitude of atrocities; more so when contrasted against the recurrent press reports from different parts of the country about the crimes on the SCs. The reasons mentioned earlier for the PCR cases also apply to this and to the large number of cases pending with the courts and ending up in acquittal.

As atrocities against the SCs are closely related to untouchability, their perpetration has to be partly explained by the persistence of untouchability and by the increasing resentment of the SCs against the social indignities emanating from its practice in different forms. These include denial of entry into public places of worship, discrimination and differential treatment in hotels and teastalls, refusal of service by washermen and barbers, and restriction on movement in certain localities, on wearing sandals, riding horses, and leading marriage processions through certain caste-Hindu localities. The other major factors listed in the various reports of the Commission/er for SCs and STs include envy of the caste-Hindus for the various welfare measures adopted by the government to ameliorate the socioeconomic conditions of the SCs, the wide economic disparities arising out of landlessness, wage labour, bondage, nonpayment of fair share of agricultural produce to the SC sharecroppers, forced harvesting of crops, forced eviction of the SC ₹ from their land and house-sites, dispute over non-payment of minimum wages prescribed by the state, and land disputes, especially as a result of land reforms and the redistribution of surplus lands.

The reports also reveal that of late many of the atrocities committed have been by some of the affluent parts of the middle caste peasantry—the so-called backward classes—,who have been the major beneficiaries of agrarian reforms and other rural development programmes and of the resultant changes in the economic and political structure in the villages.

It is important to note that, as observed in the seventh report of the Commission for SCs and STs, the incidence of atrocities is relatively lower in states where literacy rates and economic development of the SCs are relatively higher.

ABETMENT OF EXPLOITATIVE BONDAGE

Closely related to the persistence of untouchability and atrocities is the existence of SCs as bonded labourers. As the second report of the Commission for SCs and STs noted, "bonded labourers represent the extreme situation of abject prostration of landless agricultural labourers in the rural economy".

The 21st report of the commissioner for SCs and STs described the bonded labour system as follows:

- The prominent feature of the system is that a man pledges his person or sometimes a member of his family against a loan. The pledger or his nominee is released only on its discharge. Until then the man himself or the member of the family is required to work for his creditor against his daily meals. Since he gets no money, he has to depend upon someone in the family to procure the sum required for his release and this, of course, is rarely available. The relationship lasts for months and sometimes years, occasionally for an entire life time and not infrequently follows the male heir.

The Bonded Labour System Act of 1976 is intended to abolish this evil practice, and identify, free, and rehabilitate its victims of whom at least 80 per cent are reported to be SCs and STs. But its implementation has not served this purpose so far. For one thing, under this act the term bonded labour itself is defined in a limited sense. Of this the fifth report of the Commission for SCs and STs wrote: The very definition of the term 'bonded labour' restricts its meaning so much that its connotation excludes many who are virtually compelled but may not be forced to work as bonded labourers.

It is particularly difficult to establish the element of force applied by the creditors with the result that many labourers are excluded from the meaning of the term though their condition is by no means better than that of others. Because of the apparent loophole in the law, in states like Bihar systems like "attached labour" cannot be brought under the purview of the Bonded Labour System Act, 1976.

Terms like "attached labour" are nothing but a euphemism for bonded labour. For another, the implementation of the act has been far from effective even to release and rehabilitate those bonded labourers who come under its purview.

Consequently, in practice the system still persists in some form or another in many parts of the country. Data available in the eighth report of the Commission for SCs and STs reveal that as on March 31, 1986 only about 2 lakh bonded labourers were identified and freed, and of them only about 1.6 lakh were rehabilitated.

But, if the estimate of bonded labourers in the country at about 22.4 lakh as made by a survey conducted in 1978 by the Gandhi Peace Foundation in collaboration with the National Labour Institute is any indication, by its implementation the act has so far only scratched the surface.

Even going by the conservative estimate of 3.4 lakh as made by the 32nd round of the NSS, the implementation of the act has to cover a lot more ground. What is more, due to inadequacies in the rehabilitation scheme and lack of follow up action, even the freed bonded labourers are either back in or on the verge of further bondage. Of this, the fifth report of the Commission for SCs and STs wrote.

- Rehabilitation measures in many cases do not appear to be sufficient or are adopted unimaginatively. One of the reasons for unimaginative rehabilitation is that, due to poverty, illiteracy and economic backwardness, freed bonded labourers are not in a position to exercise option and preference for a particular scheme of rehabilitation. In such a situation the field functionaries have to decide for themselves the role of freed bonded labourers, taking a decision about what would be the form of rehabilitation.

As examples the report pointed out that in certain land-based schemes the agricultural land allotted was too inadequate for the maintenance of a family, and that sometimes such land itself was fallow and unfit for cultivation.

ECONOMIC DEPENDENCE

That many of the social disabilities of the SCs are because of their continuing existence as the poorest of the poor is stating the obvious. Available data also point towards this. In 1982 the SCs owned only about 8 per cent of the total land owned in the rural areas in the country as a whole, though their households accounted for about 20 per cent of the total rural households.

The index of their access to land ownership reveals that the land owned by them was virtually nil in Haryana and Punjab, and that the ratio of percentage of land owned to the percentage of households was not even one-fourth in Kerala and Bihar, was only between one-fourth and one-half in Gujarat, Andhra Pradesh, Tamil Nadu, Maharashtra, Uttar Pradesh, and Himachal Pradesh, and only between one-half and two-thirds in Karnataka, Madhya Pradesh, Orissa, Rajasthan, and West Bengal.

This low access to land, the principal resource and the main source of power, dominance, oppression and exploitation in rural India, has several implications: First, the higher percentage of landless households among the SCs compared to the rest of the population.

This is so in virtually all the states, in particular in Bihar, Gujarat, Haryana, Rajasthan, Kerala, and Madhya Pradesh. Second, the smaller area of land owned by most of the SC land owning households. In most states the SC households are conspicuous by their absence or negligible presence in the large ownership category, and by their concentration in the marginal ownership category.

In Andhra Pradesh, Bihar, Haryana, Himachal Pradesh, Kerala, Orissa, Punjab, Tamil Nadu, and Uttar Pradesh between 72 per cent and 92 per cent of the land owning households among the SCs were in the marginal ownership category as against only between 39 per cent and 58 per cent of the non-SC households in all but Bihar and Kerala. That the area of land owned by the SC households in the marginal category is too inadequate for their economic use should be only too obvious from the average size of their holdings in all the ownership categories combined. At the all India level, it is only about one-third of that among the non-SCs.

At the state level it is even less. This is especially so in Punjab and Haryana, followed by Kerala, Bihar, Gujarat, Andhra Pradesh, Tamil Nadu, and Uttar Pradesh. In fact, even most of the SC households coming under the marginal ownership category should be treated as landless, inasmuch as a large number of the landless SC households have been pushed into this category consequent on the distribution of the often barren surplus and government waste lands.

This is especially so in Tamil Nadu, where the percentage of landless households among the SCs appears smaller than that among the non-SCs. Third, the greater incidence of poverty among the SCs, and their greater deprivation by and dependence on the caste-Hindus. As the Planning Commission's Working Group on SCs and STs reported, the SCs have few assets; "are generally unable to avail themselves of the new employment opportunities generated through various economic development programmes", and "are in fact caught up in a vicious circle in which they are dependent upon their exploiters for their sustenance and are largely denied opportunities to develop the capabilities of attaining an independent livelihood".

Fourth, in the absence of access to land, as either owners or protected tenants, the SCs are forced to eke out a living mostly by working on the land of others as agricultural labourers on daily wages, by attaching themselves to landlords or cultivators, and as bonded labourers, and partly by pursuing their traditional 'unclean' and socially 'low' occupations of sweeping, scavenging, carrying 'nightsoil', leather work, and mat weaving. The 1981 Census, cultivators accounted for only about 28 per cent, whereas agricultural labourers accounted for as much as 48 per cent of the total working population among the SCs.

The corresponding percentages among the general population were 42 and 25 respectively. The composition of the SC workforce in Andhra Pradesh, Gujarat, Karnataka, Maharashtra, Orissa, and Tamil Nadu was more or less of this all-India pattern.

In the remaining states, with the exception of Himachal Pradesh and to some extent even Madhya Pradesh, that is, in Bihar, Haryana, Kerala, Punjab, Rajasthan, and Uttar Pradesh, the proportion of cultivators among the SCs was much less and that of the agricultural labourers much more than the corresponding proportions among the general population.

Between 1971 and 1981 there was not any drastic change in the composition of the SC workforce in most states. The only exception is Kerala, where the percentage of SC cultivators dropped from about 21 in 1971 to just 2 in 1981, and of agricultural labourers from 66 to 50, with many persons moving into the category of 'other workers'.

In Kerala there was considerable fall in the percentage of agricultural labourers in the general population as well from about 31 to 20. The fragmentation of agricultural holdings and their uneconomic nature, especially after the decade long land reforms implementation of the seventies abolishing landlordism and tenancy, conferring ownership rights on cultivating tenants, and distributing part of the surplus land, and the increasing scarcity of water for agricultural purposes, probably caused this major shift.

EDUCATIONAL CONDITION

As the SCs can take advantage of the measures of the third and most important category of safeguards, especially of employment and educational reservations, only with educational advancement, and educational advancement can come about only with socio-economic advancement, their educational condition can be a crucial indicator of their overall status as beneficiaries of the implementation of the various constitutional provisions.

No doubt, there has been some progress in the growth of literacy among the SCs; In 1961 the literacy percentages among them and the general population including them were 10.3, and 24, whereas in 1981 these were 21.4 and 36.2 respectively. Compared to the general population the increase is relatively more significant in Kerala, Himachal Pradesh, Maharashtra, Gujarat and Tamil Nadu. Despite this increase, the SCs are still far behind the general population in most states.

This is especially so in the case of women. While the male literacy among the SCs itself is much lower than that among the general population, female literacy is much more so. In fact, female literacy among the SCs is virtually nil or negligible in Bihar, Madhya Pradesh, Orissa, Rajasthan, and Uttar Pradesh, only about one-third of their male literacy at the all-India level, and only less than one-half in all but Kerala, Himachal Pradesh, and Maharashtra.

At the all-India level female literacy among the SCs is only about three-fourths of the female literacy among the general population. At the state level, it is even less. Only in Gujarat, Kerala, Himachal Pradesh, and Maharashtra it is above this all-India rate. What is more, literacy, understood in the census' sense of mere ability to read and write, is at best only the base of the educational pyramid, and any growth in it assumes meaning and significance only if it is sustained at the higher levels.

But, this has not happened among the SCs. The available data might give the impression that in the primary stage the SCs have almost caught up with the general population. But, this may not be true even with a steady increase in enrolment over the years. For, enrolment is just the first step in the educational process.

The report on the programme of action on national educational policy, rightly pointed out that "enrolment by itself is of little importance if children do not continue education beyond even a year, many of them not seeing the school for more than a few days". The report noted that nearly 60 per cent of the children drop out between classes I-V and 75 per cent between classes I-VIII and that nearly 22 per cent of the enrolled at the primary stage are outside 6-11 age group, mostly overaged.

For obvious reasons the corresponding percentages among the SCs must be still higher. This is partly evident from the lower enrolment ratios of the SCs at the middle stage. Here again there is considerable interregional variation. If the available data are any indication, the position is far from satisfactory at least in Andhra Pradesh, Bihar, Haryana, Uttar Pradesh, and West Bengal.

As the SCs move up further in the educational ladder, their enrolment ratio also shrinks or their drop out rate increases correspondingly: As the first report of the Commission for SCs and STs noted, for a population of about 15 per cent, at the all-India level the percentage of SC students in professional and other educational courses was only 4.3 in 1964-65, and only 5.7 in 1974-75.

At the state level, it was only in Maharashtra that their enrolment as percentage of the total enrolment in high school, undergraduate and postgraduate equalled or exceeded their population percentage in 1976-78. In virtually all other states it was below their population percentage at all the three stages.

In the high school itself the position was very bad in all but Gujarat, Kerala, and Tamil Nadu, while in the UG and PG it deteriorated even in these states. The position was especially bad in Andhra Pradesh, Bihar, Karnataka, Orissa, Punjab, Rajasthan, Tamil Nadu, Uttar Pradesh, and West Bengal in the case of both UG and PG courses.

While there might have been some change in these percentages in the subsequent years as well, it would not have been so dramatic as to equalise the educational status of the SCs with the general population. The access of the SCs to higher education is further reduced by the fact that the instructions issued by the government of India for reservation of seats are not followed by a number of states.

REPRESENTATION IN PUBLIC SERVICES

If the SCs are thus still far behind the general population in their educational attainments, it is only to be inferred that they are more so in their representation in public services. The representation of the SCs in the central services has increased over the years in all the four classes of jobs, it is only in class 4 that it has been adequate In classes 1 to 3, especially in classes 1 and 2, it has been far below their population percentage.

Comparison of the data on the representation of the SCs in the services of the states for the earliest and latest available years reveals similar shortfalls, despite an increasing trend over the years. It is only in Maharashtra that the representation of the SCs has been adequate in all but class 1; and it is only in Gujarat, and Rajasthan that it has been so at least in classes III and IV.

In all other states their representation has been well below their population percentage. Their representation in classes 1 and 2 has been especially poor in Haryana, Himachal Pradesh, Madhya Pradesh, Orissa, Punjab, Tamil Nadu, Uttar Pradesh, and West Bengal.

LIMITATIONS

As the data thus portray a dismal picture of the nation's

efforts in honouring Ambedkar's legacy, there is urgent need for streamlining the implementation of the various provisions. For doing this, some of its present limitations have to be borne in mind.

These limitations stem from at least nine sources:

- The continuing absence of social conscience, a condition so necessary for the implementation of the programmes aimed at eliminating the disabilities of the SCs. In this context it is pertinent to recall Ambedkar's observation that "rights are protected not by law but by the social and moral conscience of society", that "if social conscience is such that it is prepared to recognise the rights which law chooses to enact, rights will be safe and secure", and that if the "rights are opposed by the community, no law, no parliament, no judiciary can guarantee them I in the real sense of the word"." It is in this sense that the repeated pleas by the Commissioner for SCs and STs for creating awareness among the masses and for involving them in the implementation of the various constitutional provisions have to be understood.
- Lack of an appropriate machinery for effectively enforcing the various measures. The official status accorded, and the facilities and personnel made available, to the Commissioner for SCs and STs appointed under Article 338 have not been commensurate with the nature of his responsibility and the enormous magnitude of the problems concerning the SCs and STs. Consequently, he has not been able to function as a 'watch-dog' agency as envisaged in the constitution. It is as though realising this, and under mounting pressures, that the government of India set up the high-level commission for SCs and STs in 1978. But, as a parallel agency so far it has tended to duplicate the work of the Commissioner for SCs and Sis, who incidentally is also its ex-officio secretary. That apart, this

commission itself has observed that it is greatly handicapped in performing its functions effectively as it does not enjoy any constitutional status, that its role has been purely recommendatory, which has made it at times 'a helpless spectator of non-performance and non-compliance'. Though economic development of the SCs is well recognised as a precondition for overcoming their social disabilities, neither of these agencies is given a clear mandate in this regard, and matters pertaining to policy issues involving the SCs are hardly ever referred to them. Though both these agencies are expected to monitor the implementation of the various safeguards, even the mere monitoring has been wellnigh impossible for them, and their reports deplore time and again their inability to get the required information from the administrations in the states and union territories even after repeated reminders. The effect of their inability on the SCs is confounded by the long delay in preparing and placing their reports before parliament, leave alone any serious debates on the contents of these reports. Very often the reports themselves are very shoddy devoid of systematic presentation of any complete, reliable, and uniform data so necessary for an overall assessment of the performance of the concerned programmes.

- The *ad hoc* formulation of development schemes for SCs and STs without any long-term perspective and an operationally integrated strategy, as observed by, among others, the Planning Commission's Working Group on SCs and STs and the Commissioner for SCs and STs. Though the special component plan introduced since the Sixth Plan is expected to fill this lacunae, so far it has not made much headway.
- The meagre and woefully inadequate budget allocations in the successive five-year plans for the programmes covering the SCs. As the first report of the Commission for SCs and STs noted, during the

first 30 years of planning the SCs and STs were all along left out on the fringe, and the paltry provisions made under the sector of 'welfare of backward classes' hardly accounted for 1 to 2 per cent of the total plan outlays. The situation might not have changed dramatically in the last one decade. In this context the failure of the overall developmental efforts, problems and politics of scarcity, and like Buridan's ass the state's dilemma of choosing between its alternatives, all call for some serious rethinking.

- The misconception of the constitutional provision for taking into account the employment claims of the SCs 'consistently with the maintenance of efficiency of administration'. For preventing the abuse of this efficiency clause, the Planning Commission's Working Group mentioned earlier recommended the deletion of the clause itself. That is, however, only a desperate remedy. Consistency with efficiency has to be construed as equipping the disabled well before and even after their entry into services, to work with others on equal footing through a package of practices. The absence of such a package or its weak and inadequate presence, and the official attempt to arrive only at a crude statistical equality devoid of the much needed socio-cultural vitality which alone can eventually, if at all, equalise the social life of the SCs with that of the mainstream groups, have reduced the special safeguards to tokenism and mere concessions. In the long run the nemesis of such concessions, as Tawney rightly stated in another context, is death by dilution, if not for the administration which in any case is too big to be swayed or swatted by the small number of SCs, at least for the SCs themselves by indirectly arresting their growth potential for want of motivation and morale.
- The 'higher-echelon' nature, of the benefits and the lack of access of the SCs, especially those at the lower

levels, to the administration, to the political system, and to the judiciary.

- The absence of any mechanism for gradually excluding individuals or groups from claiming the benefits of the constitutional provisions for special dispensation once they have attained measurable self reliance in terms of inter-generational socioeconomic, educational, and occupational attainments or mobility. Such exclusion will prevent the present concentration, and result in the diffusion, of benefits, and gradually even phase out these provisions.
- The absence of any mechanism for providing special attention to the most needy by disaggregating the individual beneficiaries into groups most deserving, least deserving, and so on.
- The failure of the provisions, especially those for employment and educational reservations, to penetrate private institutions.

6

Dalit Culture and Civilization

THE MAHAR MOVEMENT'S MILITARY COMPONENT

Dr. Bhimrao Ramji Ambedkar, is famous for being "the most highly educated Untouchable in India." His education, encouraged and financed largely by the Gaikwad of Baroda, led to his role as the Untouchable's chief spokesman, the founder of a political party for Untouchables, and the moving spirit behind organizations, schools, and colleges established for their uplift. One of Ambedkar's final acts was the initiation of a Buddhist conversion movement that ultimately attracted more than 3 million Untouchable adherents. This part of Ambedkar's story is well-known. However, his family's military service in the British Raj is not widely acknowledged for creating an environment that laid the foundation for his later success. Eleanor Zelliot, an expert on Dr. Ambedkar and the Mahar movement, maintains, "[T]he hundred year period of Mahar recruitment into British armies may well have been the single most important factor, aside from economic reasons, in producing the Mahar movement."

This substance examines the importance of military service in improving the social status of Ambedkar's caste, the Mahars of Maharashtra. The focus is on their relationship with the British. The Mahars benefited from their participation in the British Army in a number of ways. First, military service became "a significant part of caste élan and mythology." The first part provides the historical evidence they use to establish their credentials as a caste with martial traditions. The documents detail the advantage, especially education that accrued from military service and discusses their access to the government that otherwise was unavailable to Untouchables.

The final part discusses the British decision to recruit only "martial races," in which the Mahars were not included, for the British Indian Army and the Mahars' efforts to gain reinstatement in the Army. The substance does not focus exclusively on Dr. Ambedkar, but uses him as a point of reference for many of the examples given.

EARLY MILITARY PARTICIPATION

Eleanor Zelliot explains that the British gave Mahars the opportunity to seek different occupations from their traditional role as a village servant. She explains that before the arrival of the British,

- Mahars had no special skill or craft, but performed necessary duties for the village as watchmen, wall-menders, street-sweepers, removers of cattle carcasses, caretakers of the burning ground, servants of any passing governmental official.... Mahar service was essential for the village; his status was low, his work menial, but his place was secure. With the coming of the British and the spread of new ways of administration and communication, the Mahar place in the village grew less important.

Military service provided Mahars with the opportunity to move beyond their traditional social position in the village. In fact, the Mahar tradition of being in armies precedes the British Raj. The recorded history of the Mahars' military achievements dates back to Shivaji's Army in the 1600s. Cynthia Enloe, a noted sociologist who has written extensively on ethnic-military relationships, states, "The best of all militaries in the eyes of a state elite is one in which the most competent soldiers are also the most politically reliable, because they have the greatest stake in the continuation of the current system. " The Mahars met this condition just as to descriptions of their loyalty. Colonel V. Longer, author of Forefront Forever:

The History of the Mahar Regiment, states:

- There were a number of useful functions which the Mahars performed. Their Argus eye; their daring tenacity and determination; their faithfulness, loyalty and honesty; their courage and candour, were inestimable qualities which were always held in respect and were for ever utilized to advantage by the village.... In course of time, their voice carried great weight when there were disputes over property as their evidence was considered most accurate, intimate, and trustworthy.

This sense of loyalty and trustworthiness led Shivaji to include Mahars as a vital component of his army. Shivaji, leader of the Maratha nation, fought for a Hindu empire, but using Untouchables did not bother him. He "found the Mahars useful, for the wily Maratha chief realised that the best way of obtaining the maximum results was to mix up various castes in his garrison forces." He used the Mahars "to watch the jungles at the foot of the hill forts, act as scouts and [they] kept the forts supplied with wood and fodder." This was the first exposure of the Mahars to an organized army that provided its soldiers with steady pay and benefits.

After Shivaji's death, Mahar units continued to serve his descendants throughout the 1700s. Their experience with Shivaji and others encouraged them to seek similar employment as sepoys of the British East India Company. Ardythe Basham, in her detailed examination of the Mahars and the military, found the perceived early martial history to be an important part of Mahar identity. She concludes, "Whether or not these incidents are historically true, they are widely accepted by the Mahars as part of their tradition, and now form part of the official history of [today's] Mahar Regiment."

The Mahars have often used this martial identity, rooted in the 1600s, to legitimate their continued presence in the military. Mahars began their service with the British in the 1750s. Stephen P. Cohen, an expert on the Indian Army, discusses the importance of Mahars in the Bombay Army in his seminal work, The Indian Army: Contribution to the Development of a Nation. He writes that Mahars were a sizeable portion of the armies of the Mahratta chieftain Shivaji, served as hereditary local policeman, and were thus a "natural" martial class. Heavily recruited in the premutiny years, the Mahars constituted a fifth to a quarter of the entire Bombay Army.

In addition to the size of the Mahar contingent, they were also praised for their conduct as soldiers. The Mahars rewarded the British with the same loyalty that Shivaji had enjoyed. The Bombay Army fought in several battles, and in most, the Mahars were recognized for their skills.

Longer proclaims:

- Much praise was showered on the Mahar Sepoys of the Bombay Army who endured the rigours of difficult marches when rations were low and disease was high among men and animals. Whether they were charging ahead or were besieged or taken prisoner-of-war, whether they were storming fortresses or making tactical withdrawals, they always stood steadfast by their officers and comrades, never letting down the honour of their Regiments.

The recorded history of their exploits, especially prior to the mutiny of 1857, supports this effusive adoration. Basham located evidence of Mahar participation in the Second and "Third Anglo-Maratha War, the Second Anglo-Sikh War and the Second Afghan War." The Mahars' exploits in these conflicts form an important part of their military lore. The Mahar participation in the battle of Koregaon on 1 January 1818 is the most famous, and also the best documented, action involving Mahar soldiers. This battle gave the British the advantage in the Third Anglo-Maratha War.

The successful defence of Koregaon by a small force of 500 men... under the command of Capt. F. F. Staunton fought without rest or respite, food or water continuously for twelve hours against a large force of 20,000 Horse and 8,000 Infantry of Peshwa Baji Rao II who was threatening the British garrisons at Kirkee and Poona. Mahars dominated Staunton's unit. The Peshwa's troops inexplicably withdrew that evening, despite their overwhelming numbers, giving the British an important victory. The men of the 2/1st Regiment Bombay Native Infantry, including many Mahars, who fought in this battle, were honoured for their bravery.

The official report to the British Resident at Poona recalls the "heroic valour and enduring fortitude" of the soldiers, the "disciplined intrepidity" and "devoted courage and admirable consistency" of their actions. Further, the action is commemorated by a monument, with the names of twenty-two Mahars killed there, erected at the site of the battle and by a medal issued in 1851. Today, the monument still "serves as a focal point of Mahar heroism." Similar anecdotes are recorded in the written histories of the Mahar Regiment and Bombay Army. All demonstrate that most Mahars soldiers were dedicated and courageous.

In addition to Army units on land, the Mahars formed a vital component of the Bombay Army's Marine Battalion. This unit's history is well documented and provides numerous examples of Mahar actions, including several acts of bravery by Mahars in the battalion. In September 1810, during the Second Maratha War, several Mahars proved their loyalty when captured by the French Navy. The French tried to induce their prisoners to enter their own service, a practice which enjoyed some success with Irish, Madrassi and Bengali troops. On this occasion, the Bombay sepoys were shown the captured Bengal and Madras Sepoys dressed in French uniforms and enjoying considerable privileges and luxuries, whereupon the Bombay Detachment started abusing them as being dead to all shame that they could forget the oath and desert their colours.

The upshot was that they were very roughly treated and some were severely wounded. To the seventeen survivors who reached Bombay a special medal was given and of this number twelve were Mahars. This is just one of many cases where Mahars distinguished themselves as a part of the Marine Battalion and is another part of the martial history that the Mahars used to legitimize their important role in the British

Indian Army. But, in the wake of the 1857 mutiny and threats from Russia, the British reexamined their recruitment policies. The Mahars were a casualty of this new thinking.

THE MAHARS DELISTMENT

Despite the Mahars' long martial history, the British ceased recruiting them in 1893. The Bombay and the other Presidency Armies were reevaluated following the 1857 mutiny. The Peel Commission first examined class composition of the armies in 1858. One report to the Commission "emphasized that `we cannot practically ignore it, so long as the natives socially maintain it.'"

This led to the discrimination against the Mahars and other low-caste groups as well as some Brahman castes which were considered unreliable. General Lord Roberts, while not originating the concept of martial races, was instrumental in implementing a strategy of building "class regiments." Recruiting policies were rewritten, and the Bombay Army "was notified that the Mahars, together with a number of other classes of the Bombay Army, would no longer be recruited to the Army." Lord Roberts recorded his rational in his autobiography, Forty-One Years in India.

He writes:

- I have no doubt whatever of the fighting powers of our best Indian troops; I have a thorough belief in, and admiration for, Gurkhas, Sikhs, Dogras, Rajputs, Jats and, selected Mahomadans; I thoroughly appreciate their soldierly qualities; brigaded with British troops, I would be proud to lead them against any European enemy.

Roberts thought that the first step to making the Indian Army was "to substitute men of the more warlike and hardy races for the Hindustani sepoys of Bengal, the Tamils and Telagus of Madras, and the so-called Mahrattas of Bombay."

He was convinced that:

- In the British Army the superiority of one regiment over another is mainly a matter of training; the same courage and military instinct are inherent in English,

Scotch, and Irish alike, but no comparison can be made between the martial value of a regiment recruited amongst the Gurkhas of Nepal or the warlike races of Northern India, and of one recruited from the effeminate peoples of the south.

The Mahars believed that their martial history demonstrated their abilities as warriors, but the British had made their decision. Mahars could only enlist as bandsmen or clerks. This would not provide the same opportunities for promotion, and allow little change in their social status. As expected, the Mahars felt the British had betrayed them after over 100 years of loyal service to the British Raj. Throughout India, there was controversy about which groups should remain in the Army.

The Mahars had support from some British soldiers, including three commanders who recommended their continued service. The commander of the 2nd Grenadiers argued that 'the Parwari is of far better fighting material than the Deccani Mussulman," and suggested that the Marine Battalion might be made a class regiment of Parwaries. The commanding officer of the 9th Bombay Infantry thought that a regiment of Parwaries, especially from the Deccan, would "give a very good account of itself."

The Commanding officer of the 19th Bombay Infantry stated that:

- "They are possessed of as much soldierly quality as many

However, their assistance was not enough to overcome the sentiments of Lord Roberts and other senior officers of the British Indian Army. Longer provides an excellent commentary on the impact of the decision on the Mahars.

He writes:

- The excellent system with its cosmopolitan composition, which had worked out over the years, was dismantled and destroyed. The Mahars, who had proudly carried the Colours of various Regiments of the Bombay Army, were crestfallen and heartbroken. For years they had provided abundant evidence of

> their courage, resolution, perseverance, constancy, and fidelity. When they bade farewell to arms there were eight Subedar-Majors, 62 Subedars, 34 Jemadars, and a host of Non-Commissioned Officers and Sepoys of the Mahar community who had served with distinction in the Bombay Army.

The Mahars would continue to fight for the right to re-enlist in the Indian Army. They were loath to lose the benefits that the military provided. Furthermore, the education provided to the soldiers had created an educated cadre that would transfer their skills into political action. However, there were few Mahars left in the Army by the beginning of World War I.

BENEFITS OF MILITARY SERVICE

Eleanor Zelliot notes that the "emergence of Mahar leaders and a new spirit of militancy in the 19th century was due in large measure to the influence of education acquired in the military."

The result was that:

- During the 19th and 20th centuries, a substantial number of Mahars removed themselves from their traditional village servant role. The establishment of British rule in Bombay Presidency provided Mahars with the opportunity for service in the army, employment in cotton mills, ammunition factories, railroads, dockyards, construction work, and as servants in British homes. The 1921 Census records that only 13.5 per cent of the Mahar working force of nearly 300,000 were employed in their traditional occupation even though most Mahars maintained strong ties with their ancestorial village.

The Mahars' ability to work among the British exposed them to Western ways, and helped them to realise that their status as Untouchables did not keep them from working in successful and satisfying occupations. They aggressively used the advantages provided by their relationship with the British. Military service provided important benefits to its soldiers.

The benefits include "pay and pensions, access to education and/or specialized training, preferential access to employment, enhanced social status, and personal satisfaction." For the Mahars, the access to education and increased social status was the most important benefits. The best example of their results was Dr. Ambedkar.

Zelliot writes that Ambedkar's experiences were "[f]ree from the traditional village role, his early life was spent among educated ex-army men, imbued with the pride of soldiers and acquainted with a more sophisticated Hinduism than that found in the village." In fact, Ambedkar extends much of the credit for the start of the movement to improve the Untouchables' place in society to contact with the British Army.

He maintained:

- Until the advent of the British, the Untouchables were content to remain Untouchables.... In the army of the East India Company there prevailed the system of compulsory education for Indian soldiers and their children, both male and female. The education received by the Untouchables in the army... gave them a new vision and a new value. They became conscious that the low esteem in which they had been held was not an inescapable destiny but was a stigma imposed on their personality by the cunning contrivances of the priest. They felt the shame of it as they ever did before and were determined to get rid of it.

It is indisputable that this access to education was helpful to Ambedkar, and therefore, to all of India's Untouchable communities. Ambedkar's family had extensive links to the military. Additionally, his mother's "father and her six uncles were all Subedar Majors in the Army," the highest rank that Indians could hold.

Ambedkar's father also was a Subhedar Major and:

- A full-fledged teacher trained at the Normal School then established by Government for turning out teachers to impart education that was then compulsory for the children as well as both male and female relations of the military servants. For fourteen years Ramji Sakpal served as Headmaster in the military school.

Undoubtedly, the accomplishments of this family were exceptional. Nonetheless, the availability of education had a positive effect on all members of Mahars in the military, including women. Consequently, Basham concludes, "The loss of this education option with the loss of their right of enlistment was therefore a real blow, not merely the loss of a theoretical benefit which few actually received." The quality of life for soldiers and their families suffered because of the loss of educational opportunities available through participation in the military. Mahars joined the military with the intent of improving their social status. They were successful in this regard.

As Basham explains:

- Within the closed circle of the regiment, caste prejudice was, if not actually absent, at least officially discouraged. Army regulations no distinction was made between soldiers on the basis of their caste or community.... Mahar officers were able to command men of other castes apparently without difficulty.

After growing up in this environment of equality it was a shock for the Untouchables to travel and live in situations away from the military cantonments. Ambedkar's biographer, Dhananjay Keer, writes of young Ambedkar's shock the first time he travelled outside the military environment while he was in school. He and his brother were travelling to meet his father in a distant village. At the railway station, they hired a bullock cart to take them to the village, but

- hardly had the cart gone a few yards when the god-fearing touchable Hindu cartman, to his wrath, came to know that the well-dressed boys in his cart were the accursed Untouchables! In a fit of rage he threw them out on the road as one overturns the dust bins;for he felt they had polluted his wooden cart and destroyed the purity of his domestic animals!

This was Ambedkar's first experience that forced him to confront his status as an Untouchable. Life in the military cantonment had sheltered him from the prejudice and discrimination for the early part of his life. After retirement, there was a period of adjustment for Mahars who lived outside the cantonment.

Basham concludes:

- As nearly as can be deduced from rather limited information, it would seem that while actually in the army, or after retired or taking other employment, while in contact with British employers and officials, the Mahar soldier was not treated in any way differently from a soldier of higher caste. Once retired and living in his native village, a Mahar soldier, although he might have a relatively high status among the Mahar community and even among caste Hindus, would nevertheless once again have to accept his untouchable status.

The important point is, even after retirement, Mahars with a military background still had access to the British government. The retired military officers were an effective lobby for Mahar rights. Retired officers also created a group of political leaders with access to the Indian government. This was especially true near military cantonments in Poona, Satara and Ahmednagar. Basham relates an incident where Mahar children were not being offered equal educational opportunities.

Local caste Hindus and low-level British education officials refused the Mahar demands for Mahar boys to be integrated into classes with caste-Hindu boys. The dispute was resolved in favour of the Mahars. Basham argues that this demonstrates they were seeking not just education for their sons, although this was obviously important, but also an improvement in their social status.

The fact that many of these parents were retired officers, and therefore could legitimately make a claim on the attention to government officials, indicates the value of military service in this respect. Clearly, the type of access available to the soldiers, active or retired, was unavailable to most Untouchables All the benefits the Mahars received were the result of their ability to develop a link with the British. This helped them overcome the obstacles erected by the Hindu social system.

Zelliot observes:

- It was their entry into the British army which proved significant for the subsequent history of the Mahar movement. It is important to gauge this significance. It consists not in any automatic elevation in the social hierarchy through military service, which indeed is ruled out in a hierarchical system governed by considerations of ascriptive status and ritual purity. It rather consists in the fact that military service at such an early date exposed them to British institutions much before the dissemination of western culture took place on a large scale.

Such an exposure socialized them sufficiently early to the new political order so that when new opportunities and alternatives became available, they were found prepared to use them more effectively than those groups which did not have this opportunity. Following the delistment of 1893, the Mahars would need all the access and knowledge they had gained to overcome the impact of being refused service in the Army.

THE FIGHT FOR RE-ENLISTMENT

The Mahars did not give up their positions in the Army easily. The British decision of Mahar "[d]elistment in 1893 had been a severe blow to them as a community, not only threatening their economic status, but also giving official sanction to caste Hindu discrimination against them." Overcoming both of these threats was the focus of two different efforts to petition the Government of India to reconsider its decision between 1894 and the start of the first World War.

The Mahars used two different strategies to influence the government; with both they tried to regain enlistment privileges in the army and an improved social status. Zelliot maintains that these efforts "show the importance of army service to the Mahars. This was clearly the beginning of their efforts to induce government to intervene on their behalf, and their questioning of their traditional inferior status." In both instances, the movement was led by educated, former military officers. The first organized attempt was in April 1895. Some of the details of the petition drive presented by Zelliot and Basham are speculative. Basham, who has completed the most recent study, states it was originally presented to the Viceroy, but was later returned for resubmission through the Bombay Government. It appears that the petition was submitted by Gopal Baba Walangkar, a retired military officer, on behalf of the Anarya Doshpariharak Mandali, the non-Aryan committee for the rightings of wrongs, an Untouchable organization. Dr. Ambedkar, following the death of his father, found a copy of the petition in his documents. Ambedkar "believed that his father had obtained the assistance of Justice M. B. Ranade in preparing the petition."

The petition compares Mahar actions to those of the higher castes and requests reinstatement in the military. The petition's pleas were simple. The Mahars believed that, in 1859, the Government had declared that the castes who fought loyally for the British were to be given due preference for military enlistment.

Therefore, they demanded:

- In view of that promise, Government should employ in civil, military and police department without any discrimination these faithful and honest persons. They should also be given education and proper opportunity for suitable posts in the department.

The case they presented for reinstatement was more complicated than their demands. Much of their argument attempts to demonstrate that their identification as Untouchables was a mistake. The 1895 petition argues that the Mahars as a group who are actually of the Kshatriya caste. This represents the Mahars attempt to change their position in the caste structure by "Sanskritization."

The petition states:

- Our ancestors were Kshatriya. In about the year 1396 there was a great famine for about 12 years which was called Durhavedi famine. That time our ancestors survived by eating whatever they could find. Therefore, they were considered low case under the Peshwa rule.

It continues by attacking the legitimacy of the higher castes. It claims, "The so called high caste and pure people's ancestors were as degraded as our people and were used to eat flesh of cow and beef. They wrote their own religious scriptures." Finally, the petition provides a "creation myth" about the high castes.

It maintains:

- The high caste people of the South are progeny of Australian Semitic Anaryas and African Negroes whereas the high caste people from North are mixture of several castes.... Several castes of foreign origin became high caste Hindus by giving up beef-eating.
- The Chitpavan Brahmins of Konkan came from the Jewish race. They fled from Africa for fear of their lives by the invaders and their ship was wrecked nearby Malabar coast. Their children and women drown and died in the sea. Those men who survived, married the native low caste women.... [W]hen they became rulers, they called themselves Brahmins.

The document's tenor shows the importance of military service to the Mahars and the use of Sanskritization tactics to show they were at least equal to the alleged high castes. This campaign was unsuccessful. The Mahars were unaware of the debate "over recruitment policy or the acceptance of Lord Roberts views on martial races" which was the prime component in the British decision.

However, Basham shows "the government of India took the petition seriously enough to request information about the Koregaon monument from the government of Bombay. Eighteen months after the initial submission of the petition, the Indian government replied that it was "unable to rescind the orders which have been issued regarding the castes to be admitted to the Bombay Army." Shortly after the turn of the century, a second attempt was organized. The second major petition was submitted to the government three times between 1904 and 1910.

The document's "signatories included forty-two military pensioners" including Dr. Ambedkar's father. Basham's research found that "[s]everal of the signatories had also written letters to newspapers or had signed at least one other petition, suggesting a long-term commitment and a willingness to agitate for change." This petition had a broader base of support than the one in 1895.

This campaign was more sophisticated than the first. The spokesman, Shivram Janba Kamble, spoke English. More importantly, the petition's "appeal for consideration was not on the basis of the Mahars' having been demoted from Kshatriyahood, but on the grounds of former service, English justice and human worth." This pragmatic approach attracted greater support than the earlier petition, and used arguments that were later refined by Dr. Ambedkar. In fact, Ambedkar took over leadership of the Mahars from Kamble.

The 1910 petition was more polite and less argumentative than the 1895 petition. The document states, "We do not aspire to high political privileges and positions, since we are not educationally qualified for them, but humbly seek employment in the lowest grades of the Public Service, in the ranks of Police Sepoys and of soldiers in the Indian Army."

It continued:

- We are making no new demands; we do not claim employment in services in which we have not been engaged before. Indeed, some few of our people do still hold positions in the Police Force, and have acquitted themselves most honourably. So also have our people been employed in the Indian Army from the very commencement of the British Raj in our country, and they have risen to the highest positions by their valour and good conduct.

Despite the reasoned arguments, this petition demands, like the first, were denied. The manpower demands of World War I had a greater effect, and beginning in 1914 Mahars, again, were recruited into the Army and given their own Regiment, the 111 Mahars. The Regiment's three battalions "were formed the towards the end of the war, but they did not see action and their martial qualities were untested." Shortly after the war, the Regiment was disbanded by the British "on the excuse of the economy." More important, however, is that the petition drives provided an organization for Dr. Ambedkar to use after the war to improve the social status of Untouchables.

Basham correctly concludes:

- Military service had been a significant factor for the Mahars in two respects. Education and skills acquired through military service created a class of community leaders, and the wish to retain the social and economic benefits derived from military service was a powerful incentive to organize behind these leaders and work for a common goal. A high level of organization and political activity in the Mahar community by the 1940s was therefore at least in part a consequence of their military past.

The long association with the military gave Mahars an issue to organize around and the movement then worked to achieve more substantial achievements than just military service.

NOW WE CAN SAY

The 120 years of service in the British military gave the Mahars excellent skills.

Basham concludes:

- Mahar soldiers were able to establish a link with the most powerful institution in India—the British Raj—and in some instances to use that link to bypass local authorities. Military service was also a way to sever the ties of village customary law which maintained the inferior status of the Mahars. Other forms of employment could take the Mahar out of the village, but none offered long-term financial security in the form of pensions.

This case study shows how military service has assisted the Mahars to fight the stigma of untouchability. Their positive experiences fighting with Shivaji encouraged them to seek similar opportunities from the British. It is clear, that in their service they received their most tangible benefits. Before delistment, Mahars in the Bombay Army received a steady wage, housing, and education. With this, many were able to retire with a pension, which, often, eliminated the need to return to the traditional Mahar occupations following their military service. These obvious benefits were eliminated following the 1893 decision. However, military service still influenced Mahar life following delistment.

As Basham argues:

- If the army system of education had produced no effects for the Mahars other than to provide an appropriate environment for Ambedkar's early life this in itself would be a significant impact on the Mahar community.

Furthermore, the petition drives provided political organizations to press for overcoming the stigma of Untouchability. There were other benefits that were accrued, even if their requests for reinstatement were refused until the beginning of the war. Kamble's work in Poona that formed the base for Ambedkar's later political movements is the best example of this. Therefore, even after military service was taken away from the Mahars, the traditions and accrued benefits continued to be an advantage to this Untouchable community.

UNDERSTAND BAHUJAN PHILOSOPHY INSTEAD OF PROLETYSING

INDIAN HISTORY

This is in response to letter from Dr. Choudhrie in DV of Sept. 1-15. I am glad to know that he is trying to study Ancient

Indian History. Not only it is illuminating, but it throws ample light on the happenings of today. One finds that from times immemorial, the struggle between the so called upper caste savarnas on one side and the rest of population on other side is going on. It had assumed different names, shapes and forms during the course of different periods of history, and the history of India is nothing but the history of conflict between these two ideologies, as is well demonstrated by Dr. Ambedkar.

The present name for this is bahujan-vad and bahujan-virodh-vad. The present day protagonists of these are Phuley, Shahu and Ambedkar on one side and Tilak, Gandhi and Golwalkar on the other. All the leaders of christians and muslims need to understand this point and explain it to the gullible ignorant and illiterate christian and muslim masses, instead of thinking in lines of proletising Dalits. These are the only two ideologies in present day India, and sooner the people understand this, earlier they will be freed from their slavery.

UNCHRISTIAN SIDE OF THE INDIAN CHURCH

In his rejoinder to Dr. Chaudhrie's letter, VTR has very aptly described the situation. If I remember it correctly, he had commented that the missionaries are educating the children of oppressors, who tomorrow will come to power and see that these very schools be closed.

It is like feeding milk to the serpents' offsprings. He had also suggested that at least 50% of seats in all christian convents must be given only to SCs and STs at no charge, and the deficit be made good by charging double fees from the children of oppressors.

AMBEDKAR'S ADVICE TO CHRISTIANS

I like to make all conversant with one of the speeches of Dr. Ambedkar, during the period of active consideration of choice of religion to adopt. May be, this might clear doubts, if any. The speech delivered to Indian Christians of Sholapur. Published in 'Janata' of 5.2.1938, reproduced from

'Dnyanodaya' "From the available religions and personalities in the world, I consider only two-Buddha and Christ for conversion. We want a religion for me and my followers which will teach equality freedom among men, and how man must behave with men and God, how child should behave with father etc. "Missionaries feel they have done their duty when they convert an untouchable to Christianity. They do not look after their political rights. I find this is a big fault in Christians. Because they have not entered into politics up till now. It is difficult for any institution to survive without political support. We, Untouchables, though are ignorant and illiterate, we are in movement. That is why we have 15 seats in the Legislative Assembly. Students are getting scholarships, there are government hostels. Such is not the case of Christian students. If an untouchable student getting scholarship get converted, his scholarship is stopped though his financial status remains same. If you were in politics, things would have been opposed.

"Your society is educated. Hundreds of boys and girls are matric. These people have not agitated against this injustice unlike the uneducated untouchables. If any girl becomes a nurse or any boy becomes a teacher they are involved in their own affairs, they do not get involved in public affairs. Even clerks and officers are busy in their work, he ignores the social injustice. Your society is so much educated, how many are District judges or magistrates? I tell you, this is because of your neglect towards politics, because there in nobody to talk of and fight for your rights...."

BSP AND KANSHIRAM

To relieve the humanity from suffering, in India, the remedy is to develop the spirit of Bahujan Samaj. We cannot progress by merely "Dalit Unity", or by only "Dalit Muslim Unity", or by only "Dalit Christian Unity", we have to build a Bahujan Samaj, which is not an easy task. One has to understand the mechanics of Bahujan Samaj. There are many misconceptions about BSP, Kanshiram and Mayavati, purposefully spread by vested interests. One has to understand

Bahujan Philosophy with all its intricacies. It is pity that Dr. Choudhrie could not get time to understand BSP while he was in Punjab. I hope he will have ample opportunity to understand it in M.P, where there is remarkable influence of BSP. BSP is not merely a political party unlike many others; it is a movement. One must read Phuley, Shahu Ambedkar and follow it with reading about Kanshiram and BSP.

SOCIAL SERVICE AND SOCIAL TRANSFORMATION

This is the important point which one must understand. Medical ethics says, prevention is better than cure. Instead of curing a disease give more attention to its prevention. To mend a fracture is social service, to create environment so that fractures do not take place is social transformation.

To give vitamin pills to malnourished Adivasi children is social service, to give their parents employment so that they can buy wholesome food for their children is social transformation. To give charity to a beggar is social service, to create social atmosphere so that nobody has to beg is social change. To give rice at ₹2 per kilo when market price is ₹7/- is social service, to raise the income of the person so that he can buy the rice at market price is social change. To feed the hungry is social service, to create situation where nobody remains hungry is social change. To teach an illiterate is social service, to destroy the social structure which made him illiterate is social change.

To open a new school in thee vicinity of an illiterate poor colony of zopadpatti could be social service, to motivate the poor hungry and illiterate man to send his child to school walking five kilometres away even on an empty stomach is social transformation. To protect a weak person by giving him weapons is social service, to make him strong enough to let him manufacture and use his own weapons is social change. To teach an egalitarian prayer to a school child may be social service, to dynamite the scriptures spreading inequality among human beings is a social change.

To assure protection to scared minorities may be social justice, to give them power so that they can defend themselves is social transformation. I have great respect for missionaries who did a tremendous amount of good work. If there were no missionaries, there would have been no Phuley, no Shahu and no Ambedkar, let alone Kanshiram and Mayawati. In my humble opinion, missionaries in India are doing social service, and are the very best at that. But still it is not social transformation. I think here lies the importance of BSP, which is not a political party alone but a movement which stands for not social service or social justice alone but for social transformation and economic emancipation.

THE NATURE OF DALIT MUSLIM UNITY

This is in response to substance by Adv. Md. Karim. It was a great misfortune that Dr. Ambedkar and Br. Jinnah could not work together, Adv. Karim says. He says Azad was a stooge. He says the anti Muslim activities are a symptoms and not a disease. He says Muslims are not a minority. He believes that population of Muslims could be more than presumed 15 per cent. He also quotes authorities to show that Islam is an egalitarian religion.

All this need not refuted and any Bahujan can agree with all these points. He avers that Muslim masses in India are in a need of allies to fight the existing system under the guidance of Islam He advises his Muslim brothers to help the Dalits in all spheres, and keep good contacts for future interaction. This is quite correct. But the main point is, what kind of unity is sought for.

He says: "The future of India lies in the unity of Dalits and Muslims-not under the banner of this party or that because no party is aiming at providing an alternative to the existing social, political and economic setup but under the invigourating and revolutionary message of Islam..." Why no political party is thought to be neccesary? Is it an invitation for the Bahujans to adopt Islam?

Is it a proletising work? If it is, well and good; nothing wrong in that; only that perhaps DV is not a forum for it. Our experience of mixing religion with politics is always counter productive. The combination does neither promote the religion nor the politics. The political meetings of RPI used to start with Buddhist prayers, the non Buddhists in the party, gradually, faded away.

The religious sermons to Budhists used to end with request for support to RPI work, the non-RPI Buddhists stopped comming. I feel the two must not be combined, the religion and politics. I hope Adv. Karim does not wish to propagate religion from political platform.

WHAT IS THE SPIRIT OF ISLAM

Do the Muslims consider Dalits as non-hindus? I think, it is the first neccesity that they must make a distinction between "Hindus" and Dalits. Dalit leaders have time and again declared that. Leaders of all Dalit parties, of all shades and colours. But Muslim leaders do not think about this. I think this is the main hurdle. No doubt, Islam is a great religion. Also it can not be gainsaid that meeting of Ambedkar and Jinnah could not bear fruits.

If the unity has to bear any fruits, today, it has got to be based on secular points. The basis has to be non-religious. It should be purely on political ideology. What is that ideology? I believe, that ideology could only be Ambedkarism. Our Muslim brothers have got to get themselves aquainted with Spirit of Ambedkarism, which is different from Spirit of Buddhism

HINDU MUSLIM RIOTS AND DALITS

A letter by Dr. Ambedkar sent from England at the time of Third Round Table Conference published in "Janata" of 24.12.1932, "When Hindus and Muslims fight among themselves, the Untouchables tend to incline towards Muslims. They feel, they would be benefitted if they develope friendship with Muslims. But Untouchables should keep in mind that it is not all that true as it appears and so they should be very careful. What I experienced at the time of Sarada Act about the Muslim policy, can not called satisfactory.

I got first severe jolt when I found that almost all the Muslims got ready to oppose the essential Act like Sarda Act along with the obsolete and puranic, fundamentalists and revivalist orthodox Hindus. And at the time of Round Table Conference, I got second experience now that their attitude can be how narrow and retrograde, like that of sanatani orthodox Hindus.

A special telegram from the Brahmin President of Varnashram Brahman Sangha was received recently by a Muslim delegate, Mr. Gazanavi. It was a message that Muslims should cooperate with orthodox Hindus in opposing the Untouchables temple entry movement. It was also suggested that, if India gets freedom, it would be dangerous to the religion of both Hindus as well as Muslims, and so the religious Muslims should be careful about the swaraj like religious Hindus.

The sanatani brahmins also requested Mr. Gaznabi to put forward the side of sanatani Hindus by the Muslim delegates in the RTC! Thus, it could be said that these arthodox brahmins have materialised the proverb that 'we are orhtodox brahmins and our relatives are muslims'. Mr. Gazanabi has published this telegram in 'Times' here. The fact, that the orthodox Bengali Muslim like Mr. Gaznabe should be entrusted the job of preserving the religion of Hindus, by the orthodox Hindus, and that he should accept it, should be borne in mind by all the reformists in India.

It is an execlent example of how an orthodox sanatani Hindu is ready to pray even an 'yavan' or a 'mlenchha' when he finds the life of his 'dharma' is in danger. And the 'dharma' of Hindus is such a provokative one, that whenever any thing new happens, or due to time any change takes place in traditional customms, they shout that, dharm' is in danger. Just like a sanatani Hindu, the Indian Muslim also is a strange object. He is averse to all social reforms. His corelegionists outside India have turned to be social revolutionaries.

A Muslim patriot like Kemal Pasha has quashed all customs and traditions which are hurdles against the progress of nation and human life. I have great respect and affinity for Kemal Pasha. But the Indian Muslims, even the patriots and nationalists like Shaukat Ali, do not like Kemal Pasha and

Amanullah. Because they are reformists, and in the eyes of a Indian Muslim, reform is a sacrilege."

SUB-CASTES WITHIN THE SC/ST

This has reference to the substance on rivalry of subcastes Madigas and Malas among the SCs, and a frank debate welcomed by our editor.. Our editor has welcomed the rivalry among the subcastes in these words: "There is nothing to be ashamed of or worried about the inter-Dalit bickering. Rather this should be welcomed." This attitude is quite in keeping with his old known notion that if you could strengthen each jati and make them strong enough to demand their rightful share just as to their population from the 'evil' jati people, then the system of jatis will crash.

Unfortunately I beg to defer with him. Some time back Bhoja Tarakkam from Hyderabad had argued that it is against Ambedkarite principles to think of strengthening any jatis. I fully agree and endorse his view. Dr. Ambedkar had specifically advocated that the process of abolition of castes must not start with abolition of subcastes. He averred that if the process stops at that level, as suggested, end up by strengthening the caste system. What applies to subcastes equally applies to castes within the SC/ST group. Annihilation of castes was what Dr. Ambedkar wanted.

It could only be achieved through social amalgamation by inter caste marriages, and to promote that the sanction behind the sastras must end. This was what was intended. Your contention is that, when castes, individually, become strong enough, will fight with BSO and get their rightful number of positions, and thereby reduce the power of BSO. Unfortunately this does not happen in practice. When Ambedkar said educate, agitate and organize, he meant agitate against BSO oppressors.

We took it to mean struggle amongst ourselves. We fight amongst ourselves for every thing and we beg for favours from others. We have become subservient dummy stooges of others, popularly termed 'chamchas'. Though we do not have enough strength to get elected in Parliament, we rush to the feet of men in power, and that too individually and separately, ignoring the so called unity, and beg for a berth in ministry for self and get kicked out. All our self respect vanishes that time. This is the state of affairs. How do you expect that such a people will be able to fight with the oppressors for the rights of masses, they can only beg for self prosperity.

First we have to increase our strength, then and then alone we can bargain. Power is something that can not be obtained by begging, begging only budgets petty alms. Why some castes among the SC/ST could not progress? This is the question one must answer with some clear vision and self introspection. It must be agreed that, in spite of equal opportunity given by the reservations which started at the same time for all SC/STs, the progress made by different castes among the SC/ST is not uniform. There are many reasons, which must be understood before we devise ways and means to bridge the gap of disparity among the SC/ST castes. The main point is that, Dr. Ambedkar had given a call to denounce old ways of earning a subsistence and embark on mass scale education. Some people followed his ways were Ambedkarites, and some followed Gandhi's ways and were called 'harijans'. They did not change.

Those people who abandoned their ancestral calling and gave up the dirty means of livelihood, which they were ordained to follow by the Brahmnical social order for centuries, progressed faster and those who stuck to their old professions lingered behind. Why there is dissatisfaction? The main reason is that there is supposed to be a restriction imposed by Supreme Court to limit reservations to 50 per cent.

Under what circumstances Supreme Court has given this ruling and what are legal ways to counter it, must be debated by the legal luminaries from among the bahujans and people should take steps legal or legislative to amend the constitution, if needed, to ensure that every caste must get their rightful share in running of government, *i.e.* in legislature and executive, including judiciary, as Kanshiram says "jisaki jitani sankhyaa bhaari, usaki utani bhaagidaari". I consider this is the only method, by which dissatisfaction among the various castes can be reduced. When there is enough for everybody, nobody should grumble.

There is now grumbling because share of 50 per cent people is appropriated by 15 per cent. Reservations must not be on economical grounds Shri T.P.Kamala- nathan has given, in the same issue of DV, the instances of people against caste based reservations. Everybody knows that manuvadis are behind this. Unfortunate part of this is that, even the OBC people, who are co-sufferers, are brain washed to support this argument. They are made to believe that the OBCs can't get jobs because of SC/ST reservations.

They should be explained that,

- Even after half a century, SC/ST strength is not complete as per their quota, and SC/ST are not responsible for grabbing OBC's share.
- OBC's share is grabbed by those from 15 per cent, who rightfully deserve only 15 per cent and are now holding about 70 per cent.
- We find even today it is not very difficult for higher caste people to obtain a certificate of being SC/ST by corrupt means.

When they can obtain false caste certificates, how much easy it will be to obtain a false income certificate of low income for these people, and how much corruption will be there to prevent SC/ST poor people from obtaining their rightful share. The question of enlightenment of OBCs is rather crucial.

They have been brain washed by upper castes for centuries to be against Dalits. Their ignorance is phenomenal and their prejudice is outstanding. In spite of countrywide movement by BSP for Mandal Commission, there are many among OBCs who believe that it is something which is meant for upliftment of Dalits alone and not of OBCs. If we succeed in convincing the OBCs that caste based reservations are good for them, most of bahujan's problems will end and a strong bahujan samaj will emerge.

What is our aim? Our editor is fighting for Dalit Muslim BC unity for a long time. This is same thing what Kanshiram calls bahujan samaj taking this word from old Buddhist literature. It is simple formula of 85 per cent versus 15 per cent. But what is the meaning of unity. When different groups live in physical proximity, and have desire in them to come closer and unite, the ultimate step is social unity where whole society becomes one and there is full harmony and rapport with matrimonial relationships between groups which were differing to each other and may even be antagonistic.

This is the ideal state and should be the ultimate aim. That is annihilation of castes, as Dr. Ambedkar envisaged. But it takes centuries to achieve and has to pass through various stages. Religious harmony is an earlier stage, and that also takes tremendous will power to unite and strong urge for it and is also a lengthy process. The first stage is, of course, political unity, which must be achieved before there is any kind of dialogue possible within the groups. When we talk of unity, we only mean political unity at this early stage of understanding. If we can develop among all these groups goodwill and friendship even on only political lines, it will be a great achievement.

At the movement these groups are warring groups, there is not even a dialogue, let alone sense of common belonging. On 14th October 1956, Dr. Ambedkar converted half a million Dalits to Buddhism. Next day there was a meeting of selected workers only in Hotel Shyam in Nagpur where Babasahib was staying, and I was fortunate to be present there as one of the three student workers. That was Babasahib's first speech in Hindi, I heard. He expressed his anguish for infighting among the workers and expressed his desire to launch a party which will have people from all castes.

He asked the workers to develop readiness to work in association with others. Also on his last day, he wrote some letters to leaders like Lohia and P. K. Atre etc. But we find that, the party of his vision, could not go beyond its scope of one single caste. Even whatever people from other castes were in the party, they gradually left and now it has an image of one caste party. Hopes and aspirations expressed by our saviour are shattered to make a united party. Only hope now seems to be Kanshiram, who has not only paved the way of political unity among the various groups but also started a campaign of jati todo samaj jodo and tried to assimilate people of different castes, an aim which was very dear to our beloved saviour Dr. Ambedkar.

What is to be done? One must accept that when schedules of castes and tribes were made to be incorporated in the constitution, there was a tremendous hurry. Many were left out and many were superfluous. This was known to the founding fathers of constitution, so an arrangement was made to review the schedule periodically. This should be taken in spirit of adjustment and not of antagonism. But at the same time we should prevent categorization within SC/ST. I endorse the view of D. Venkateswarlu that this will weaken the masses and perhaps that is what the BSO wants.

We must not play in their hands. We get only those reservations which are pleasing to BSO For decades RPI was demanding abolition of political reservations of SC/STs. But they are forced on us. Whereas nobody demanded reservations for women, but they are granted in a hurry and when some people wished to link caste based questions with it, the bill is shifted to select committee.

We, thus get what is good for them, without any consideration for what we want. For last fifteen years or so Kanshiram has brought forward the theory of 15 per cent versus 85 per cent. You yourself have sup- ported this theory many times.

Now if you advocate different castes among these 85 per cent to get consolidated separately instead of together, then how are we going to struggle against the 15 per cent. After all, at this stage of our development we are not asking for social unity, we are not asking for religious unity, we are asking only for political unity.

BAHUJAN SAMAJ AND THE EUROPEAN KNOWLEDGE

India lost these Equality and fraternity also.

The learned author points out:

- "At a still later point of time, in the long meandering

> course of our history, the society got divided into innumerable castes and sub-castes. The evil of discrimination as high and low among men, on the basis of birth, hereditary avocations and other considerations raised its head and the pernicious practice of untouchability with all its degrading implications."

After the demise of Equality and fraternity in India it took its birth in Europe. The rights of citizens mentioned in the preamble of the Constitution are taken from the declaration of the rights of Man pronounced by the French Constituent Assembly. The concepts of three varieties of Justice, Liberty, etc were also foreign to the caste-ridden society of India. The principles of socialism were borrowed from the economic and political thoughts of the West and USSR.

So much was the debt of the nation to European knowledge, not to speak of European Science and Technology. How did India come in contact with the European Knowledge? As in other parts of the world enquiry in this part of the world was also speculative. The attempt was to explain the reasons for various occurrences in nature. It was observed that there were evil effects during solar and lunar eclipses. Why? It required an explanation. It was attributed to the emission of poison of the snakes, which was swallowing the Sun or the Moon. Similarly Aristotle wanted to explain why the fire when it was lit went up and the stones thrown up returned to the Earth. Aristotle every object had its natural resting-place and it desired to go to its resting-place, whenever it was displaced. Heaven is the resting-place of fire and therefore whenever fire was lit it went up.

The stones had the Earth as its resting-place. So whoever it is lifted returned to the earth. The intensity of the desire of an object to go back to its resting-place depended on its size. The greater is the size the stronger is its desire of an object to come to its resting-place. So bigger objects returned earlier than smaller object. Galelio wanted to know whether it was really so. He climbed Leaning Tower of Pisa and dropped from there two objects of the same material but of different size and observed whether it fell simultaneously on the ground or whether the bigger one due to its stronger desire to come to its returning place fell earlier than the other.

He found that two objects fell simultaneously on the ground disproving the Aristotelian concept. This type of activity led to the growth of a new branch of knowledge. The specialty of this type of knowledge was that it could be tested by anyone anywhere in the world and its truth could be established beyond any doubt. This knowledge attained universal acceptance. This type of experimental knowledge came to be known as science and it made rapid progress encompassing all departments of life and natural phenomena. Europe was the centre of this activity. It had its impact on India also.

During the first half of nineteenth century, in the field of education, there were two schools of thought in India; one wanted only the traditional education in Arabic. Persian and Sanskrit and the other advocated elementary education in vernacular and higher education in English. It was at that time MACAULAY reached the shore of India. It marked the turning point of India's intellectual progress. On 10th July 1833 speaking on the India Bill in the House of Commons MACAULAY said "It may be that the public mind of India may expand under our system till it has outgrown that system; that by good Government we may educate our subjects into a capacity for better Government; that having become instructed in European knowledge they may, in some future age, demand European Institutions.

Whether such a day will come, I know not. But never will I attempt to avert it. Whenever it comes, it will be the proudest day in English history." MACAULAY came to India as Law Member of the Executive Council of the Governor general of India. He in his celebrated minute dated 2-2-1835 placed before the Supreme Council strongly defended those who advocated English education. His arguments were supported by the following two illustrations.

- "The first instance is the great revival of letters among Western nations at the close of the 15th and the beginning of the 16th Century. At that time almost everything that was worth reading was contained in the writing of the ancient Greeks and Romans. Had our ancestors acted as the Committee of Public Instruction has hitherto acted; had they neglected the language of Ciero and Tacitus; had they confined their education to the old dialects of our own Island; had they printed nothing and taught nothing at Universities but the chronicles of Anglo-Saxons and romances in Norman-French, Would English have been what she is now? What Greek and Latin were to the contemporaries of More and Ascham our tongue is to the people of India."

- "Within the last hundred and twenty years, a Nation which had previously been in a state as barbarous as that in which our ancestors were before crusades, has gradually emerged from the ignorance in which it was sunk and has taken its place among civilised communities. I speak of Russia. There is now in that country a large educated class, abounding with persons fit to serve the State in the highest functions and in no way inferior to the most accomplished men who adorn the best circles of Paris and London_ How was this change effected? Not by flattering national prejudices, not by filling the mind of the young Moscovite with old woman's stories which his rude fathers had believed—But teaching him those foreign languages in which the greatest mass of information had been laid up and then putting that information within his reach. The languages of Western Europe civilized Russia. I cannot doubt that they will do for the Hindu what they have done for the Tartar."

The Government of India accepted the view of MACAULAY and on 7th March 1835 announced that "The Great object of British Government ought to be the promotion of European Literature and Science among the Natives of India. "Prsuant to this declaration three Universities were established in 1857 one at Bombay and others at Calcutta and Madras. Within a period of about 30 years the new system of education produced highly educated Indians and a desire for better existence generated in them. It was at that time that Allan octavian hume took initiative to establish an organisation came to be known as the Indian National Congress. Here again it was left to a European to take the lead. He wanted the most highly educated of the nation to meet each year and chalkout programme for the purpose of securing greater freedom, more impartial administration and a larger share in the management of the country.

The first session of Congress was held in Bombay in the year 1885. The Indian intellectuals started comparing the administration of India with that of England and started feeling dissatisfied with the shortcomings in Indian administration. They started demanding European Institutions culminating in a movement for independence and ultimately asked the British to QUIT INDIA. At last India became free. The proudest day of English history as Macaulay said in 1833 dawned on 18th July 1947 when the Indian Independence Act 1947 was passed by the British Parliament as follows:

- As from the fifteenth day of August, nineteen hundred and forty-seven, two independent Dominions shall be set up in India, to be known respectively as India and Pakistan,
- The said Dominions are hereafter in this Act referred as "the new Dominion", and the said fifteenth day of August is hereafter in this Act referred to be as "the appointed day".

The Indian National Congress had passed resolutions to reorganise the states on the basis of languages. But after independence the Government of free India run by the Indian National Congress did not evince much interest in the formation of linguistic states.

Therefore, late P.Sriramulu started his fast unto death demanding formation of states on the basis of languages in accordance with the resolutions that had been adopted by the Indian Congress. He was not satisfied by the oral assurances given to him and he continued his fast and sacrificed his life.

Immediately after his death the Jawaharlal Nehru Government at the centre announced the constitution of a State Re-organisation Committee for the demarcation of the States based upon various languages spoken in different parts of the territory of India and as per its report the linguistic states were formed on 1st November 1956.

The regional languages became the official languages of the respective states and it gave tremendous impetus and encouragement to the regional languages for it's all round developments. 42 long years have rolled by after the formation of linguistic states. But the Indian languages are yet to attain the standards of European Languages in so far as science and technology are concerned.

There is no progress except in collaborating with European countries. The question therefore is whether it is time to discontinue the education in European literature, science and technology, which brought about so much of revolutionary changes in all departments of Indian life. No doubt for administrative expediency the states have been reorganised and linguistic states has been formed.

Does it mean that thereafter all educations must be only in regional languages? Will it elevate the knowledge of the people to the international standard or will it draw them back to pre-MACULAY period? The Bahujan samaj has a great stake in this matter. The European educated Upper Castes led the Independence Movement and secured freedom from the yokes of the British.

It was the European education that helped them to achieve it. What about the Bahujan Samaj, which is still suffering under the iron yokes of the Upper Castes? They too will require European education to free themselves from the yokes and shackles of those who enjoy freedom today so that they may also live human beings with dignity and self-respect. Every year there should be a meeting of highly educated intellectuals belonging to the deprived and neglected parts of the people as what the Indian National Congress was doing before independence. These meetings should consider how to shape the destiny of their people, how to alleviate their sufferings and how to take them to a prosperous new life. There should be a Second Independence Movement for the purpose and it should be the responsibility of the highly educated intellectuals of these communities to lead such a movement.

SOCIAL STATUS QUO

In June this year, a Dalit panchayat chief, Adiamma was removed from her office in Karnataka. Her only crime was that she continued with her toilet cleaning job even after becoming president of the panchayat. A few years back a Dalit youth was forced to swallow human excreta in a Karnataka village. Similarly, in southern Tamil Nadu, a Dalit MLA was shoed away, abused and humiliated publicly, when he visited his constituency, simply because he was a Dalit and yet he had audacity to visit his constituency and hear people s grievances. In most parts of rural Andhra Pradesh, Tamil Nadu, and Karnataka, hotel/tea shops maintain two-glass system one for Dalits and other for non-Dalits. In all the three States, practice of untouchability is rampant in its crudest form, uncomparable to rest of the India.

The pattern of violence in this part of India contains medieval era characteristics, and is comparable only to the pattern of violence in western UP, Haryana and parts of Rajasthan bordering UP. A few years back, in district Mathura of UP, a Dalit youth and Jat girl were hanged from a banyan tree. This gory crime occurred in day time, witnessed by some 20,000 people.

Their only crime was to enter in a wedlock, defying the caste norm. About an year back, Gujjars of district Dholpur, Rajasthan caught hold of a Dalit youth, punctured his nose, and put a thin rope, meant for stitching jute bags, through it. The bleeding victim was paraded in the village streets. The victim, Rameshwar Jatav ran a small grocery shop, and had demanded ₹50 from Kamlesh Gujjar, who had bought items on credit.

There is no dearth of such incidents to show the point. Every year, during the marriage season, we come across news items how a Dalit bridegroom was attacked for riding a mare. Also, the Dalit panchayat chief elected from reserved seats in this region, face similar social handicaps as witnessed in the southern States. What is common to both the regions? Climate, cropping pattern, language, dress and food-habits are all radically different.

It should have been only natural that the pattern of violence in both the regions was either radically different from each other, or similar to the pattern as witnessed at all-India level. Contrary to that, both the regions have a distinctly similar pattern of violence, distinctly dissimilar to the rest of India. Why? If there is any commonality in the two regions in question, distinct from the rest of India, it is the social composition of the ruling castes. In both the regions, Brahmins have a thin presence, and Kshatriyas are virtually non-existent. Traditionally, the upper Shudras have owned agrarian assets, but were subjected to politico-cultural dominance of Brahmins. In post-Independence period, slowly but steadily, they consolidated their political power as well, replacing Brahmins decisively. Despite that, at cultural level, their dominance lacked socio-cultural legitimacy, neither Brahmins and nor Dalits, for their own different reasons, accepted them as the ruling castes. Traumatised by this unique varnal-caste logic of power and legitimacy, the upper Shudras tended to invoke fundamentals of the Chaturvarna value system, as it existed earlier.

Since a social order of the medieval era cannot be enforced today, it only adds to frustration. In order to gain an upper varna-like dominance, violence is the most reliable and the final tool that the upper Shudras know. In both the regions in question, there exists a parallel system of governance, where regulatory authority of the modern State is subjected to the antiquated laws of Chaturvarna order.

If in a couple of decades, migration of upper Varna population from rural India to urban India is accomplished, and the upper Shudras take full control of rural India, the

Italian fascists, in their graves may feel ashamed of being amateurs. The Dalits and the artisan OBCs, who together constitute about 57 per cent of India's total population, and who are the real proletariat, have a tough task at this juncture of history. While the struggle for a democratic social order has to fight the upper Shudras in rural India, it has to oppose the upper Varnas in urban India. As if that is not enough, its also has to fight the intellectual hegemony of both the ruling social blocks.

And the progressives expect the people to believe in the following:

- That it is not the social conflict or varna/caste dominance which is the fundamental crisis of Indian society, but the religious conflict;
- That the varnashram system is not a social order, but a religious system called Hinduism, and a party like the BJP, by invoking Hindus religious passion, is planning to install communal fascism, which we must prevent by bringing the Congress back to power;
- That an upper varna party like the BJP will use violence as the political weapon to suppress opposition, and the upper Shudras parties, will use democratic methods to deal with opponents and;
- That fascism as a political doctrine, as it evolved in Italy, can be more atrocious, more violent, more vicious than the ideology of the varnashram social order, and therefore we must all adopt a new phrase of fascism to define the anti-democracy doctrine. The intelligentsia of the country must understand that this is not the closing years of 18th century when a Shankaracharya would come and redefine charging elephant as mithya, and the people of India will lap it as reality. Much changes have occurred during past over one millennium. There is Amedkarism also for the Dalits to shape a vision. When Dr BR Ambedkar was raising the caste question, he was being told that Independence of the country was more important than the social question, and once

freedom was accomplished, the caste question would be addressed. When Independence was achieved, Dr Ambedkar joined the Nehru Cabinet with the hope that the caste question will be addressed then. But he was told then that national reconstruction was more important, and once this was achieved, the resolution of caste question would be accompanied.

More than five decades have passed since then, but the varna/caste dominance remains. Once again, when the question of social transformation is being raised, people are being told that they must join secular brigade first to defeat communal fascism; probably they mean that the social questions can be tackled later. This is unacceptable. One cannot fight something which does not exist. The varnal-caste conflict is the fundamental question of India, and the agenda of communal fascism is only a mischievous construct, scripted only to retain the varnal-caste hegemony, and to ensure the social status quo.

SUB-CASTES AMONG DALITS

INHUMAN QUALITIES OF HINDUISM

Graded inequality, Ban on inter dining, forced endogamy, polluting touch, and restriction on occupation are enumerated as evils of Hindu caste system, and it is claimed that these are absent in castes of SCs, STs and BCs. Dr. Ambedkar's theory of "Genesis of Castes" is quoted to support this view. Bojja Tharakam has dealt with this at length. Let his 'tributes to DV' be construed as a courtesy and not as change of his views. In any case, I feel, to concentrate on genesis of caste, is to divert our attention to a wrong direction. The main question is whether the castes among avarnas and savarnas, today, belong to different categories. Unfortunately, the features are seen also in avarna castes. Avarna castes are no less dangerous to society than savarna castes. And Ambedkar's Annihilation of Castes applies equally to both.

KANSHIRAM'S WORK

The rosy picture painted by the editor about chamars of

UP is, I am afraid, not all that true. Whatever is achieved politically is not because of strengthening of chamar jati, but due to cooperation of all the various small castes. You only have to see the caste structure of seats of MPs contested by Kanshiram during last Loksabha elections, or for that matter even in recent Vidhansabha elections. Kanshiram and Mayavati have not tried to strengthen only chamar caste, as is presumed by our editor.

They have asked to strengthen all bahujans to come together and work for common good of all bahujans including dalits. They never worked for "separate but equal" castes. Neither Dr. Ambedkar, nor Shahu, nor Phuley worked on the lines mentioned by our editor. They always worked to bring all together, demolishing walls among the castes, never ever, they advocated salvation of any individual caste or that of an individual person within a caste.

WHAT IS KANSHIRAM'S 'JATI TODO SAMAJ JODO'

Dr. Ambedkar confirmed in 'Annihilation of Castes', that the sanction behind the sastras must end. He had given special emphasis on the 'Manu' a smriti said to be written by a brahmin pundit Sumati Bhargava at the time of counter-revolution started by Pushyamitra Shunga about 185 BC. This is the main book, Dr. Ambedkar attacked. It must be understood that though it is said to be religious scripture, Dr. Ambedkar considered it to be a political book, rather a law book, or you may call it the Constitution of Ancient and Medieval slave India.

Only in Ambedkar's India a new Constitution is provided to this country, and that too not entirely to the satisfaction of its maker. So the fundamental way is to make the bahujan samaj understand that they are not Hindus and hence they must stop considering themselves as Hindus. They shall not follow the tenets of Manu smriti. This is happening gradually, You find that the Adivasis, though they are being coerced by the manuvadis into believing that they must follow Hindu gods and Hindu religious worship etc, are talking freely of Ambedkarism and are turning gradually away from BSO. This process is the process of 'Samaj jodo'. This can be attributed to the work of Kanshiram in post Ambedkar era. Again I have to make it clear that at this stage, without jeopardizing stand for religious and social unity, we can only strive for political unity; the religious and social unity will have to wait. I feel, our editor, also means to achieve only political unity at this time, when he says, "What we need is not the 'unity' that destroys any identity, but an understanding and harmony which would help maintain and foster such identities to fight the oppressor."

DALIT UNITY IS NOT ENOUGH

Without in any way denigrating the efforts of those who are striving for Dalit Unity, I feel, even if all the Dalits of India, of all castes, shades and colours, unite, they cannot achieve any power without the help of other oppressed castes, as they are only about 16% or so. And if there is no power, caravan of Ambedkar will be on retrograde journey. Many non-dalit castes are realizing the mischief done by Caste system, they are having dialogue with Dalits and uniting with them, as is seen in North Indian states. To think that those who talk of 'Unity' belong to a 'dominant caste' and so have an unfair vested interest in 'unity', will rather be an injustice to their efforts. The dominance they achieved is not the cause of their 'Unity talks', but it is the result of it. Before Phuley, Shahu and Ambedkar thought of Unity, the condition of all dalit castes was more or less same, none was dominant and all were subservient to BSO.

SHOULD WE NOT DESTROY OUR IDENTITY?

Are various leaders ready to give up their identity on argument that Dalit liberation must get priority over all other demands? One does not have to give up ones identity, if we are talking at this stage of only political unity. But if we unite only politically at this stage, a time will come, when we have to unite religiously and socially also. At that time, I would like to ask these leaders, "Can they afford not to dissolve their identities?" If they did, their castes would be wiped out by the BSO. One has only to see the way these sub-castes are fighting among themselves just for crumbs, they have forgotten that their real enemy, BSO, is safe and secure in its own citadel. Even at this stage, infighting among the sub-castes is counter productive and injurious to the interest of their own caste.

It is the leaders of BSO, who make them fight by showing a carrot to the stooges. It is a post Poona pact situation of proliferating chamachas, big and small. The members of Ambedkarite public have by now acquired enough knowledge and experience to identify these stooges and keep away from them. If some one likes to remind the people of this situation, let him not be labeled as selfish and his warnings condemned as being of "educated- meaning brain washed", person of a 'dominant' caste.

7

Ambedkar's Works for Dalits Education

INTRODUCTION AND PURPOSE STATEMENT

From the moment a Hindu child is born in India, his or her opportunities for social and religious freedom are shaped through the influence of the caste system despite laws passed 50 years ago to abolish such discriminatory practices. Many children at the bottom of this caste system face a future of poverty, unemployment, illiteracy, abuse, sickness, and for girls, even rape and prostitution. Stemming from its 3000-year-old origins, the caste system is one of the world's longest surviving forms of social stratification.

People are divided by birth just as to one of four main castes, with yet another estimated 200 million categorized beneath this caste system. Many in society consider these people to be unclean and unworthy of basic human rights and label them "The Untouchables" or Dalits. In 1955, the Indian Parliament passed the Untouchability Offences Act, making the practice of castes illegal, however, it may take generations to remove the stigma and change the views and traditions of an entire society.

This lack of social justice for many, coupled with the desire to promote fair and equal treatment of the people within a country that is quickly gaining influence in the global market and economy, has made this topic one of extreme interest. Although many of these longstanding traditions continue to hold fast, India has also experienced significant changes during the last several decades. With the advancement of technology, some researchers no longer consider India to be classified as a developing country, but as a newly industrialized country. This classification includes several nations, such as Mexico and Thailand, with economies more advanced and developed than those in the developing world, yet without the full indicators that would classify it as a developed country.

With the rapid increase of major global corporations choosing to outsource large portions of high technology jobs to India, the need for quality English medium education is vital if the country intends to continue to compete in that particular market. Yet India continues to struggle with the needs of its individuals, especially in rural areas, with limitations that inhibit the ability to make the desired changes in a timely manner. Not only has the current government been unable to increase the number of schools and teachers needed to rectify the situation, but society itself has been resistant in some areas to the change of the social order embedded in the caste system. In an effort to affect change in a social structure that consists of an interdependent set of roles and norms, Dalit leaders have joined forces to demand what they refer to as a holistic reformation for their own people.

They describe this as a concern for the whole individual's physical, mental, emotional and spiritual development through education, economic support, health aid, and legal advocacy. By accepting the outside resources of International Non-Governmental Organizations, they feel they can make the changes necessary to reduce the educational and socioeconomic gap between the castes. The Dalit Empowerment International, a Non-Government Organization based in the United States, formed in 2002 in response to this corporate uprising of the Dalit people. The Dalit leaders at that time challenged the organization with a twofold request: to offer their children an English medium education, and to include Christian principles in the hope of transforming their worldview to one based on human dignity and self-worth, in an effort to create a new future. Working together with the already established All India Christian Council and other partners, the DEI uses its resources from the United States, Canada and the United Kingdom, to educate the western world about the situation of the Dalits and to gather financial and human resources to support ongoing work in India.

The AICC is a coalition of over 3,000 Indian organizations and federations and proactively protects the interests of Christians, Muslims, Dalits, Tribals and Backward communities. Also, by joining together with AICC as well as another national overhead organization with four decades of educational experience, they feel they can use the expertise and experience to make a significant impact. Having volunteered with several non-profit and faith-based organizations, studying education and its societal role around the world has become an area of extreme interest for me. I chose to study the field of international comparative education in order to examine the effectiveness of such programmes in diverse cultural contexts.

Having met the president of the DEI at a symposium in the United States, I was intrigued by the overall approach and methods of their model. The organization situates the educational component within a framework of three other elements, human rights advocacy, health and medical needs, and economic development. I wanted to study in depth the effectiveness of this approach, and specifically this programme, and its religious implications within the established caste system. A substantial amount of research has been done to define quality education to confirm the educational inequities within the caste system and to acknowledge the addition of many INGOs in the global effort to create access to quality education for all.

However, little research examines the effectiveness of faith-based INGOs and their impact on an educational situation that is affected by another religious system. This study will add to the current literature by providing an evaluative look at one particular programme, which can add to our understanding of how such educational faith-based programmes could aid disadvantaged and stigmatized groups. In order to gain insight into the strategies of this organization, I used qualitative research methods including ethnographic evaluative techniques to conduct a formative programme evaluation. A programme evaluation of this sort seeks to appraise the quality of the education and the achievement of the stated goals, which is not only useful to the DEI programme administrators, but to other programmes as well. The purpose of a formative evaluation is to examine each of the components of a programme in such a way that specific changes could be made to enhance the programme, not to judge the overall worth or value of the programme.

My role as an evaluator is to present the specific findings to the leaders of the organization such that the appropriate stakeholders and decision makers can use it to guide future implementation.

Using the following questions, I evaluated four out of the DEI's 62 schools:

- How does this education programme plan to improve the future quality of life for Dalits?
- Does the DEI programme meet its proposed goals?
- What further areas of research will address the long term societal change that will be necessary for this programme and others to be effective?

To be as objective in my evaluation as possible, given the timeframe, resources and the fact that I would be the only evaluator, I used methodological triangulation by interviewing administrators, teachers and students, reviewing the program's literature and observing in the classroom. This process allowed me to compare the goals with the actual implementation practices in order to examine effectiveness of the programme in the schools observed.

This study focuses on both the practical application and logistics of this education as well as the religious aspect. Introducing educational practices which promote religious choice and enhance India's efforts towards a worldview of human dignity may be of key importance in providing information for future aid in the urgent educational needs within India today. The following parts present the research and the findings.

To begin with, the background surrounding the disparity in education for the Dalit child, as well as the governmental policy, anti-conversion laws, and the specific goals of the DEI are described. Next, a series of questions that guided the research are discussed. Following this is a review of current literature on subjects that formed the foundation for this evaluation.

This includes topics such as the inequities in education, NGO involvement, the use of English medium, the future implications of education for the Dalits, the paucity of similar studies evaluating other programmes, and finally educational programme evaluation theories.

This is followed by a detailed explanation of the data collection and methods that were used to gather the information to evaluate the programme. The findings are then analysed and the results of the evaluation are discussed. In the conclusion, the findings are summarized such that programme developers can use this material in the future to benefit the programme, as well as to inform readers of the issues and future implications of this research.

BACKGROUND

UNDERSTANDING CASTES

The plight of the Dalits must be understood, in order to have the cultural sensitivity needed to bring in an outside organization and use the resources effectively. The goal of closing the gap in education, so entrenched in thousands of years of religious or cultural practices will require time and skill, and much of it will have to do with teaching from a platform of education based on human rights. As I began this study, it quickly became obvious that I could not ignore the religious element of the education, as it is so enmeshed in the cultural differences and discriminatory practices which lead to such a gap in achievement and attainment in the first place.

As one director in India said:

- In the United States, you had discrimination between blacks and whites, and it was a social justice issue, which can be changed by laws over time. People were free to choose to be Christians, but were discriminated against because of their colour. In India, though, it is far deeper. It is a religious issue, if people remain Hindu, they are discriminated against, if they convert, they are fined and even persecuted. To try to change the discrimination, one must face the religious issue of caste.

It is historically understood that Hinduism was first established by an amalgamation of three different religious sects, Arayanism, Dravidianism and Animism and the four caste levels were a method of establishing social order, whereby each person had an occupational function. Traditionally, for example, the top level, the Brahmins, were considered the highest level and held the positions of priests and teachers. The next group included the Kshatriyas, who held positions as the warriors and royalty.

Then, the Vaisyas were given positions as moneylenders and traders. Finally, considered the lowest of the four levels, the Sudras carried out the menial jobs in society. The Dalits, or untouchables, or ati-Sudras were actually considered beneath all of these levels, performing the jobs that other members of society would not. To be touched or even crossed by the shadow of a Dalit made any other caste member unclean and ritualistic cleansing was required.

Though much of this structure has changed over time, as governmental order and economic models changed, the concept of social stratification has remained, in some areas more so than others. Through several grass roots efforts to empower individuals, the Dalits are now seeking societal change. The DEI, as one of these efforts, feels that by eliminating discriminatory practices in the classroom, and changing the beliefs within the family and the community, there can eventually be actual change at the government and societal level.

From their literature, they intend to be involved at all of these levels:

- Serving as an international advocate for Dalit rights is the heartbeat of the Dalit Empowerment International. Beginning with the United States government in Washington DC, DEI seeks to bring an end to caste-based discrimination and the resulting oppression the Dalit community experiences. DEI also represents Dalits internationally in the United Nations and at major conferences on human rights and religious liberties. Additionally, DEI seeks funding to underwrite legal fees for Dalits actively pursuing political and social change through the Indian legal system and all necessary constitutional means.

Therefore, educational practices can become a crucial part in this path towards change.

GOVERNMENTAL VIEWS

The people of India respect Gandhi as the founding father of the modern Indian nation. However, there is controversy as to his approach to try to abolish the caste system. Some feel that he merely tried to eradicate the practice of untouchability but did not do enough to touch the foundations of the stratification of caste. He believed that "caste as it exists today is no doubt a travesty of the original fourfold division which only defined men's different calling". Gandhi attempted to teach by example that doing the menial labour of a Dalit should be considered as honourable as any other trade.

It was actually Dr. Bhim Rao Babasaheb Ambedkar, a former Dalit, who founded the Indian Constitution in 1949 and attempted to abolish the foundation of the caste system itself in an effort to bring about the commitments made in the Constitution to promote equality. Despite the strong beginnings, Dr. Ambedkar expressed his concerns that such an undertaking may seem impossible without a change in the thinking established by caste when he stated:

- There is no doubt; in my opinion, that unless you change your social order you can achieve little by way of progress. You cannot mobilize the community either for defence or for offence. You cannot build anything on the foundations of caste. You cannot build up a nation, you cannot build up a morality. Anything that you will build on the foundations of caste will crack and will never be whole. The only question remains to be considered is ... How to abolish caste? This is the question of supreme importance

Other countries, though not affected by caste, also recognized the need to change societal norms and in 1974, UNESCO began to lay the foundations for human rights education.

By 1978, the participants in the International Congress on the Teaching of Human Rights created specific and practical definitions by stating that human rights education and teaching must aim at:

- Fostering the attitudes of tolerance, respect and solidarity inherent in human rights
- Providing knowledge about human rights, in both their national and international dimensions, and the institutions established for their implementation
- Develop the individual's awareness of the ways and means by which human rights can be translated into social and political reality at both the national and international levels.

Following these efforts more than forty years after the creation of India's constitution, the UN Decade for Human Rights Education began in 1995 and has been influential in raising global awareness of educational inequities. It will continue to take time, however, to create curriculum based on practices that will change the thinking of the individual as well as the society.

The DEI intends to support his effort. India has become a central focus as various countries attempt to eradicate discriminatory practices through these educational efforts. For example, the United States House of Representatives just passed House Concurrent Resolution 139 on July 23, 2007, that addresses the ongoing problem of untouchability in India. The resolution is the first of its kind from the United States Congress and the DEI has been involved at several levels of global awareness. Juxtaposed with this global awareness, however, is the continued effort by the Indian government to implement more anti-conversion laws in order to protect people from coercion and manipulation by what is considered any minority religion in India. Anti-conversion laws have been passed through much controversy in eight of the 28 states and the specific language states:

- No person shall convert or attempt to convert, either directly or otherwise, any person from one religion to another by use of force or by inducement or by any fraudulent means, nor shall any person abet any such conversion.

Although these protective efforts are well founded due to past practices by different religious groups pressuring people to convert by way of inducement through education or medical aid, they create a dichotomous message that goes against the Constitution's Article 25 that promises free choice:

- Freedom of conscience and free profession, practice and propagation of religion.- Subject to public order, morality and health and to the other provisions of this Part, all persons are equally entitled to freedom of conscience and the right freely to profess, practice and propagate religion.

Though it is too complex a topic to discuss in this document, as the debate over coercion and choice through new knowledge can be subjective, one must be aware of the conflict in attempting to use any other religious educational foundation within various states in India.

GOALS OF DALIT EMPOWERMENT INTERNATIONAL

From the literature established by the DEI and through interviews with individuals involved in the education, it is clear that their goal is to accomplish each of the human rights agendas by including the egalitarian practices of Christianity as they build their curriculum. With this in mind, this study will attempt to compare the following mission statement and all of its underlying elements with the actual practices. Their holistic efforts focus on four main areas.

- Education through English-based curriculum with trained national teachers
- Medical resources of vaccinations, healthcare, and medical interventions
- Economic Development by offering micro-loans and vocational training programmes
- Human Rights and Social Justice by serving as an international advocate for social change and new governmental policies

To incorporate each of these areas into the development of a community, the DEI establishes what it calls Community Education Centres as a central location for all four aspects of their charter. Though each of these areas is crucial to the advancement of developing societies, this document will focus specifically on the educational efforts. For the purpose of this document, the term CEC or DEI school will be interchangeable. To date, 62 CECs have been established in 13 states, serving over 10,000 students, through DEI's efforts to coordinate a global interest in the situation of the Dalit people.

The DEI provides an excellent example to use for this study, because, unlike several other faith-based organizations such as World Vision and Compassion International, the DEI focuses strictly on the needs of the Dalit people. The DEI also has many collaborative sources with churches and other organizations within India. These organizations are in agreement as to the strategic importance that an English and faith-based education brings to the Dalits, as a gateway to eradicating injustice, illiteracy and overcoming poverty.

They have determined that some of the greatest opportunities for education and employment within India and around the world are given to those who are literate in English as well as their own state language. Also, since one of their main charters is to teach from a worldview based on human dignity and self-worth, the issue of faith is a key component in this study. Dalits are choosing to convert primarily to the egalitarian beliefs of Buddhism, Islam and Christianity as a way out of a system that still holds great power, not only in India, but in other countries as well. The regions for developing schools are selected through careful research conducted by the DEI national leaders to locate areas of Dalit majority with the greatest needs, where no other comparable facilities exist, and no other full time holistic development projects are functioning. The schooling is subsidized by the organization, but a nominal fee is charged to create a sense of ownership and accountability for the students and their families.

DEI's child sponsorship programme brings in funds from around the world to provide the uniforms, books, a meal where needed, and to cover the teacher's salaries, the cost of the facility and other administrative costs. I was told that, "Many of these children are introduced to education for the first time, and the enthusiasm spreads as they take home what they have learned and share it with their families."

A statement from the literature given to me by the director explains:

- To teach a Dalit is social service, but to destroy the social structure which made him illiterate, is social transformation. To open a new school in a Dalit village is a social service, but to motivate the Dalit hungry and illiterate parent to send his child to school even if it meant less income for the household is social transformation. To provide free food to a Dalit is a social service, but to educate and empower him to earn his own food is social transformation.

This document will evaluate the DEI's approach of holistic transformation within a group of people in order to shed light on the goal of accomplishing global awareness and support for the struggle for freedom through education.

CRITICAL LITERATURE REVIEW

In order to lay the foundation that guided the planning and design of this research, the following part will review current literature on four essential subjects. First, it discusses established discrimination and inequities in education for Dalits and the need for human rights education. This is followed by studies about involvement of INGOs and their participation in education or social justice worldwide, as well as the paucity of studies evaluating similar programmes. Third, it discusses global debates over whether to teach from an English medium of instruction. Finally, it establishes the framework of educational ethnography and programme evaluation theories that were used as the foundation of this study.

DISCRIMINATORY PRACTICES AND THE NEED FOR HUMAN RIGHTS EDUCATION

Numerous studies have been done to understand the level of disparity between the treatment of the Dalits and their upper caste peers. Education inequality is merely a portion of the complex nature of what Prime Minister Singh acknowledges as "India's hidden apartheid". Despite the Constitutional Directive of universal elementary education and Education for All goals, the gap in educational access and achievement between the Dalits and the general population in India is still quite large and continues to increase, which is of great concern in the globalizing world today.

Dalits, also referred to in the Constitution as the Scheduled Castes make up approximately 16.2% of the population of India, yet only 41.5% of Dalits in rural India were considered literate compared to the national literacy rate of 64.8%. Using econometric estimates on data gathered from 16 states and 33,000 rural households, in 1765 villages, Borooah and Iyer found that Dalit enrollment was lower than for Hindus for various reasons such as income, psychological factors, and access. For Hindu boys and girls, the enrollment rates were 84% and 68% respectively, but for Dalit boys and girls it was 70% and 55%.

Parent and community attitude, as well as religion and caste, are intertwined and have much to do with a child's education. Even though states such as Kerala have been involved for years with anti-caste reform, findings show that there is still statistically significant disparity between the Scheduled Caste and Scheduled Tribe groups and all other groups, suggesting the continued existence of an elite group despite years of effort to eradicate the discrepancies.

In an effort to uncover the reasons behind the continued disparities, a group of researchers began a first-ever study examining the practice of untouchability in 11 states, specifically in 565 rural villages between 2001 and 2002. Investigators conducted an 18 month survey, spending several days in each village using observations, interviews and focus groups to gather their data.

Though there has been improvement over the past decades, they found that practices of untouchability and discrimination do indeed still exist, though at different levels in each state and region. For example, one third of the villages still keep separate glasses and plates for Dalits, and refuse them entry into the shops. Purchases must be made from outside, without touching or examining the merchandise.

They found that 64% are not allowed in public places of worship, and 48% are not permitted to use the village water facilities for fear of their contamination. In order to understand the level of degradation many of the Dalits still face today, it must be noted that investigators found that "in every state, despite legal bans, Dalits continue to manually remove human excreta from public and private latrines, often with their bare hands".

Most often, they are required to perform tasks that relate to human waste, and death, all without pay, as an expected role in their existence. In terms of educational practices, Nambissan and Sedwell state that "the perspective within which the educational concerns of Dalit communities should be addressed must be one of social justice as Dalit communities have suffered from social discrimination and have traditionally been denied access to learning."

They contend that unless the discrimination is acknowledged, and confronted by teachers, parents, community leaders and educational institutions, the gap will continue to widen. For example, currently 38% of the village schools practiced separate eating arrangements, and 22% separate seating arrangements in the classroom. Shah found that "rural schools impress upon young minds and bodies the principles of segregation and discrimination, reproducing the hierarchies of caste and untouchability."

Many feel that these practices must stop in order for the message of equality to be heard and incorporated into the thinking of the individuals. If the community, and society at large, does not change this way of thinking about Dalits and other marginalized groups, merely creating more sensitized teaching practices and more educational opportunities may not be enough.

Studies show that despite the increased sense of dignity that education alone can bring, many still have a difficult time converting this cultural capital into actual long term employment due to discrimination within the job market. These studies depict a new crisis, where Dalit youth are becoming frustrated due to their lack of opportunities, even if they are educated, and parents are becoming less willing to invest in the education they thought would make a difference for their whole family.

If education access does increase, yet society does not accept the change in thinking of these Dalits, then developmental initiatives simply focusing on increased formal education may not be as successful as hoped in raising the social standing of the Dalits.

Therefore, if outside organizations enter into a community, some find that it may be important that they teach not only with a cultural sensitivity, but with the goal of diffusing egalitarian thinking and practice throughout the entire community in order for long term effects to take place. Although such debate over the best approach cannot be examined fully in this document, these issues do become foundational in this programme evaluation as it examines both the implementation of the goals of the DEI schools, as well as how these schools are situated within the current efforts for societal changes.

Analysing the efforts towards creating quality education, taught with a holistic approach through a faith-based egalitarian foundation of human rights could be an important starting point as India attempts to educate the next generation.

NON-GOVERNMENTAL ORGANIZATION

As a newly industrialized country, India's government has found it difficult to keep up with the demand for quality education. Each state within India has widely disparate needs in educational funding, but for most, bringing in outside resources by working together with NGOs becomes a key factor in advancement for the people. Obtaining additional sources of financial aid, as well as creating effective ways of expending them, becomes even more critical if a society is expected to improve and develop. This especially becomes significant with the growing trend of dissatisfaction with the poor quality of education offered through the existing government schools.

Dalit parents have dreams for their children to become engineers, doctors and government officials, yet they realise that quality education is necessary to achieve these dreams. Many are turning to an alternate private schooling for their children. In this "differentiated demand" for education that is considered of "good quality" this began a mushrooming increase in private unaided schools in the past decade alone. However, quality becomes difficult to maintain here as well, as many of these private schools hire poorly trained teachers, with lower pay, creating schools for the Dalits that are of substandard nature with a poor reputation.

It is also difficult to gain official statistics on private schools in India, and the affects of NGO involvement, as many private schools are not granted official recognition by the government for a variety of reasons. Singh's initial studies show through preliminary tests of achievement, that performance of children in the PUA unrecognized schools did not differ much from the scores of children studying in the government schools. Current research is needed to examine these trends and possible progress over time. With both international and national NGOs willing to step in to help fill this demand, evaluating specific programmes to determine the quality and type of education provided and whether it is effectively implemented is essential if funds are to be used to their fullest potential.

Although there is plenty of literature discussing the need and involvement or NGOs, there is a paucity of literature studying the effectiveness of specific programmes and practices. With India's goals of Education For All, NGOs will continue to play an important role, working along with the government to come up with creative ways to motivate people towards further education, with a holistic approach, but without creating dependency, ultimately effecting a change in society.

ENGLISH MEDIUM OF INSTRUCTION

Even if funding and other resources are available, however, there is still much debate over the pedagogy and curriculum that must be chosen by the key actors. Currently, there is global discussion over whether classes should be taught in the more traditional style of rote learning and classroom order, or in the more recent trend towards child centred pedagogies, with interactive classroom involvement. Also included in this debate for India is the question of whether classes should be taught through an English medium of instruction, the native language of each state, or the national language, Hindi.

These decisions are being made on a state-by-state basis within India, which has 22 state languages, and continued controversy over whether Hindi should still be considered the national language as the Constitution allows for the use of both Hindi and English in varying circumstances. As an example of the difficulties in these decisions, the state of Kerala began to make some of these changes in style and curriculum in 1998. The state planned to adopt a new experimental approach that was designed to be "child-friendly and to deemphasize rote learning lectures in favour of guided learning and playful interaction".

This District Primary Education programme met with controversy, however, as people feared even further stratification between the Kerala students: those who would be able to afford to choose private schools, or those who would become "guinea pigs" in the government schools under this new method.

Along with changes in style not English. Although the native tongue of Malayalum was already being used for instruction after a controversial decision to drop the universal English medium in 1987, it was still a difficult transition to make.

Some continue to pose that teaching in the mother tongue or first language for most of the day with English being taught as a separate subject is the most effective method, as children will understand the subject matter better. Others feel that by starting English younger, the children will become more proficient and will catch up with the subject matter as needed. Although the controversy continues, it must be noted that Kerala, due to a variety of factors, does hold the highest literacy rate in the country at 90.9% compared to the national rate of 64.8%.

The dilemma in this decision is that although each state is requiring that all government schools will teach using the local language up through the 10th grade, all testing and education after that is in English. Thus, children who go to the local government schools, especially in rural areas where no English is used, are by default eliminated from attending upper education that would qualify them for the jobs being reserved for them under affirmative action laws.

Also, without quality English education, these children cannot compete for the jobs in the rapidly growing sectors of the Indian economy, such as technical support and sales for major corporations. Although it is not within the purview of this document to determine the positive and negative ramifications of these decisions, it helps to provide a foundation for the decisions that organizations such as the DEI must wrestle with in determining what they consider to be best educational practices for the Dalit children.

EDUCATIONAL ETHNOGRAPHIES AND PROGRAMME EVALUATION

In order to evaluate an educational programme, such as the DEI provides, it is important to understand first the terminology as well as the overall intent. Popham to evaluate something is to appraise its quality and ultimately, to determine its worth. One approach in educational research is to focus on quantitative measures, such as achievement, assessments, levels of attainment, and so on.

Although I did query these particular areas, and future long term studies would be necessary to discern improvement and success, this study will use qualitative ethnographic methods, focusing on the purpose of the education, the effectiveness, and its position within a view towards societal change.

Using ethnographic methods allows a more descriptive approach, seeking to understand actual situations in context, providing the reader with a far more "meaningful picture of educational undertakings than would be possible from a more traditional scientific paradigm".

As Cronbach so eloquently puts it, "Intensive local observation goes beyond discipline to an open-eyed, open-minded appreciation of the surprises nature deposits in the investigative net". It is understood that, with the ethnographer as the human instrument, there will be some influence by the personality and background of the ethnographer. Being able to study a situation in its natural context, and gather data from a range of sources such as observations, and conversations with key actors to gain their perspective, brings together a valuable collection of information.

This approach is usually accomplished in a less structured way, and the analysis of the data involves interpretation through descriptions and explanations, with any form of quantifiable analysis taking a supportive role. One of the differences in most ethnographic educational evaluations, is that there is less time spent on site than a typical ethnographic study because so much is already known about the expectations of an educational environment. Also, for the purpose of this study, there are a few differences between research and evaluation that require clarification. Although both seek to gain new or additional knowledge, a researcher aims to reach a conclusion, and evaluators are more interested in affecting decisions, whether made by the evaluators themselves, or those who have requested the evaluation. Also, generalizability is a crucial difference between the two. Ideally, results from research can be generalized to fit a larger scope of similar situations that are being studied.

However, educational evaluations tend to focus on a specific educational programme with no intent to generalize to others. The gathered knowledge can be useful to the stakeholders and key decision makers as they seek to improve the programme. Since DEI. working with the AICC, intends to expand these 62 schools to 1,000, placed all over India, the information gathered in this method, can be useful to a larger scope within the organizations and even other organizations evaluating similar issues in their programmes. One difficulty in any kind of evaluation stems from determining the level of judgment the evaluative ethnographer can or should make in assessing the results of his or her study, what Scriven refers to as the recommendation problem. Theorists do not agree as to whether an evaluator should simply present the findings and leave it up to the programme administrators and decision makers to take it to the next step of modifying policy or implementing change, or whether the evaluators should be the ones to lay out a series of recommendations based on their findings. Cronbach's approach would be that of a minimalist, holding to the first view that an evaluator should collect the facts about the programme being evaluated, but not place any sort of value on the results, leaving that to the programme administrators.

Others, such as Scriven, would take it further, making actual judgments on "value, merit or worth" and using a team of experts to make specific recommendations that could be implemented. Finally, the term formative evaluation must be clarified. Once again, different theorists disagree on the role of the evaluator. In 1967, Scriven created the terms formative and summative that are currently used today to distinguish two specific roles in educational evaluation. Formative evaluations apply to programmes that are still capable of being modified. That is, they are still malleable, and even slight modifications to different components can be made as the programme continues to be implemented. If there are some components that are considered deficient, they can be improved upon towards a better overall programme.

Summative evaluations on the other hand are generally focused on more complete and established programmes and are being assessed as to the overall worth of the programme and whether it should continue. This type of evaluation has more of a final judgment approach, versus the modification approach of formative evaluations. This concept is useful in understanding the overall intent and expectation in any particular evaluation. Having reviewed the various approaches, I have chosen to use qualitative ethnographic methods to conduct an educational formative programme evaluation using a minimalist approach. To begin with, though I have background in education, and have studied the situation with the Dalits, I am not an expert nor am I fully knowledgeable in the cultural context.

As such, the value judgments should be made by both the national and international elected and paid officials of the programme who are held accountable to the budgetary considerations as well as overall strategy and outcomes. Also, there is not enough time in this study to delve fully into the data gathering phase in the field to make necessary recommendations. This study can be useful however, as I am coming in with as objective an eye as possible, knowing that I am not a stakeholder, but am interested in the global efforts to affect change in a society through education. With this approach, I can collect data at the micro level and present this information to the programme developers of the DEI to discuss some of the changes that could be made, and how these changes would affect the overall programme. In summary, there has been much research on the educational gap, and discriminatory practices against the Dalits, and the need for quality education based on equality and human rights. However, little research exists that specifically evaluates the various approaches of NGOS such that best approaches and methods can be implemented by others.

Specifically, there is little research, if any, that evaluates faith-based NGOs as they work within a delicate balance between conflicting worldviews, societal norms and government policy. This document will add to the future foundation for such in depth research on various programmes that could aid other organizations in the continued quest to eradicate the gap in education for the Dalit children.

DATA AND METHODS

The purpose of this formative educational programme evaluation is to examine each element of the programme, focusing on individual aspects of the intended goals and actual implementation.

Looking at these elements at each of the four individual sites allows for separate examination as well as some comparison and vision towards future implementation. Even though the time frame was limited to only ten days in Andhra Pradesh, I used qualitative methods, drawing largely from the ethnographic tradition of in-field research, gathering documentation, conducting interviews and observing the situation in context. Ideally, I would have had access to some of the typical quantitative information such as test scores, attainment, and teachers' experience levels that can be used to support the findings. However, due to time constraints at each site, I had to limit the investigation to the self-report of the participants, combined with my own observations, understanding that much of this involves individual perceptions. As an evaluator, I will present the findings in such a way that they can be used by the programme developers for the purpose of shaping and refining the programme, as well as guiding further research.

Many of these findings will involve fiscal decisions, and strategic plans for future implementation, which are beyond the role of the evaluator in this case. The following four parts clarify the various points of how the data was collected as well as the methods used. The first part describes the preparation prior to departure which is followed by the in-field set up and constraints. The third part describes the interviews and limitations of this process, followed by an explanation of the observation methods.

PRIOR TO DEPARTURE

Several months prior to departure, in preparation to conduct this evaluation, I briefly outlined the intended purpose for my study and contacted the DEI in the United States to discuss feasibility of this type of research over a ten day period in the spring. The United States based administrators contacted the programme directors in India and gained permission for me to travel to Andhra Pradesh in March, 2007, to observe in classrooms and interview various programme participants at multiple sites. Although the DEI has established schools in 13 states, this location was purposely selected by the DEI for its easy access to transportation and lodging as this area contains a college campus of a partner organization, as well a medical clinic. It was also centrally located to four different schools, one in an urban setting, and three others in surrounding rural villages which added to the diversity of the sample. I recognize that this is just one region and these schools may not be indicative of the overall programme, however, safety, cost and time were constraints that made some of the other schools too difficult to consider.

The DEI was supportive and eager to have this programme evaluated. Even though they clearly believe in the effectiveness of their programme, they encouraged having an outside observer review it from an academic perspective. Also, these particular schools have been established for at least three years, and they felt that they were stable enough to be implementing the original objectives, yet far enough along to look for continued improvement, creating a perfect opportunity for a formative approach. One of the constraints that I faced was the confidentiality issues that needed to be addressed before permission could be granted to conduct interviews and, more importantly, write up the findings to be available on the internet. Along with the typical anonymity of the participants, I needed to commit to the leaders of the DEI schools in India that they would have permission to read the material before it became available to others to help avoid any risk of exposure to individuals.

Although each school is recognized by the government and has permission to function in full academic capacity, families in these Dalit communities still suffer from discrimination and outright persecution from those in society who either do not want them to receive equal rights and quality education, or to be attending a school with faith-based ideology. Thus, any identifying details of the organization, leaders, students and locations had to be removed, including references to their website. To begin the evaluation process, I reviewed the goals as stated in the DEI documentation and on their website and then formed semistructured interview questions that would allow the programme implementers and participants the opportunity to confirm effective implementation, and suggest improvement.

This would also allow flexibility in the interview process to follow up on topics that the participants found important to discuss. Due to the time constraints and expense, I was not able to conduct a pilot study, so I discussed and revised the questions several times with the DEI administrators, as well as colleagues who received their prior education in India.

Both suggested adjustments to the questions that would help the participants better understand the questions without my leading them to certain answers. Next, a particular advantage in programme evaluation is for the evaluator to have background knowledge and some level of expertise in order to more accurately observe and document what is seen, as well as probe deeper through the interview process.

To prepare for this, I read a collection of essays and written by the president of the organization to better understand the background and issues that the families face, as well as the overall goals of this organization, and its partnership with established organizations in India. I watched their DVD and read newsletters, and other documentation. Reading news articles about current discriminatory practices as well as academic journal articles discussing the educational gaps faced by Dalits also helped to gain corroborative evidence of current difficulties that are not just the opinions of the DEI leaders.

To gain a better understanding of India's historical context and current practices, I also read parts of the Indian Constitution, the Affirmative Action Laws and Anti-Conversion Laws. Rounding out this preparation was my own background teaching and volunteering in classrooms from kindergarten to 12th grades in the United States, observing first-hand the classroom environment and the expected ability levels of each age group. As Wolcott states, "we know the school setting so well that, unknowingly, we become our own best informants".

IN THE FIELD: INTENTIONS AND PRACTICAL CONSTRAINTS

Having prepared through readings and communication with the field, I then traveled to India to begin the interviews and observations. Originally, the DEI coordinator in India had committed to introducing me to the principals of the schools for interviews followed by a "snowball method" to select further participants. That is, the staff would ask for volunteers, and those who participated would recommend more volunteers, and so on. In order to maintain as much validity as possible, I had intended to interview both students and their parents as well. Also, to avoid selecting only avid supporters, I intended to ask to interview people who may have some negative views about the education, teachers and school, as this could lead to clarification and a balance of perspectives. Typical of many evaluations, things did not go smoothly in the field. When I arrived in Andhra Pradesh, I found that the key actors who would be coordinating all of the interviews had not been notified of my plans, or the purpose of the study. However, one advantage of the individual sites not being notified in advance was that it added a level of credibility to what I observed in that they did not have time to prepare or alter the situations in any way that would place them in a more favourable light.

This lack of preparation, coupled with the fact that a school holiday was suddenly added to the schedule by the Ministry of Education, something that apparently happens periodically without prior notice, as well as the shift in schedules to a half day summer schedule that week, led to several changes in plans.

So despite the number of days allocated for this evaluation, five days were lost due to logistical problems alone. Also, having to travel four to five hours each way to two of the schools made it such that I could only spend one or two hours at each, making it impossible to schedule meetings with the parents.

For greater validity, this study should have included several days at the same site, with the opportunity to interview parents as well as community leaders involved in establishing the programme. While waiting for the coordinators to establish plans to visit the sites, I immersed myself in the daily life of the campus, finding as many opportunities to meet with people in the community, travel in the area, experience life in India, and observe activities that would create a better cultural context for my study.

I attended a college graduation which was especially interesting as many of these students had spent their internships teaching in the DEI schools and had earned their credentials with the goal of becoming full time teachers at various locations throughout India in the following year. Next, a pastor who volunteers with some of the local youth who attend the DEI schools, and one of the school managers took me to visit an area they commonly refer to as "the slums," where a large number of Dalit families live in abject poverty. They also took me to what they call the "pipe village" where approximately 150 families live in concrete pipes joined together.

Although there was not enough time to start any interviews at this point, it gave me insight about their living conditions, and when I observed some of these children days later in their classroom, they had met me before with men they already trusted. This is extremely important in participant observer research.

INTERVIEWS

Finally, with only five days left, I was able to begin visiting the school locations and start the interviews and observations. In order to protect the locations of each of the schools, I will identify them as School A, B, C and D. Each school has been established for a different length of time and depending on funding and site constraints, have a different number of grades from Lower Kindergarten through 8th.

By the time we arrived at the rural schools A and B, there was only one hour remaining for observations before school let out at 12:30. Because of this, my original plans to interview individual teachers had to be revised to a focus group format after school hours.

For simplicity, and due to literacy and translation issues in the more remote areas, I prepared oral consent for all participants, even though all that I actually interviewed read English well. The total interviews throughout all four sites included two principals, three managers, two teacher focus groups, a 6th grade and 8th grade class focus group and finally the national administrator for the DEI schools. In India, and at these schools in particular, a manager has the role of evaluating a teacher's performance at the end of the year, and is responsible for purchasing materials, student enrollment, as well as moral training activities.

The principal is responsible for academics, government standards, time schedules, lesson plans and exams. One interesting constraint to note was that in the focus groups, each responded differently depending on whether their teacher or principal was present. For example, the eighth grade class was very formal with their teacher present. When I asked the questions, one by one, around the room, each student would stand in place and answer politely. In some of the more subjective questions, it was difficult to know if some were simply responding to peer pressure by giving responses that others had already said or if they would have chosen the response on their own.

Many times, when a student was hesitant, trying to think of an answer, others would give them suggestions. With the sixth grade class however, the teacher left me in charge and I made the mistake of trying to relax the more formal classroom standards, due to time constraints. They immediately became very animated, loud, changing seats, asking questions and so on. It took quite a while to get the class back under control, but they were candid in their responses.

The teacher focus groups were at first reserved, but as I explained the purpose of the study, they became more cooperative and answered more readily, as many of them had just finished their own studies and wanted to support my research.

However, when they did answer a question, the principal or manager often modified their answer, softening it, or adding to it. I was aware that I would not be able to get fully candid responses with a manager or principal present. Another reason that teachers were hesitant to open up I found, was due in part to the sensitivity of the topic of Dalit discrimination.

As an evaluator, I needed to establish a level of trust with the interviewees in order for them to be as open as possible. Though each one that I spoke with displayed a respect for my role as university researcher, I found that when I either explained my background, or that I had met the organization's president and studied the background of the Dalits, they quickly opened up with passionate enthusiasm for what they do and why.

As I needed to remain as objective as possible, I did not want to disclose too much information about myself that would direct their answers, but at the same time, establishing this relaxed atmosphere allowed them to more openly discuss the children, the difficulties, or the religious element of their teaching.

Having more time to interview individuals would have allowed deeper probing of the issues resulting in more complete data. One last interview constraint is that due to schedules, many of the interviews with management had to be conducted in the car, one time with the principal himself driving through four hours in traffic that I have only experienced in India. The conversations were interspersed with horns honking continuously, cell phone call interruptions, barking dogs and shouts of children playing in the streets. The recordings were difficult to hear when I tried to transcribe the notes each night.

Also, two of the interviewees said that they felt constrained being recorded, because they were self-conscious about their grammar, pronunciation and word usage, knowing that I would be quoting them in a research document. I found that they became much more relaxed, open and even fervent about their goals and implementation without the recordings. Therefore, most of the quotations are paraphrased from my notes.

OBSERVATIONS

As I did not know in advance exactly how many schools I would observe, or what the age levels and abilities would be, I did not develop a formal observational protocol with a list of specific events or behaviours that I intended to analyse. My observation methods were therefore unstructured, and because there was no way to observe the students completely unnoticed, I conducted my sessions as a participant-as-observer interacting with the children, tape recording and writing notes as often as I could using a journaling method.

Two of the schools, with a one day warning of my arrival, prepared a formal greeting with the traditional flower lei and special presentations, greeting me in the language of their original state as well as in English and Hindi. I was reminded of the complexity of the educational dilemmas in India. It is such a diverse land, of many languages and high illiteracy in many states, which gave me an understanding of the desire for many to learn English as a shared tool of communication and opportunity for future educational attainment. As I was escorted through each classroom, from the Lower Kindergarten to their highest grade on campus, the students were excited and eager to welcome me and perform recitations, songs and ask questions.

The children displayed their coursework, and their writings in all three languages, English, Telugu and Hindi. I spent approximately five to ten minutes in each room, as we had to complete the entire campus within an hour. I recorded the greetings, songs, and poetry, which were also performed in all three languages, as well as the questions of several of the children which I later used to evaluate the level of ability and pronunciation.

After collecting the data, I read through the notes and listened to the recordings and coded for themes to evaluate the responses to the specific questions and to create as complete a picture as possible of the matching of goals with effective implementation. Although not all data that would be useful in a full educational evaluation could be gathered in a short timeframe under the various constraints, the data that was collected allows me to answer each of the research questions to varying degrees, depending on the location and the interview participants.

Ethnographic evaluations begin with a desire to understand, with the next step being to appraise and assess what is understood, in such a way that the results can guide the decision making process of key actors.

FINDINGS AND DISCUSSION

An ethnographic formative programme evaluation differs from a strictly qualitative approach, in that my role as an evaluator is to examine the implementation of each of the stated goals of the DEI at the four sites, not to judge the overall values, assumptions or decisions in establishing these goals. Generally, a formative evaluator gathers information at each of the sites that can be used by programme staff to assess and improve their programme as necessary. As the DEI did not request this evaluation, or guide the specific research questions, the overall value in this analysis rests in gaining a better understanding of the educational situation of the Dalits, such that future research can be pursued. In order to create a logical flow of the findings and discussion, I divide the following parts just as to the three original research questions. I then further separate the findings into the same categories of the DEI stated goals that I initially used to formulate the interview questions for the students, teachers and DEI leaders.

The reader throughout these findings. It begins with the over arching question of how this programme is situated within India's overall plans to affect change for the future of the Dalits. This includes the holistic approach to addressing the needs within the local and the global contexts, followed by the specific topics of English medium of instruction and teaching from a human rights perspective based on a Christian worldview. Although economic development and health needs are addressed briefly in context of the holistic approach, the dashed arrows show that they will not be a main focus of this document.

In the second part, based on the rest of the stated goals of the organization, each of the specific elements is examined to see how these goals are being implemented. Finally, the third question deals with future research to be addressed in the conclusion. Each of the findings is examined and discussed based on an analysis of the documentation, interviews and observations where applicable.

CONTEXT

India is a land of vast diversity and yet in that diversity, extreme disparity. As I rode through the streets I saw stores filled with exquisitely woven saris and expensive jewelry while children begged for coins at the corners. Oxcarts meandered through the streets next to expensive vehicles, and cows stood side by side with motorcycles, waiting to cross the street creating an interesting backdrop of both ancient and modern. From rural to urban and from state to state, there are marked contrasts that create a daunting task as India strives to educate an estimated 20 to 30 million children who are not attending primary school as the country presses towards the goal of education for all by 2015. In this type of evaluation, it is extremely important to understand the context in which each of the schools is situated as it becomes necessary in analysing the findings. For example, had I simply seen the children at each school location, well groomed, dressed in uniforms and speaking English, studying math and science, I would not have had any understanding of the level of accomplishment of the programme. These schools choose to compare their achievement levels to private schools in the area, whose children generally come from entirely different socioeconomic backgrounds and home environments. They explained that each of the schools has unique constraints that must be addressed as they make decisions on the best approach that will impact the community.

LIVING CONDITIONS

To begin with, one must understand the children's living conditions and the affects this can have on their education. As I walked through the narrow crowded streets of the slums, with over 150,000 people separated by just one wall from the airport runway, I could smell the open sewage draining in an infrastructure not designed to handle the amount of people living there. The children clustered around wearing tattered and dirty clothing but with eager curiosity, smiling shyly and asking questions using gestures if I could not understand them.

Most were barefoot and the smaller children wore no clothing at all, or simply a shirt. Stepping carefully around the pigs, cows, dogs and goats all rummaging through the trash heaps piled around the slum, I saw the "rag pickers," a name given to the women who sort through trash all day looking for glass or articles of clothing to sell.

The pastor and the school manager who were escorting me through the slums introduced me to a woman who sits all day, sorting this glass into piles for recycling.

One of the families invited me into their home, which was approximately seven feet across, with a tiny door leading to another room. I was surprised by the shiny, modern looking shelving mounted on the wall for all of their neatly arranged dishware, pots, and utensils.

The pastor said it was not always this clean and orderly in these homes but that he works together with the school in their holistic efforts to teach families about hygiene, cleanliness and health, despite their living conditions. The other area that I visited prior to the school interviews was the area nicknamed the "pipe village" where people have been brought out of rural villages as bonded laborers for a concrete pipe manufacturing company.

Bonded labour is described as a "slave-like form of attachment to a particular employer, often the result of usurious personal loans". These people must stay and work for the company until they have paid off their debt. The company allows them to live in the discarded segments of pipe, where, for the past 30 years, they have built up a whole village, formed by connecting pieces of pipe and bricking off the ends and creating openings for doors. They cook outside while chickens and pigs roam freely in and out of the homes. I was told the villages used to have electricity that the company intended to be used for lighting only.

However, when people started using it for televisions, irons, radios and so on, the company considered that an abuse of the privilege and turned it off completely. Inside the pipes, it was dark and crowded, yet this is where the children read and do their homework by candlelight. Even within this village, however, there is a contrast in conditions. Walking through the village, I noticed that while one half was cluttered and dilapidated, the other half was very orderly, with cleanly swept dirt, and pipe homes lined up in rows, with all personal belongings neatly stored inside. When I asked the pastor about the difference, he said that it depends on which part of India the villagers come from.

He said that there are some stereotypical differences between the education level and hygiene of the northern and southern villagers that they see in the pipe village. We had invited one of the DEI teachers along, a Swedish intern who had not yet visited where the children lived. One little girl, excited to see her teacher in her village, motioned for us to follow her. She scampered ahead, and we could see through the opening of her five foot diametre pipe home, that she was quickly scooping up a piece of clothing from the floor and stuffing it into the corner of their neatly ordered space. She giggled at us and spread her arms in a gesture of welcome and pride to her home.

The rural areas face different types of difficulties. Transportation is not readily available and the children often have to walk for miles in the stifling heat. This affects attendance as they either arrive tardy, or end up not coming at all. Due to the types of jobs available in these areas, generally related to seasonal farming, children often either move to where the jobs are available for their parents, or some are needed to help with the family income.

This affects the ability of the children to stay in school for a full year, as well as the ability of the parents to financially support any of the education on a month by month basis if fees are required. The managers said, however, that there are some positive factors in rural living, specifically that children are not exposed to "dangers and too much knowledge about life" that is seen in the close quarters of the slum areas, and they often have better access to food.

One village had small one or two room concrete homes built by the government placed neatly on individual lots. Walking past the open doors, I saw no furniture and some people were sleeping during the heat of the day on the concrete floors. I met several adults sitting on the floors hand rolling up to 1,000 cigarettes a day for a wage of approximately one dollar per day. The manager said that the DEI is working within these communities to set up training opportunities such as embroidery, tailoring, and computers and creating self-help groups using microenterprise concepts that establish cooperative loan efforts in small groups to begin businesses within the communities. This holistic approach once again, aims not only to assist in the children's education, but to affect the community in which they live. These children, whether in urban or rural settings, have many obstacles to overcome in their path towards education. Whether it is their noisy or crowded study conditions, lack of parent education and support, distance of travel, limited days in attendance, lack of food and clothing, or even just the stress of everyday living due to limited access to water, electricity, and medical treatment, these conditions can have an overall affect on their achievement and attainment through the programmes offered.

Understanding how they live is necessary for me as an evaluator to fully comprehend the observations and interviews in context, but I recognize that it is crucial for the programme developers as well as they make decisions regarding how the funds are best spent, whether it be for curriculum, lunch programmes, uniforms, supplies, transportation, or after school homework assistance.

SCHOOL CONDITIONS

In the rural School A, the children actually meet in a condemned building while waiting for a new facility to be built. The fifth grade class is conducted outside under a tree as there is no room for a classroom and the children wanted to continue after fourth grade. Many of the rooms have no tables, chairs or play equipment for recess. There is no electricity at this school, and the water has to be carried 200-300 feet. There is also no phone service or e-mail access making it difficult for staff to communicate with other DEI locations. With no bus service, some of the children travel over six miles to get to school. They showed me the property for the new building, but the lack of infrastructure will make it difficult to build. This adds to the time the children have to wait for better facilities and for additional grades to be added. The DEI brings in a medical clinic before school starts to assist with some of the basic medical needs within the village. They also had sewing classes for village women. School B is also in a rural setting with brightly painted murals of flowers on the front giving it a welcoming presence.

Some of the grades had desks and chairs while others sat on concrete floors. Many of the children either walked home or shared rides on the small autorickshaws that come by after school each day. The management would like to add more rooms in order to add grades to the school, as well as more rooms for the sewing classes that I visited for the women in the community. Several people referred to School C as their model and I could quickly see why.

It is also in a rural setting but the facility was markedly neat, well painted, with brightly coloured playground equipment and flowers landscaping the front. The children had desks and chairs and though they, too, would like to add more rooms, the facility was very well maintained. Instead of the typical hand printed postings on the other bulletin boards this school had computer printouts of calendars, rules and daily schedules. I visited the sewing and computer classes in session where both young men and women attend who have either had no formal education or were older than 10th grade so were beyond the formal school setting. School D, the one urban school that I observed, was located within a larger campus with other facilities nearby. In the classrooms where I conducted focus group interviews, they had desks and chairs and they did have some playground equipment to be shared by all classes.

These children have access to public transportation and several students have bicycles. They have plans to add two stories to this facility as they are limited by land space. With this foundation of context laid, the following parts present specific findings relating to the research questions. Throughout the rest of the findings, since each site is unique in its setting and stage of development, if a finding is specific to a school, I will report it separately, otherwise I will refer to overall findings on given topics.

DETAILED FINDINGS

The research question being addressed and the specific claims of the DEI, followed by a summarized list of the types of interview questions that I used to examine how the areas are being addressed. This first question helps to understand the overall goals of the DEI and their plans for societal change.

I found two specific areas that they address beyond the obvious educational components. One is the desire to teach English such that the children can gain access to higher education through the country's English medium universities, as well as increased job opportunities.

Although many countries struggle with the topic of how English should be taught, the fact remains that there is an ever increasing global market that requires English proficiency. The second desire is to teach a new sense of self-worth and equality that traditionally has been denied them. The organization feels that a significant way to change the thinking of the society is to teach through the children, their parents and community leaders that each individual has value, and that all should be given equal opportunity through values commonly established as human rights. Their intent is to use a holistic approach as they seek to change the future for this group of people. Although I will focus primarily on their approach to education as it interrelates with human rights and social justice, it became clear throughout the interviews and observations that they address more than these areas through economic development and medical aid in an attempt to change the framework in which these children learn.

Research shows that India has made inroads in the educational process, but the disparity still exists and simply offering education or even changing their way of thinking about their self-worth, will not guarantee a more prosperous future for these children. That is why the organization is eager to make changes at a societal level. Though it is a very large undertaking and beyond the scope of this document, it needs to be acknowledged in order to understand how these particular schools fit into the overall framework This objective was expressed well in the conversations with two leaders. One asked me, "What do you believe, who influences the child's career most, the teacher or the parent."

I said, "I'd like to think the parent." He said, "Yes, for you, you would want that, but you are not in their world. For these children, if the parent is illiterate, the only goals will be to be the same as the parent–a street sweeper or a rag picker. At the CEC's we want to improve their education, career, and their future. DEI plans to use this education to improve the whole community." Another said, "Our duty is to help the deprived, they must have an education to be empowered, enlightened and equipped to face the challenging world." As a faith-based NGO, with a mission to aid this poor and oppressed people, they have chosen to use the egalitarian teaching of Christianity based on moral stories and concepts found in the Bible.

To examine whether the claims are being practiced, I asked a variety of questions of the children, teachers and administrators regarding the importance of English education, as well as how it is taught, what the children intend to do with the education, and how this will help reach that goal. Although the term "quality" is difficult to gauge without actual test scores and proficiency levels, I will address what was at least observable regarding this statement.

ENGLISH MEDIUM INSTRUCTION

As an English medium form of instruction, all subjects are conducted in English throughout the day, but they also learn Hindi and Telugu in separate language classes each day. Their level of achievement was really quite impressive considering that especially in rural areas, most have absolutely no access to English outside of school. Schools in the urban areas may hear it in the stores or on the streets and can practice what they learn, but in the rural areas, with no English spoken at home or in the community, there is no opportunity to hone the language skills.

In an effort to improve the children's abilities and to invest in the whole community, some of the schools are even beginning to add parents' language courses. Each of the principals and managers spoke English well, and I understood them easily, although it did take the first few days in India to adjust to the variety of accents, as many came from different parts of India, where their first language or dialect is specific to that state. Interacting with the teachers, I found some of the accents were a little more difficult to understand, but we adapted to each other quickly during the focus group interviews. The children spoke eagerly with me in English so there was no need for the interpreter that was provided. In their villages or in their homes, they speak Telugu, as that is their state language in Andhra Pradesh. Most do not speak Hindi as I was told the southern states prefer not to use this for various reasons.

The children are not allowed to speak other languages at school at any time, either in class or on the playground. In the focus group interview with 6th grade students, I asked the children if there was anything they did not like about their school. One boy said that he did not like it when others broke the rules and spoke Telugu at school on the playground as he wanted to practice only English. Several children nodded in agreement. I did find that their accents were more difficult for me to understand, as mine was for them. One girl was explaining that her favourite subject was what sounded like "shasho shtudies." When I looked puzzled, the teacher clarified by enunciating "social studies," and then I was able to understand more clearly their future pronunciations. They responded to their teachers' requests of them in English, showing recognition of her questions. Their written proficiency was noted as they enthusiastically showed me their notebooks filled with writing in all three languages, very neatly done, even in the younger grades.

As I observed in each classroom, the youngest children recited poems and sang songs for me in English but I was not able to assess how much beyond rote memorization they had learned yet. These children were in their first year of exposure, and the recitations as opposed to full conversations were typical of that level of achievement. The first grade class could recite the Psalm 23 and the Lord's Prayer which are both about 12 lines long, which for length alone, was an accomplishment for that age group. In some classrooms, they had individual children recite greetings for me, and some classes chanted in unison, carrying the struggling students through it together. One thing I would like to have delved into further would be the records of the students' backgrounds before attending a DEI school. I would like to know if they learned English at another school before coming to these locations, especially those in higher grades, or if the school is solely responsible for their English achievement.

For example, several in the 8th grade at School D said they had received English education prior to the opening of this school, so I would like to have discussed this with the parents and the teachers, or be able to look at the records and create some analysis of number of years of education before attending these schools. Three in that class had come to this school for their first year with no prior English education. The teacher said they were doing very well and all students in that class were able to answer my questions, though sometimes it took two or three attempts. Another area of concern for the future for these schools is that some states are beginning to force the decision in favour of mother tongue education. One CEC in another state for example has been warned that they have one year to stop teaching from an English medium or they will be "de-recognized by the government." This will prove to be very difficult for private schools who want to maintain government recognition, yet believe in their choice of English medium as their main form of instruction, rather than as a separate language course.

The national director said that a school would have to apply to the state to be given a "no objection certificate" and would be charged huge fines in order to maintain the Central Board Secondary Education standing within the federal government. This is the higher standard curriculum and the one that the DEI schools would like to be recognized under. Without these restrictions, they can qualify to be recognized under the National Open Schools curriculum but they consider this a lower standard, and the DEI schools feel the quality would suffer under that recognition.

The leaders are concerned that if children have to go to the government schools which teach only in the local language of Telugu, with a small amount of English, then the issue of what will happen after 10th grade, when all tests are presented in English, has serious implications. The DEI recognizes the need for these children to continue into upper education, but feels that with the limitations on access to English will be a detriment to their future prospects.

Maintaining quality standards of curriculum from state to state while complying with government restrictions creates conflict for the leadership which will continue to be addressed under this disagreement regarding approach. With these concerns in mind, I wanted to understand the overall affect an English education had on the goals and dreams of the children. Although I had to resort to a focus group format, rather than a personal interview with individual children and their parents, I did have a chance to interact with two classes in a lively discussion about their future plans, favourite courses, and what they would do if they could not go to this school. Some of their responses reflected their desire for education in general and some pertained specifically to English. One boy, who was still fairly new to the English language said, "It is good education in this school, I am become learned, studying English." When I asked what they would do if they could not go to this school, several said they would find another English school to go to, but two eighth grade girls, both wanting to become doctors said, "I don't know what I would do, my parents cannot send me anywhere else, and then I could not learn," and, "I would miss my education and my goal to become a doctor."

I visited the home of one of these girls the previous week in the pipe village, so I asked the manager more questions about them. He told me their scores are good and with sponsorship, they have every possibility of fulfilling that dream in the years ahead. Addressing the impediments to the quality of the English education, the director shared that it is difficult to find enough teachers who have excellent English abilities who are willing to live in such difficult environments. He said the teachers rate themselves on a scale of 1-10 at about a six or seven. He said they cannot expect children to learn any higher than a six or seven if they have no higher example. When asking the teachers for what they wish they could have to improve their ability to teach, several of them asked for

English tapes or CDs to play so that they and the children could hear clear pronunciation of non Indian English with its mix of accents from different dialects.

Since these rural locations make it very difficult to attract quality, well educated teachers, one of the ideas the leadership is considering is to offer opportunities for nine month internships for people from the United States, Canada or the United Kingdom to come and teach each age group every day, in order for them to hear it spoken by those whose first language is English. One of my particular areas of interest in this English education stems from my career as a database consultant for a major computer corporation based in the United States.

Currently working with their customer service department, which has outsourced all sales, technical support and customer service to various cities in India within the past three years, we recognize a huge demand for English proficiency. Customers express frustration when the accent cannot be understood, and corporations in India are struggling to find qualified employees with strong educational background and English skills. Thus, both factors are important in the children obtaining higher education leading to openings in the global market. In this part, the interview questions relate to areas of human rights, current discrimination, issues of self-worth, and the situation within the community.

Recognizing that there is a direct conflict between the two religious beliefs, I also examine how the DEI uses a Christian worldview to achieve these goals.

UNDERSTANDING THE GLOBAL EFFORTS

First, acknowledging the need to accomplish more than simply the education and change of thinking of the individuals, I needed to understand how the DEI addresses the issue from a macro level within the international efforts towards social justice and human rights. As the review of literature shows, even when the Dalit children do obtain an education, society will not necessarily allow them to fully utilize this and create change for themselves and their families. I interviewed the social justice coordinator with the DEI to discuss their efforts to raise global awareness on these very issues. He explained that the DEI president travels extensively, along with other spokes people from India, the United States and the United Kingdom, in a concerted effort to advocate for the Dalit people. Using documentary screenings and research gathered from current sources, the DEI joins with others to present in committee meetings, hearings and briefings in several arenas such as the United States Congress, State Department and the United Nations.

The recent passing of the US HCR 139 shows marked solidarity in the global efforts to eradicate continued discriminatory practices.

HUMAN RIGHTS EDUCATION USING A CHRISTIAN WORLDVIEW

Along with these efforts, many of the sources on the DEI's philosophy and work emphasize that social change comes not just from government rulings, but requires grassroots social activism as well. The sources further emphasize that there must be a change in thinking of the people in order for these new changes in societal order to take place.

Their mission statement asserts that "The DEI exists to empower the Dalits in their quest for social freedom and human dignity by networking human, financial, and informational resources." Acknowledging the disparate thinking between the two belief systems, I asked how they planned to teach their stated values, within the framework of the government restrictions and societal opposition. The DEI considers the education a secular education using a government standard curriculum, yet taught from human rights framework based on Christian ideology.

Their intention is to establish egalitarian thinking along with the moral principles that promote equality in society. The managers and director said that through songs, moral stories, and even some Bible verses, as well as the behaviour and expectations modeled by the staff, they feel they can help the children and their parents engage in a new way of thinking, promoting self-worth, fair treatment and future hope.

They have labeled this approach as "holistic transformational activities." However, in order to be careful to separate actual Christian doctrinal religious teaching, from the moral and egalitarian principles taught on a weekly basis, they said they also offer a traditional Christian "Vacation Bible School" during the week just after school lets out for the summer.

This is an optional week, offered to the children and any of their friends who are interested. Parents choose whether to have their children attend with an explanation that it is not part of their educational curriculum but will be a series of children's activities based on Christian teaching.

This allows a careful division between the holistic transformational activities throughout the school year and specific religious teaching in the summer. Each of the leaders and managers I spoke with articulated specific messages that they wanted to get across to the children and families through their teaching which seemed to divide well into two main categories:

- Each individual has value and self-worth
- All are created equal, with equal rights as a citizen of India

I address each of these, as well as the use of a Christian worldview to accomplish each goal.

INDIVIDUAL VALUE AND SELF-WORTH

Effectively teaching and measuring the construct of "value and self-worth" is difficult but they feel that by daily reinforcement, encouragement and modeling, they can begin to affect change. To teach a sense of value, the staff said they find a variety of ways from the time children are in the LKG to encourage the development of their understanding of who they are as human beings. For example, through songs and verses, the schools teach that God loves each child and values them, which differs, the director said, from the Hindu traditions that Dalits are considered God's waste product and therefore unworthy of the benefits that others receive. The president states in his writings that he would like for the children to at least hear that they are loved by God, which he feels brings a sense of dignity and self-worth.

It is typical of Dalit children, as with most children, to assume they might do the same job that their parents do some day. Only with Dalits, these jobs often entail the most menial and repulsive tasks imaginable in society perpetuating the concept that this is their only value to society. To combat this type of thinking, some of the schools hold activities such as a Career Day, where the children dress up in costumes that the school has for different career choices. These include nurses, doctors, policemen, engineers, musicians, judges, lawyers, athletes, and so on.

Not only do the children participate in this, but the parents are invited to the event, to encourage them to see the potential in their child with this education. I asked one of the managers if the parents are happy with the education, as I could not interview them directly. He said the parents at his school have expressed excitement over the changes they have seen in their children because the "growth and learning gives them hope." To follow up on this in my focus group sessions with the sixth and eighth grade classes, I asked them what they would like to do for a career when they finished school.

It is common for children to pick a goal that sounds glamorous or popular, but for these children, who have been impressed with the concept of taking on the least desirable jobs in society since birth, their responses indicated a different hope. The school said they work very hard to stress the options for their future, and these children reflected that in their responses.

Each selected specific career paths, with the most popular being "children's doctor," "software engineer" and "police officer." Although only one had actually worked on a computer they had definitely been exposed to this idea for a career. When I pressed them on some of their specific answers such as cardiologist, or eye doctor, they explained that each had family members who had benefited from these particular fields and they wanted to be able to help someone like that someday.

These results are important in that they seem to reflect that these children are not making any assumptions based on their parents' job choices, as none of the children interviewed had parents in any of these fields.

ALL ARE CREATED EQUAL AND HAVE RIGHTS

Promoting the second concept that all are created equal, the DEI said that the education is offered to all faiths, races, and genders with no restrictions or need to convert in order to obtain the benefits of education.

For specific examples of how they use Christian ideology to show egalitarian beliefs, the staff said that they have moral classes on Fridays or Saturdays using commonly accepted books in India that teach moral values, and some simple biblical teaching throughout the week such as the verse, "All men and women are created in God's image". The director said this differs significantly from the traditions of Hindu teaching that each of the caste levels stems from a different part of God, such as the Brahmin caste from God's head, down to the lowest caste from God's feet. The children recited these verses and poems for me, as well as songs about how "God created you and me."

In the hand-motions that accompany this song, the children pointed first to me-a white, American woman and then to themselves. The fact that they could perform these gestures as a perfectly natural act, without hesitation, was quite remarkable when one understands the cultural background. Teachers and students must demonstrate this equality as well.

They said they are very careful that no caste or discriminatory practices are shown among the staff, or in their treatment of the children. In School D for example, if children show discrimination in any way, they are made to publicly apologize and parents are told that if this continues, the child will be removed from the school. Each of the schools offers community involvement with the parents, such as parent meetings, parades in the community and even clean up days in one.

In order to teach these concepts to all, one school said that at each of the four parent meetings per year, they "remind the parents that each child is an Indian citizen and therefore entitled to all rights and privileges belonging to every member of society, that all people are created equal, and that no caste treatment is allowed." To continue this in the community, they held a Children's Day parade, where all teachers and children marched throughout the village carrying banners stating, "Drive out castism to open equality," and "Education opens the doors for future life." Every two months, they hold an evaluation and planning meeting where they question how they are doing academically, and how well they did in the community at passing the vision on from the manager, to the teachers, to the children and to the parents.

As they teach these concepts, they said they are fully aware and respectful of the government restrictions on certain states, or even resistance within particular communities. For example, one of the main restrictions that some states face is the anti-conversion law discussed previously. Although the four schools I visited are not in one of these states, several of the other DEI schools are. Anti-conversion laws state that no one can pressure others with financial resources or gifts, or through threats of divine displeasure, in order to convince someone to convert. They take several precautions in offering this education, such as clearly explaining to the parents that while it is a government recognized school it is based on a Christian worldview, as well as making sure that the community leaders are supportive of this and that there are no coercive practices.

When I asked the managers if there are any difficulties with this method of teaching, which goes against Hindu beliefs, one school told me that some parents chose not to have their children attend because of the Christian influence. He said this makes it difficult for the children as many of them want to come and be with the other children and learn, but the parents do not want them to be taught another religion. Another manager said that there was some difficulty when parents complained to the leader of the village about the Christian teaching.

He said the village leader did not want to upset the school, as he valued the education for the community, but he did not want to upset the parents, as they are the ones who elect him to office as leader. So he resolved it by reprimanding a local teacher at a public meeting, telling him not to teach these songs and verses. The manager asked the leader to encourage all parents to come to him directly in the future if they have any concerns, but he said that none of the parents removed their children from the school. In their efforts to teach equality and human rights, several managers said they are aware that some of the children are too young to understand the concept of inequality. One said they all live in a Dalit community, so at a young age, they are not exposed to the idea that anyone is any different. However, by fourth and fifth grade the schools want to begin an active strategy beyond the daily teaching, that will engage them in awareness of their rights as an Indian citizen and to develop critical thinking skills.

One school said that they will be starting debate teams, where they divide up the upper grades into four groups or "houses," and assign them an "awareness topic" topic such as AIDS, equality and so on. The school would assign teachers to help the children prepare and a judge for the event. The idea is to have schools join together for a special day, and have all children present so that they can learn from the skills practiced and topics discussed.

He said, "This way, their language will improve, their thinking will improve and they will learn to ask other people and prepare." Each of these collective practices is used to continue their efforts in "holistic transformation" throughout the communities. By approaching it from both the global level and the classroom level, and even into the homes, they aim to affect change throughout India. In order to gain information regarding the vision for future schools as well as current statistics.

SELECTION OF SCHOOL SITES

So far, there are 62 CECs in 13 states with an average of approximately 200 students each. At the time that I started this research, there were 54 CECs with 7,000 students enrolled, and now, less than one year later there are over 10,000 students enrolled in the schools. The goal is to eventually have other organizations join through the AICC to establish 1,000 CECs nationwide. I was told that selecting the locations of the CEC's involves several steps. First, the DEI must be invited into the village. "The overhead organization that the DEI works with is very popular," just as to one of the managers, and village leaders have heard that they are building schools to help the Dalits. If a leader expresses a desire to have a school built within the community, the DEI responds by sending a team to survey the area to determine whether it is a match for the criteria.

The village or area must show a specific need, that is, there must be a high enough concentration of Dalits, without a similar English speaking school within walking distance. There must also be government cooperation with vaccinations, and healthcare for the children, and finally, the leader within that village must be motivated and cooperative as he will have direct influence on the parents and the community to affect change. The village leaders and the parents are informed that it is an English medium school, following government standards of curriculum, using a Christian worldview. Village leaders have found that the level of violence is lower with more education and they desire an opportunity to see a hope for the future of their children.

Gaining the trust and participation within the community is a key element in establishing effective intervention. The issue of anti-conversion laws is also carefully addressed in each state in order to protect the individuals from any fines. This part lays out the quality of the education, as well as academic placement within the surrounding communities. Once again, although "quality" is difficult to measure without specific quantitative measures, I will address their goals and observable efforts.

QUALITY OF EDUCATION

Each of the schools currently has government permission to operate and recognition from the Ministry of Education. Twice a year, the ME inspects the teachers, children. From LKG to fifth grade, the schools may choose their curriculum and still be recognized, but from the sixth grade on, the schools must follow the government curriculum and timetables of testing under the Centralized State Board Exams and India Centralized Standard Education.

Board exams from the state are required at seventh and tenth grades. As one principal stated, they also give their own exams each trimester and if the students are not performing well, they approach the teacher and help the teacher with the subject matter to improve for the next testing round.

Although I was not able to gather quantitative data on test scores, and compare them to statewide results, the director said that they prefer to compare themselves to private schools which have a higher level of standard than the government schools. He said they compare very well and students from some schools are even beginning to win prizes in local extra curricular competitions for drawing, singing and sports. While I was there, an annual review was in progress, where managers and principals of all the southern campuses had gathered to discuss strategies, dreams, difficulties, goals and successes.

If this were a more complete evaluation, this would be the perfect forum where future improvements would be discussed, based on findings, especially if I were able to conduct the parent interviews, and individual student and teacher interviews.

EQUAL OPPORTUNITY FOR EDUCATION

The children and adults all stated that any child could go to the school, however, the managers and director confirmed that preference is given to the Dalit children if there is a capacity limit. Most of the schools reserved 60% for Dalits. To determine whether this was actually in practice, and to see if it appeared that many children convert either because of the education, or in order to obtain the education, I asked two of the schools if they knew the attendance rate based on religious beliefs or practices. The records from School B, the percentage of the students' faith background is 92% Hindu, 6% Muslim and 2% Christian.

School D had 10% Muslim and the rest mostly identified themselves as Hindu. Most areas, they said, have very few Muslims or Christians, which fits with their overall strategy to establish schools in the areas with the greatest need for education for the Dalits.

As these schools are at least three years old, there does not appear to be any high conversion rate, just as to their records. One of the difficulties mentioned by several with regard to allowing all children to attend is the transience of the families who work with seasonal jobs.

One school said that parents will sign their children up and begin school for the first two months, but then leave with the uniform, shoes and books, following job availability. The school does not want to turn these children away, or discriminate in any way based on what they think might happen, but at the same time, they recognize the reality that the student may leave, and take the supplies with them that would have benefited another child coming in.

Also, another school has parents who are trying to get their children into a boarding school facility, which would provide for all of their needs. As soon as any opening becomes available, they will remove their children from the DEI school. To accommodate this, one school requires a beginning of the year fee, knowing of the particular problems in that area. Then, as the year progresses they continue a monthly payment schedule.

For this subject, I discussed with the management some of the issues commonly discussed in attempting to evaluate overall quality of the teaching staff. I then questioned two focus groups of teachers regarding their educational background and years of experience. I asked the management how they train the teachers in the "holistic transformational activities." This part also discusses the teacher's level of satisfaction with the teaching experience, and what they wish they could change, as well as perceived obstacles to their ability to teach or to the overall educational experience.

ACCOUNTABILITY

A key component in the success of any educational programme has been shown to be the accountability of the teachers. One particular aspect is teacher absenteeism. Students cannot be educated if the teacher is not present, and India holds one of the higher rates of teacher absenteeism with 25% absent in government primary schools on any given day. There are several reasons for this, including the lack of repercussion if a teacher does not show up to class.

The CECs address this by allowing eight "casual days" which are used for vacations and eight "sick days." Anything beyond that, they do not get paid for. The school day runs from 8:00 a.m. to 3:30 p.m. Teachers are permitted three "tardies," but anything beyond that is disciplined by a reduction of pay or removal of a vacation day. The principals claim that this has not been an issue with their staff, partly due to the rules and accountability established and partly due to the commitment of the teachers to help these under-privileged students.

STAFF EDUCATION

As I was not able to interview the staff at each of the four schools, I summarize the findings regarding the years of experience and education level from schools A and B. As these schools have only been open for two years and five years respectively, the average teaching time of 16 months at School A and 2.7 years at School B is low, but not surprising.

Part of this is due to the fact that the schools are very new, and part to the difficulty they have in maintaining staff in rural areas with lower pay. The four schools had an average ratio of 22 students to one teacher. Of these two schools, School A had less educational background among the staff. Three were still completing their degrees remotely, and two held Bachelor of Science in Education degrees, one a Bachelor of

Science in Education with a credential of a Bachelor of Education and two held other certifications.

School B, the more established school, had more degreed staff, three with BA or BSc degrees, five with BEd credentials in addition to their BA or BSc or MA degrees, and two with specific training in nursing and Hindi. There are several reasons that the leadership faces difficulty attracting well educated staff, however. One is the lack of equipment and materials that these teachers have been trained to expect in order to do an excellent job of educating. They have been trained in many cases with full degrees in education, but in the rural areas, there are not enough resources for science laboratories, computers, audio visual equipment, libraries, musical instruments, sports equipment and so on.

They feel they cannot do as good a job as they were trained to do without the necessary resources. Also, as the principal reported, the living conditions are much harder than these teachers who have lived in the cities have ever experienced and being far from their families and friends creates a lonely environment. However, those educated through a partner organization have already experienced many of these conditions because part of their education contains a service component, where they have spent as much as a year in the field, working in very difficult conditions, such as the slums or remote villages. The leadership foresees difficulties, however, in maintaining continuity with the staff in these conditions.

I asked if they ever hire teachers who are non-Christian, and the principal said it would be very rare. They want teachers to be able to teach from a Christian perspective, with the DEI's approach to holistic transformation so there is no confusion in practices.

It is hard to recruit teachers into the villages, however, as the government pays more for a BEd, making it hard to attract the quality teachers who could choose the government city jobs instead. Despite facility differences and varying educational backgrounds, one other point that was notable as I observed in these schools was the order and discipline. School A, the newest of the schools where many children are being exposed to formal education for the first time, had far less structure and order than School C, the model school. When School A lined up to greet me and have their photo taken, the children clustered close together, in no particular order while the children in School C, also with very little warning of my arrival, filed out of their classrooms in perfect order, separated by one arm's length, standing at attention, ready for the salute and pledge.

It was a very impressive sight to see each row, perfectly aligned by grade, with teachers standing in the back. Children had previously memorized greetings that they used as well as their daily pledge routines. I am told by colleagues from India that this is the standard routine for the elite private schools in India.

It was a very interesting observation to see the difference between a newly formed school, and one that is more established. It would be useful to discuss further with the staff whether these differences in the schools are due to the length of time since they were established, the expectation of the leadership, or the children's background, or a combination of the three.

JOYS AND OBSTACLES

I asked the teachers what the enjoyed most about teaching and though it did take some time at first to think of an answer, several said that they enjoyed seeing the changes in the students, and watching them learn about their rights as human beings and about Christian principles through Bible verses and stories.

After even a small amount of education, they see improvements in health and hygiene, and they hear the children speaking English in society. The teachers agreed that watching the children gain confidence as they learn provides the impetus for many of them to continue. One of the difficulties they face is that it is hard at first to get the families to take learning seriously and to cooperate together with the school, or to even have their child enroll. One school went door-to-door, explaining the cost, the value and what would be provided. Students would start to attend, but since many walked for some distance, they would often come in late.

This caused disruptions in the classroom and in their learning. Also, the children did not know how to treat a teacher, and the parents had never been to school themselves so had little expectation for their children's behaviour in school.

Recognizing this, one manager conveyed that he felt that, "Discipline comes first, then education will come out of it." To aid in this, the school created a policy for the parents, showing what was expected of the children on holidays, weekends and in the evenings, such that what they were allowed to do at home would match with the school's expectations. If the child was going to be absent for more than three days due to illness, the parent needed to show a doctor's excuse.

In order to handle the "tardies," one school warned the students and parents that they would start locking the gate when school began at 9:00 a.m. When parents and children came late, they were turned away. The manager shared that when one little boy cried and begged to be allowed to come in, it "broke his heart," and he allowed him to come, talking to him about correcting one's mistakes and learning from them. He said that after two days of these methods, none of the children have had difficulties with tardiness.

FUTURE DREAMS

Every programme has some room for improvement regardless of current successful application so I asked the managers, teachers and students if there is any one thing they would like to add to their school. Interestingly enough, their answers all coincided with similar categories.

The following is a list of the five most common answers and a summary of the participants' comments:

- *Transportation*: They would like a bus or large van for the children, staff and even parents when they come in for meetings with the teacher. With no public transportation in the rural areas, the distance is often so far that if children walk, as was noted before, they are often late to class or do not come at all.

- *Music*: Even though most of the 6th grade focus group had already given me their answer, when one student said they would like musical instruments or singing classes, two-thirds of the class instantly raised their hands in agreement and wanted me to add that to their previous answer. Teachers also wanted to have music and to be included in the community-wide events that some of the DEI schools are competing in successfully. In some of the classes, I found it interesting that the children did not hold a tune very well, but sang in more of a chant. Although it is typical for several children out of a class of 30 to not be musically gifted, I found this lack of ability to sing to be noticeable. I asked how much exposure they have to music and I was told there is very little due to where they live in rural areas, the lack of electricity, and so on. There is little that would train their ear from a young age while forming foundational musical abilities.
- *Science Labs*: Science in general seemed to be very important to these students and their teachers. Several students said their favourite subject was science, and they listed specific topics, with ten out of 23 saying biology. Other students listed chemistry, physics and botany. Teachers wanted to be able to offer these science classes that utilized their full expertise and to include hands-on laboratory experience for the children.
- *Libraries*: Every group wanted to add a library that would be available to check out material such as history books, general knowledge books, science books and stories. Some of the schools are going to be able to add this soon.
- *Sports Programmes and Equipment*: Each school generally had one or two barrels with play equipment to be shared by all classes at recess time.

> In receiving the gifts sent from the United States, one teacher said, "Thank you for the gifts, you have just doubled our jump rope supply!" I had only delivered one per school. The children wanted organized competitive sports, and the teachers and managers said that having an actual Physical Education teacher would help with discipline issues as there would be an incentive to behave or else miss out on something they enjoyed. Also, they said that PE teachers are trained in techniques of order and discipline

Surprisingly, chairs and desks, even though many of the classrooms had no furniture. At the time, I did not think to question whether they considered this an obvious goal they were already working towards or unnecessary compared to the other items they could not substitute with any other object or method, such as sitting on the floor. There were several other needs listed, such as manipulatives, audiovisual equipment, computers and craft supplies. In this part, I summarize the interviews with staff regarding fees that parents pay for their child to attend, and how it is handled if they cannot pay. Also discussed are the school's provision of books, supplies, uniforms and the availability of a midday meal, as well as facility issues.

COST OF EDUCATION

As is stated in their goals, and through interviews, the DEI leadership has found that having the parents pay for part of the education creates a sense of ownership and accountability. Each of the schools charges fees on a different scale, based on the surrounding community, the average wage and availability of jobs for the parents.

Once this is determined, the fee is collected from the parents on a monthly basis, with the rest being subsidized by the DEI funding. There is a problem with the transience of some families due to the type of seasonal labour they are employed in. Therefore, the fees are adjusted by school depending on these issues.

School D, for example, charges an initial fee of 50-100 rupees with the monthly remainder supplied by the DEI which covers the costs if a family leaves and takes the supplies with them.

For Schools A, B and C, the parents pay fees ranging from 25 to 30 rupees per month with the remainder of the cost of approximately 75 rupees per month being subsidized by international funding through the DEI. The managers, most parents are able to supply the fees, but if they cannot, the DEI pays the full fee. An average salary in the rural area of School A is 1,000 rupees per month which is approximately 25 dollars.

BOOKS, SUPPLIES AND UNIFORMS

Each of the schools supplies at least one uniform per student, which usually included shorts for the boys, a jumper for the girls, one shirt, socks, shoes, and a belt and tie for both. One of the schools supplies two uniforms. These children come from such poverty, that they have found that having one complete clean outfit brings a sense of pride, belonging and unity.

It also levels all sense if inequality, as each has equal opportunity to look the same at school. I noticed the children generally came with carefully groomed hair, the girls in pony tails and braids, sometimes wearing bracelets and barrettes. When one school was notified that morning that I was coming to evaluate the school, the principal, knowing it was wash day in the community, quickly sent the local children back home to put their uniforms on for their "inspection." When I arrived, some were in uniform and some in "street clothes," and the principal explained the situation, wishing they each had two uniforms so that all week long, they could look clean and well groomed.

As a way of combining efforts within the community, the women who are learning to sew, create the uniforms for the children, so it is a matter of funding more than availability. Each school, after carefully evaluating the needs within the community, supplies at least the school books required, and some schools add a book bag, writing utensils and other supplies. The children carry an average of over 20 small text books and writing books each day, similar to the size of a bluebook used for exams. People from the United States had donated one suitcase of gifts for the schools, including Frisbees, blow up balls, pencils, vitamins, and so on.

One of the teaching interns was excited about the pencils. She explained that one day, one of the young boys got up to leave the classroom after she asked them to write down an assignment. She told him to sit down and follow directions. He said, "I can't, I have to go see my brother." She reminded him that this was class time, and he could see his brother later. After some interchange, he finally explained, "I have to go see my brother, he has our pencil!" Most of the younger children use chalk and a slate board for in-class work such as math calculations.

This school provides all the supplies needed for any science fair projects or materials needed to join in local school competitions as they have found that parents cannot afford these additional expenses.

MIDDAY MEAL

Two of the schools no longer provide a midday meal of eggs and fruit because they did not have enough resources and had determined that this was a programme that would have to be cut rather than cut resources to any other part of the programme.

One school is still planning to initiate this programme when they have a new building as there is no kitchen facility at their current site.

One of the schools gives one egg per day for each student. Although the director acknowledged that research shows that children at this level of need could do better in school with a meal provided, he felt that these particular children would get some sort of a meal from home, but that parents would not be able to, or would not choose to buy books or school supplies. This decision is made individually for each school depending on the needs within that community.

FACILITIES

One of the needs most commonly mentioned is to have separate bathroom facilities for boys and girls. Several adults that I interviewed explained that these children are "exposed to way too much information about life," living in the conditions that they do.

They explained that Dalits are usually expected to use open fields, or that girls, especially in the slums, are exposed to even dangerous conditions, being made to wait until evening to use the facilities, which puts them at risk of attack or even rape. By adding separate facilities, they felt they could add to the community education about health and hygiene.

Also, if a lunch programme is to be provided, they would need a room in which to store and prepare the food. Each of the schools I visited was using every room available, sometimes for multiple purposes such as after school programmes and self-help groups, with no place for teachers to store their materials, join for meetings, study or prepare. They said that all schools will need to expand, not only to supply these needs, but to even have enough rooms for each grade level as the schools grow each year to meet the demand.

Some of the most common requests for improvement that I heard were for a teachers' room, computer lab, library, science lab and enough rooms to at least go through the eighth grade. However, as one principal shared, the DEI and partner organizations are continuously putting money into new schools, which then limits the resources available to existing schools. This dilemma will be discussed in the conclusion as I look at future goals.

OVERALL SUCCESS OF THE PROGRAMME

Each of the findings show clear accomplishment of the overall goals of the DEI, with each school at a different level of achievement due to location, years since establishment, availability of resources as well as background of the children.

Although there are areas that each could improve if given additional resources, seeing the difference in these children's lives, knowing the environment and background from which they approach this educational experience, is remarkable. UIdeally, I would like to continue to follow the success of this programme over time, and to interview the parents, students and community leaders to assess the long term positive influence for these children and their whole community.

8

Proceedings and Movements of Dalit

POONA PACT

During the first Round Table Conference, when Dr. Bhimrao Ramji Ambedkar favoured the move of the British Government to provide separate electorate for the oppressed classes (Dalit), Gandhi strongly opposed it on the plea that the move would give power to the oppressed classes (Dalit).

He went for an indefinite hunger strike from September 20, 1932 against the decision of the then British Prime Minister J.Ramsay MacDonald granting communal award to the depressed classes in the constitution for governance of British India. In view of the mass upsurge generated in the country to save the life of Gandhi, Ambedkar was compelled to soften his stand. A compromise between the leaders of caste Hindu and the depressed classes was reached on September 24,1932, popularly known as Poona Pact. The resolution announced in a public meeting on September 25 in Bombay confirmed -" henceforth, amongst Hindus no one shall be regarded as an untouchable by reason of his birth and they will have the same rights in all the social institutions as the other Hindus have". This landmark resolution in the history of the Dalit movement in India subsequently formed the basis for giving due share to Dalits in the political empowerment of Indian people in a democratic Indian polity.

The following is the text of the agreement arrived at between leaders acting on behalf of the Depressed Classes and of the rest of the community, regarding the representation of the Depressed Classes in the legislatures and certain other matters affecting their welfare.

- There shall be seats reserved for the Depressed Classes out of general electorate seats in the provincial legislatures as follows:-Madras 30; Bombay with Sind 25; Punjab 8; Bihar and Orissa 18; Central Provinces 20; Assam 7; Bengal 30; United Provinces 20. Total 148.
- Election to these seats shall be by joint electorates subject, however, to the following procedure All members of the Depressed Classes registered in the general electoral roll of a constituency will form an electoral college which will elect a panel of tour candidates belonging to the Depressed Classes for each of such reserved seats by the method of the single vote and four persons getting the highest number of votes in such primary elections shall be the candidates for election by the general electorate.
- The representation of the Depressed Classes in the Central Legislature shall likewise be on the principle of joint electorates and reserved seats by the method of primary election in the manner provided for in clause for their representation in the provincial legislatures.

BATTLE OF KOREGAON

THE MARATHA WARS

While I can understand the desire of Dalits to home into that skirmish and claim that to be the be all and end all of all, skirmishes like this have to be grounded in the greater framework. The Maratha Empire brought to life by Shivaji attained its greatest strength by 1760.

And I should point out that Shivaji was not a Brahmin. While they claimed Kshyatriya status later on, there are some arguments that he was originally a Dalit, a Shudra to be precise. Finally, Shivaji's army was largely composed of people like him, so it was a Dalit Army anyway which got promoted, so to say. Then comes the first Anglo Maratha War 1777-1783 where first the Maratha's won and then the British won. In both cases, native soldiers were far too frequently Dalits. Anyway, more land was captured by the Brits and the power of the Maratha's was further reduced.

Peshwa Baji Rao II and his father basically got up to no good. In 1802, BajiRao went and sucked up to the British after being defeated by Holkars in the Battle of Poona. This pissed off the other Maratha warlords and they got into a bit of a fight with the British which ended with more loss of territory for the Marathas. Then comes the crucial 3rd War which our Dalit friends might now appreciate.

This relates to the 3rd Anglo Maratha War 1817-1818 or the Pindari War. The Pindari's were highly mobile cavalry units which were not on the payroll of any ruler but associated with rulers in return for protection and permission to plunder. Guess what? These Pindari's were low caste, Ladul and also had quite a lot of Muslims (mainly Afghans and Pusthun). Anyway, all this plundering was not good for the British and a really very big army of 120,000 men and 300 artillery pieces was put into gear by Lord Hastings to exterminate these Pindari's. The attacks happened from the east in Bengal, from the South in the Deccan and from the west from Gujarat and Bombay.

THE IMMEDIATE PREDECESSOR TO THE 1ST JAN 1818 BATTLE OF KOREGAON

Once the British invaded Maratha territory to go after the Pindari's, there were skirmishes between the Peshwa's forces and the British forces such as the sack of the British Residency in Pune, and then the British routed another Peshwa force at Khirki. Then the main battle was fought in the Battle of Khadki on November 5, 1817 where the Peshwa Baji Rao was routed pretty much comprehensively and then the British took over the Peshwa's seat at Shaniwarwada by November 17, 1817. The Peshwa, by this time, was running ragged. There was another battle between the Nagpur forces and the British at Sitabalsi on November 27 1817. The next battle to be fought was the Battle of Mahidpur on 20th December where the Holkar's fought and lost to the British, after being betrayed by one of the Pindari (who killed Tulsibai).

THE BATTLE OF KOREGAON

A good description of the battle can be found here. This is a book by WC Taylor, A Popular History of British India published in 1847. Sounds like a pretty good bash. Taylor says that the Peshwa's forces numbered about 25,000 although it should be noted that counting was pretty vague at that time. Still, it wasnt 50,000. But here's the crucial thing, the Peshwa's forces then retreated not because they were defeated by Captain Francis Staunton's forces, but because they got to hear that British reinforcements were coming over. The British forces lost 200 soldiers out of 500, and 6 out of 7 British officers. Good defensive battle without food or water at this village.

THE SOLDIERS

The soldiers who did most of the dying were Mahars. And again ironically, they got their start in being soldiers by no other than Shivaji to become scouts and fortress guards. They were highly mobile light infantry, which is the reason why they were in the 2nd Battalion, 1st regiment of 'Bombay Native Light Infantry' as part of the Maratha Light Infantry. The Peshwa's soldiers were also by and large lower caste soldiers including Mahars, in any case, not Brahmins.

So the fighting basically was between lower castes, only the people who were ordering them around were the British and the Peshwas. This Mahar Regiment still exists and has provided two of the most brilliant Indian Army Chiefs: Gen (Retd) K V Krishna Rao and Gen (Retd) K Sunderji. Also, there is no caste element to the regiment from 1963 onwards and it is now a fully mixed regiment.

THE AFTERMATH OF THE BATTLE OF KOREGAON

There was another fight between the fleeing Peshwa's

forces and the British at Ashti on February 20th 1818 and he remained under pressure till he surrendered to Sir John Malcolm on June 3, 1818 and was given the pension of an annual payment of 8 lakhs rupees. The Battle of Koregaon was celebrated by raising of an Obelix which commemorated this.

So all in all, I am afraid what my research threw up was in sharp variance with the mythology is being provided. It was frankly a small battle/skirmish in a much bigger war, the Peshwa's forces were not defeated in this skirmish, the British Army did not fight this battle expecting the worst because they had been winning every battle in this war, this battle of Koregaon was not really that important as fighting kept on happening for months after this battle and I am afraid there is absolutely no evidence that any kind of caste based ideology was involved in the fight.

So all in all, good myth but a rather more calm reading of the historical record tells differently. I can also see why the Dalit hotheads want to use this battle to burnish their credentials. After all, all revolutions need their battles. If they do want to celebrate the success of lower caste soldiers, they should celebrate Shivaji, the Indian Soldier, the bravery that these soldiers showed to whoever paid them.

SELF-RESPECT MOVEMENT

The Self-Respect Movement was founded in 1925 by Periyar E. V. Ramasamy (also known as Periyar) in Tamil Nadu, India. The movement has the aim of achieving a society where backward castes have equal human rights, and encouraging backward castes to have self-respect in the context of a caste based society that considered them to be a lower end of the hierarchy. The movement was extremely influential not just in Tamil Nadu, but also overseas in countries with large Tamil populations, such as Malaysia and Singapore. Among Singapore Indians, groups like the Tamil Reform Association, and leaders like Thamizhavel G. Sarangapani were prominent in promoting the principals of the Self-Respect Movement among the local Tamil population through schools and publications. A number of political parties in Tamil Nadu, such as Dravida Munnetra Kazhagam (DMK) and All India Anna Dravida Munnetra Kazhagam (AIADMK) owe their origins to the Self-respect movement, the latter a 1972 breakaway from the DMK. Both parties are populist with a generally social democratic orientation.

THE TENETS OF SELF-RESPECT

Periyar was convinced that if man developed self respect, he would automatically develop individuality and would refuse to be led by the nose by schemers. One of his most known quotes on Self-Respect was, "we are fit to think of 'self-respect' only when the notion of 'superior' and 'inferior' caste is banished from our land". Periyar did not expect personal or material gain out of this movement. He used to recall in a very casual manner that as a human being, he also was obligated to this duty, as it was the right and freedom to choose this work.

Thus, Periyar opted to engage himself in starting and promoting the movement. Periyar declared that the Self-Respect Movement alone could be the genuine freedom movement, and political freedom would not be fruitful without individual self-respect. He remarked that the so called 'Indian freedom fighters' were showing disrespect of self-respect, and this was really an irrational philosophy.

Periyar observed that political freedom as conceived by nationalists not excluding even Gandhi and Jawaharlal Nehru did not cover individual self-respect. To him neither revival of the original spirit of Hindu religion and ancient traditions which formed part of Gandhi's conception of freedom, nor complete liberation from the British rule which was considered by Nehru to be the meaning of freedom or both of them together could ensure individual self-respect or remove the ills from Indian societies.

In his opinion the task of fulfilling the need for self-respect would have to be faced whatever be the extent of political freedom gained. Pointing out that even the British monarch in a sovereign independent nation had no freedom to marry a person of his choice and had to abdicate his kingdom, Periyar raised a question whether Gandhi's vision of freedom or Nehru's concept of independence contained even an iota of individual self-respect.

Periyar believed that self-respect was as valuable as life itself and its protection is a birth right and not swaraj ('political freedom'). He described the movement as Arivu Vidutalai Iyakkam, that is, a movement to liberate the intellect. The terms tan-maanam or suya mariyadai meaning 'self-respect' are traceable in ancient Tamil literature considered a virtue of high valor in Tamil society.

Periyar once claimed that to describe the ideology of his movement, no dictionary in the entire world, implying that no other language, could provide a word better than or equal to suya mariyadai.

Started as a movement (Iyakkam in Tamil) to promote rational behaviour, the Self-Respect Movement acquired much wider connotation within a short period of time. Periyar speaking with M.K. Reddy at the First Self-Respect Conference held in 1929, explained the significance of self-respect and its principles.

The main tenets of the Self-Respect Movement in society were to be: no kind of inequality among people; no difference as rich and poor in the economic life; men and women to be treated as equals in every respect without differences; attachments to caste, religion, varna, and country to be eradicated from society with a prevalent friendship and unity around the world; and every human being seeing to act just as to reason, understanding, desire, and perspective, and shall not be subject to slavery of any kind or manner.

Equality with stress on economic and social equality formed the central theme of the Self-Respect Movement was due to Periyar's determination to fight the inequalities ingrained in the caste system and religious practices. Working on the theme of liberating the society from the baneful social practices perpetrated in the name of dharma and karma, Periyar developed the idea of establishing this movement as the instrument for achieving his objective.

ANTI-BRAHMANISM

Tamil Brahmins (Iyers and Iyengars) were frequently held responsible by followers of Periyar for direct or indirect oppression of lower-caste people on the canard of "Brahmin oppression" and resulted in attacks on Brahmins and which among other reasons started a wave of mass-migration of the Brahmin population.

Periyar in regards to a DK member's attempt to assassinate Rajagopalachari, "expressed his abhorrence of violence as a means of settling political differences". Eventually, the anti-Brahmanism subsided with the replacement of the DMK party by the AIADMK.

SELF-RESPECT MARRIAGES

One of the major sociological changes introduced through the self respect movement was the self-respect marriage system, where by marriages were conducted without being officiated by a Brahmin priest. Periyar had regarded the then conventional marriages were mere financial arrangements and often caused great debt through dowry.

Self-Respect marriages encouraged inter-caste marriages and arranged marriages to be replaced by love marriages. It was argued by the proponents of self-respect marriage that the then conventional marriages were officiated by Brahmins, who has to be paid for and also the marriage ceremony was in Sanskrit which most people did not understand, and hence were ritual and practices based on blind adherence.

MANDAL COMMISSION

The Mandal Commission was established in India in 1979 by the Janata Party government under Prime Minister Morarji Desai with a mandate to "identify the socially or educationally backward."

It was headed by Indian parliamentarian Bindheshwari Prasad Mandal to consider the question of seat reservations and quotas for people to redress caste discrimination, and used eleven social, economic, and educational indicators to determine backwardness. In 1980, the commission's report affirmed the affirmative action practice under Indian law whereby members of lower castes (known as Other Backward Classes (OBC) and Scheduled Castes and Tribes) were given exclusive access to a certain portion of government jobs and slots in public universities, and recommended changes to these quotas, increasing them by 27% to 49.5%.

SETTING UP OF MANDAL COMMISSION

The plan to set up another commission was taken by Mr. Clooney and the Morarji Desai government in 1978 as per the mandate of the Constitution of India under article 340 for the purpose of Articles like 15 and 16. The decision was made official by the president on 1 January 1979. The commission is popularly known as the Mandal Commission its chairman being B.P. Mandal..

CRITERIA TO IDENTIFY OBC

The Mandal Commission adopted various methods and techniques to collect the necessary data and evidence. The commission adopted 11 criteria which could be grouped under three major headings: social, educational and economic in order to identify OBCs.

Social

- Castes/classes considered as socially backward by others.
- Castes/classes which mainly depend on manual labour for their livelihood.
- Castes/classes where at least 25 per cent females and 10 per cent males above the state average get married at an age below 17 years in rural areas and at least 10 per cent females and 5 per cent males do so in urban areas.
- Castes/classes where participation of females in work is at least 25 per cent above the state average.

Educational

- Castes/classes where the number of children in the

age group of 5–15 years who never attended school is at least 25 per cent above the state average.

- Castes/classes where the rate of student drop-out in the age group of 5–15 years is at least 25 per cent above the state average.

Economic

- Castes/classes where the average value of family assets is at least 25 per cent below the state average.
- Castes/classes where the number of families living in kuccha houses is at least 25 per cent above the state average.
- Castes/classes where the source of drinking water is beyond half a kilometre for more than 50 per cent of the households.
- Castes/classes where the number of households having taken consumption loans is at least 25 per cent above the state average. Also known as "Creamy layer," this criteria of separation is ignored by the government which is known as the most controversial issue of reservation.

Weighting Indicators

As the three groups are not of equal importance for the purpose, separate weightage was given to indicators in each group. All the Social indicators were given a weightage of 3 points each, educational indicators were given a weightage of 2 points each and economic indicators were given a weightage of 1 point each. Economic, in addition to Social and Educational Indicators, were considered important as they directly flowed from social and educational backwardness. This also helped to highlight the fact that socially and educationally backward classes are economically backward also. It will be seen from the values given to each indicator, the total score adds up to 22. All these 11 indicators were applied to all the castes covered by the survey for a particular state. As a result of this application, all castes which had a score of 50% (*i.e.* 11 points) were listed as socially and educationally backward and the rest were treated as 'advanced'.

OBSERVATIONS AND FINDINGS

The commission estimated that 54% of the total population (excluding SCs and STs), belonging to 3,743 different castes and communities were 'backward'. The commission used 1931 census data to calculate the number of OBCs. The population of Hindu OBCs was derived by subtracting from the total population of Hindus, the population of SC and ST and that of forward Hindu castes and communities, and it worked out to be 52 per cent.

Assuming that roughly the proportion of OBCs amongst non-Hindus was of the same order as amongst the Hindus, population of non-Hindu OBCs was also considered as 52 per cent.

- Assuming that a child from an advanced class family and that of a backward class family had the same intelligence at the time of their birth, it is obvious that owing to vast differences in social, cultural and environmental factors, the former will beat the latter by lengths in any competitive field. Even if a backward class child's intelligence quotient was much higher as compared to the child of advanced class, chances are that the former will lag far behind the latter in any competition where selection is made on the basis of 'merit'.
- In fact, what we call 'merit' in an elitist society is an amalgam of native endowments and environmental privileges. A child from an advanced class family and that of a backward class family are not 'equals' in any fair sense of the term and it will be unfair to judge them by the same yard-stick. The conscience of a civilized society and the dictates of social justice demand that 'merit' and 'equality' are not turned into a fetish and the element of privilege is duly recognised and discounted for when 'unequal' are made to run the same race.
- To place the amalgams of open caste conflicts in proper historical context, the study done by Tata institute of Social Sciences Bombay observes. "The

British rulers produced many structural disturbances in the Hindu caste structure, and these were contradictory in nature and impact .... Thus, the various impacts of the British rule on the Hindu caste system, viz, near monopolisation of jobs, education and professions by the literati castes, the Western concepts of equality and justice undermining the Hindu hierarchical dispensation, the phenomenon of Sanskritization, genteel reform movement and militant reform movements from below, emergence of the caste associations with a new role set the stage for the caste conflicts in modern India. Two more ingredients which were very weak in the British period, viz, politicisation of the masses and universal adult franchise, became powerful moving forces after the Independence.

RECOMMENDATIONS

The report of the commission was submitted in December 1980. Following are the recommendations as stated in the report. It may appear the upliftment of Other Backward Classes is part of the larger national problem of the removal of mass poverty. This is only partially correct. The deprivation of OBCs is a very special case of the larger national issue: here the basic question is that of social and educational backwardness and poverty is only a direct consequence of these two crippling caste-based handicaps.

As these handicaps are embedded in our social structure, their removal will require far—reaching structural changes. No less important will be changes in the perception of the problems of OBCs by the ruling classes of the country.

Reservations

One such change in the attitude of the ruling elite pertains to the provisions of reservation in Government services and educations institutions for the candidates of Other Backward Classes. It is generally argued that looking to the large population of OBCs (52%), recruitment of a few thousand

OBCs every year against reserved vacancies is not going to produce any perceptible impact on their general condition. On the other hand, the induction of a large proportion of employees against reserved vacancies will considerably impair the quality and efficiency of the Government services. It is also stated that the benefits of such reservations will be skimmed off by those parts of OBCs which are already well off and the really backward parts will be left high and dry. Another argument advanced against this approach is that the policy of large scale reservations will cause great hurt burning to those meritorious candidates whose entry into services will be barred as a result thereof. All the arguments are based on fairly sound reasoning.

But these are also the arguments advanced by the ruling elite which is keen on preserving its privileges. Therefore, like all such reasoning, it is based on partisan approach. By the same token, while illuminating some immediate areas of concern it tends to ignore much larger issues of national importance. It is not at all our contention that by offering a few thousand jobs to OBC candidates we shall be able to make 52% of the Indian population as forward. But we must recognise that as essential part of the battle against social backwardness is to be fought in the minds of the backward people. In India Government service has always been looked upon as a symbol of prestige and power. By increasing the representation of OBCs in Government services, we give them an immediate feeling of participation in the governance of this country. When a backward class candidate becomes a Collector or a Superintendent of Police, the material benefits accruing from his position are limited to the members of his family only.

But the psychological spin off of this phenomenon is tremendous; the entire community of that backward class candidate feels socially elevated. Even when no tangible benefits flow to the community at large, the feeling that now it has its "own man" in the "corridors of power" acts as a morale booster. In a democratic set-up every individual and community has a legitimate right and aspiration to participate in ruling this country. Any situation which results in a near-denial of this right to nearly 52% of the country's population needs to be urgently rectified. Apprehensions regarding drop in the quality of Government services owing to large-scale induction of S.C./S.T. and O.B.C. candidates against reserved posts may be justified only up to a point. But is it possible to maintain that all candidates selected on merit turn out to be honest, efficient, hard-working and dedicated? At present, top echelons of all the Government services are manned predominantly by open competition candidates and if the performance of our bureaucracy is any indication, it has not exactly covered itself with glory.

Of course, this does not imply that candidates selected against reserved posts will do better. Chances are that owing to their social and cultural handicaps they may be generally a shade less competent. But, on the other hand, they will have great advantage of possessing first hand knowledge of the sufferings and problems of the backward parts of society. This is not a small asset for field workers and policy makers even at highest level. It is no doubt true that the major benefits of reservation and other welfare measures for Other Backward Classes will be cornered by the more advanced parts of the backward communities. But is not this a universal phenomenon? All reformists remedies have to contend with slow recovery along the hierarchical gradient; there are no quantum jumps in social reform.

Moreover, human nature being what it is, a "new class" ultimately does emerge even in classless societies. The chief merit on reservation is not that it will introduce egalitarian amongst OBCs when the rest of the Indian society is seized by all sorts of inequalities. But reservation will certainly erode the hold of higher castes on the services and enable OBCs in general to have a sense of participation in running the affairs of the country. It is certainly true that reservation for OBCs will cause a lot of heart burning to others. But should the mere fact of this heart burning be allowed to operate as a moral veto against social reform.... When the higher castes constituting less than 20% of the country's population subjected the rest to all manner of social injustice, it must have caused a lot of heart burning to the lower castes. But now that the lower castes are asking for a modest share of the national cake of power and prestige, a chorus of alarm is being raised on the plea that this will cause heart burning to the ruling elite.

Of all the specious arguments advanced against reservations for backward classes, there is none which beats this one about 'heart-burning' in sheer sophistry. In fact the Hindu society has always operated a very rigorous scheme of reservations, which was internalised through caste system. Eklavya lost his thumb and Shambhk his neck for their breach of caste rules of reservations. The present furore against reservations for OBCs is not aimed at the principle itself, but against the new class of beneficiaries, as they are now clamouring for a share of the opportunities which were all along monopolised by the higher castes.

Quantum and Scheme of Reservations

Scheduled Castes and Scheduled Tribes constitute 22.5% of the country's population. A pro-rata reservation of 22.5% has been made for them in all services and public sector undertakings under the Central Government. In the States also, reservation for SCs and STs is directly proportional to their population in each State.

The population of OBCs, both Hindu and non-Hindu, is around 52% of the total population of India. Accordingly 52% of all post under the Central Government should be reserved for them, but this provision may go against the law laid down in a number of Supreme Court judgements wherein it has been held that the total quantum of reservations under Articles 15(4) and 16(4) of the Constitution should be below 50%.

In view of this the proposed reservation for OBCs would have to be pegged at a figure which, when added to 22.5% of SCs and STs, remain below 50%. In view of this legal constrain, the commission is obliged to recommend a reservation of 27%. States which have already introduced reservation for OBCs exceeding 27%, will remain unaffected by this recommendation. With the general recommendation regarding the quantum of reservation, the Commission proposes the following overall scheme of reservation for OBCs:

- Candidates belonging to OBCs recruited on the basis of merit in an open competition should not be adjusted against their reservation quota of 27%.
- The reservation should also be made available to promotion quota at all levels nitika goyal (3) Reserved quota remaining unfilled should be carried forward for a period of three years and deserved thereafter.
- Relaxation in the upper age limit for direct recruitment should be extended in the same manner as done in case of SCs and STs.
- A roster system for each category of posts should be adopted by the concerned authorities in the same manner as presently done in respect of SC and ST candidates.

The scheme of reservations in its toto should be made applicable to all recruitment to public sector undertakings both under the Central and State Governments, as also to nationalised banks. All private sector undertakings which have received financial assistance from the Government in one form or the other should also be obliged to recruit personnel on the aforesaid basis. All universities and affiliated colleges should also be covered by the scheme of reservation. To give proper effect to these recommendations, it is imperative that adequate statutory provisions are made by the Government to amend the existing enactments, rules, procedure, etc., to the extent they are not in consonance with the same.

Educational Concessions

Our educational system is elitist in character, results in a high degree of wastage and is least suited to the requirements of an over-populated and developing country. It is a legacy of the British rule which was severely criticised during the independence struggle, and yet, it has not undergone any structural changes. Though it is least suited to the needs of backward classes, yet, they are forced to run the rat-race with others as no options are available to them.

As 'educational reform' was not within the terms of reference of the Commission, we are also forced to trend the beaten track and suggest only the palliative measure within existing framework. Various State Governments are giving a number of educational concessions to other backward class students like exemption of tuition fees, free supply of books and clothes, mid-day meals, special hostel facilities, stipends, etc. These concessions are all right as far as they go. But they do not go far enough. What is required is, perhaps, not so much the provision of additional funds as the framing of integrated schemes for creating the proper environment and incentives for serious and purposeful studies. It is well known that most backward class children are irregular and indifferent students and their drop-out rate is very high.

There are two main reasons for this. First, these children are brought up in a climate of extreme social and cultural deprivation and consequently, a proper motivation for schooling is generally lacking. Secondly, most of these children come from very poor homes and their parents are forced to press them into doing small chores from a very young age.

Upgrading the cultural environment is a very slow process. Transferring these children to an artificially upgraded environment is beyond the present resources of the country. In view of this it is recommended that this problem may be tackled on a limited and selective basis on two fronts. First, an intensive and time bound programme for adult education should be launched in selected pockets with high concentration of OBC population.

This is a basic motivational approach, as only proper motivated parents will take serious interest in educating their children. Secondly, residential schools should be set up in these areas for backward class students to provide a climate specially conducive to serious studies. All facilities in these schools including board and lodging, will have to be provided free of cost to attract students from poor and backward homes, separate Government Hostels for OBC students with the facilities will be another step in the right direction. Abeginning on both these fronts will have to be made on a limited scale and selective basis.

But the scope of these activities should be expanded as fast as the resources permit. Adult education programme and residential schools started on a selective basis will operate as growing-points of consciousness for the entire community and their multiplier effect is bound to be substantial. Whereas several States are extended a number of ad hoc concessions to backward class students, few serious attempts have been made to integrate these facilities into a comprehensive scheme for a qualitative upgradation of educational environment available to OBC students.

After all, education is the best catalyst of change and educating the backward classes is the surest way to improve their self image and raise their social status. As OBCs cannot afford the high wastage rates of our educational system, it is very important that their education is highly biased in favour of vocational training.

After all reservation in services will absorb only a very small percentage of the educated backward classes and the rest should be suitably equipped with vocational skills to enable them to get a return on having invested several years in education.

It is also obvious that even if all the facilities are given to OBC students, they will not be able to compete on an equal footing with others in securing admission to technical and professional institutions. In view of this it is recommended that seats should be reserved for OBC students in all scientific, technical and professional institutions run by the Central Government as well as State Governments. This reservation will fall under Article 15(4) of the Constitution and the quantum of reservation should be the same as in the Government services, *i.e,* 27%. Those States which have already reserved more that 27% seats for OBC students will remain unaffected by this recommendation. While implementing the provisions for reservation it should also be ensured that the candidates who are admitted against the reserved quota are enable to derive full benefits of higher studies.

It has been generally noticed that these OBC students coming from an impoverished cultural background, are not able to keep abreast with other students. It is, therefore, very essential that special coaching facilities are arranged for all such students in our technical and professional institutions. The concerned authorities should clearly appreciate that their jobs is not finished once candidates against reserved quota have been admitted to various institutions. In fact the real task starts only after that special coaching assistance to these students, not only these young people will feel frustrated and humiliated but the country will also be landed with ill-equipped and sub-standard engineers, doctors and other professionals.

Financial Assistance

Vocational communities following hereditary occupations have suffered heavily as a result of industrialisation. Mechanical production and introductions of synthetic materials has robbed the village potter, oil crusher, blacksmith, carpenter, barber, etc. of their traditional means of livelihood and the popularization of these classes is a well-known phenomenon in the countryside. It has, therefore become very necessary that suitable institutional finance and technical assistance is made available to such members of village vocational communities who want to set up small-scale industries on their own. Similar assistance should also be provided to those promising OBC candidates who have obtained special vocational training.

Of course, most State Governments have created various financial and technical agencies for the promotions of small and medium scale industries. But it is well known that only the more influential members of the community are able to derive benefits fro these agencies. In view of this, it is essential that separate financial institutions for providing financial and technical assistance are established for the backward classes.

Some State Governments like Karnataka and Andhra Pradesh have already set up separate financial corporations etc, for OBCs. Cooperative Societies of occupational groups will also help a lot.

But due care should be taken that all office-bearers and members of such societies belong to the concerned hereditary occupational groups and outsiders are not allowed to exploit them by infiltrating into such cooperatives. The share of OBCs in the industrial and business life of the country is negligible and this partly explains their extremely low income levels. As a part of its overall strategy to uplift the backward classes, it is imperative that all State Governments are suitably advised and encouraged to create a separate network of financial and technical institutions to foster business and industrial enterprise among OBCs.

Structural Changes

Reservations in Government employment and educational institutions, as also as possible financial assistance will remain mere palliatives unless the problems of backwardness is tackled at its root. Bulk of the small land-holders, tenants, agricultural labour, impoverished village artisans, unskilled workers, etc. belong to Scheduled Castes, Scheduled Tribes and Other Backward Classes.

"Apart from social traditions, the dominances by the top peasantry is exercised through recourse to informal bondage which arises mainly thorough money-lending, leasing out of small bits of land and providing house-sites and dwelling space to poor peasants. As most of the functionaries of the Government are drawn from the top peasantry, the class and caste linkage between the functionaries of Government and the top peasantry remain firm.

This also tills the socio-political balance in favour of the top peasantry and helps it in having its dominance over others." The net outcome of the situation is that not with standing their numerical preponderance, backward class continues to remain in mental and material bondage of the higher castes and rich peasantry. Consequently, despite constituting nearly 3/4th of the countries population, Scheduled Castes, Scheduled Tribes and Other Backward Classes have been able to acquire a very limited political clout, even though adult franchise was introduced more than three decades back.

Through their literal monopoly of means of production of higher castes are able to manipulate and coerce the backward classes into acting against their own interests. In view of this, until the stranglehold of the existing production relations is broken through radical land reforms, the abject dependence of under privileged classes on the dominant higher castes will continue indefinitely. In fact there is already a sizeable volume of legislation on the statue books to abolish zamindari, place ceilings on land holdings and distribute land to the landless. But in actual practice its implementation has been halting, half-hearted and superficial. The States like Karnataka, Kerala and West Bengal which have gone about the job more earnestly have not only succeeded in materially helping the Backward Classes, but also reaped rich political dividends into the bargains.

It is the Commission's firm Conviction that a radical transformation of the existing production relations is the most important single step that can be taken for the welfare and upliftment of all backward classes. Even if this is not possible in the industrial sector for various reasons, in the agricultural sector a change in this nature is both feasible and overdue. The Commission, therefore, strongly recommends that all the State Governments should be directed to enact and implement progressive land legislations so as to effect basic structural changes in the existing production relations in the countryside. At present surplus land in being allotted to SCs and STs. A part of the surplus land becoming available in future as a result of the operation of land ceiling laws etc. should also be allotted to the OBC landless labour.

Miscellaneous

- Certain parts of some occupational communities like Fishermen, Banjaras, Bansoforas, Khatwes etc. still suffer from the stigma of untouchability in some part of the country. They have been listed as O.B.Cs. by the Commission, but their inclusion in the lists of Scheduled Castes/Scheduled Tribes may be considered by the Government.

- Backward Classes Development Corporations should be set up both at the Central and State levels to implement various socio-educational and economic measures for their advancement.
- A separate Ministry/Department for O.B.Cs. at the Centre and States should be created to safeguard their interests.
- With a view to giving better representation to certain very backward parts of O.B.Cs like the Gaddis of Himachal Pradesh, Neo-Buddhists in Maharashtra, Fishermen in the Coastal areas, Gujjars in Jand, it is recommended that areas of their concentration may be carved out into separate constituencies at the time of delimitation.

Central Assistance

At present no Central Assistance is available to any State Government for implementing any welfare measures for Other Backward Classes. The 18 States and Union Territories which have undertaken such measures have to provide funds from their own resources.

During the Commission's tours practically every State Government pointed out that unless the Centre is prepared to liberally finance all special schemes for the upliftment of OBCs, it will be beyond the available resources of the States to undertake any worthwhile programme for the benefit of Other Backward Classes.

The Commission fully shares the views of the State Governments in this matter and strongly recommends that all development programmes specially designed for Other Backward Classes should be financed by the Central Government in the same manner and to the same extent as done in the case of Scheduled Castes and Scheduled Tribes.

Regarding the period of operation of the Commission's recommendations entire scheme should be reviewed after twenty years.

We have advisedly suggested this span of one generation, as the raising of social consciousness is a generational progress. Any review at a shorter interval would be rather arbitrary and would not give a fair indication of the impact of our recommendations on the prevailing status and life-styles of O.B.Cs.

IMPLEMENTATION

All the recommendations of the report are not yet implemented. The recommendation of reservations for OBC's in government services was implemented in 1993. As on 27 June 2008 there is still a backlog of 28, 670 OBC vacancies in government jobs. The recommendation of reservations in Higher educational institutes is implemented in 2008.

CRITICISM

The National Sample Survey puts the figure at 32%. There is substantial debate over the exact number of OBC's in India, with census data compromised by partisan politics. It is generally estimated to be sizable, but lower than the figures quoted by either the Mandal Commission or and National Sample Survey.

There is also an ongoing controversy about the estimation logic used by Mandal commission for calculating OBC population. Famous Indian Statistician, Mr.Yogendra Yadav who supports Reservations agrees that there is no empirical basis to the Mandal figure. According to him "It is a mythical construct based on reducing the number of SC/ST, Muslims and others and then arriving at a number."

National Sample Survey's 1999-2000 round estimated around 36 per cent of the country's population is defined as belonging to the Other Backward Classes (OBC). The proportion falls to 32 per cent on excluding Muslim OBCs. A survey conducted in 1998 by National Family Health Statistics (NFHS) puts the proportion of non-Muslim OBCs as 29.8 per cent L R Naik, the only Dalit member in the Mandal Commission refused to sign the Mandal recommendations. He said that there are two social blocks among the OBCs: upper caste (Jat and Gujjar) and upper OBCs (Yadavs, Kurmis, etc.) and Most Backward Classes (MBCs). He feared that upper OBCs would corner all the benefits of reservation.

Here we shall present the study of the Mandal Commissions's list of the OBC for the state of West Bengal only for the sake of brevity. In this list, Urao (along with its synonyms Bandot, Haro, Karkata, Luidu, Shitheo, Tigga and Tirki) has been listed as an OBC (OBC No.176). On the other hand, it is already in the list of Scheduled Tribes for the state with a slight difference of spelling "Oraon" (ST 33).

Similarly, Scheduled Tribes Kharia (OBC 105; synonym of Lodha, ST 23 in the ST List), Kherwar (OBC 107; ST 17, with a spelling Kharwar), Koda (OBC 113; ST 20, spelled Kora), Bhotia (OBC 33; ST 5, spelled Bhutia), Brijia (OBC 39, ST 7, with a spelling Birjia), Gonda (OBC 68; ST 12, spelled Gond) and Lakra (OBC 123, and Lakar OBC 122, which is actually a surname adopted by many members of the Scheduled Tribe Munda), which are already declared STs for the state. Tharu (OBC 171) is a widely studied scheduled tribe.

Thapa (OBC 170) is a synonym of ST Sherpa (ST 5, same as Bhutia, Tota, Dukpa, Kagatay, Tibetan, Yolmo). Many famous ST surnames have been listed as OBC Mahato (OBC 129), etc. Other anthropologically famous scheduled tribes listed as OBC are Kuki (OBC 118), Lushei (actually Lushai; OBC 124), Koli (OBC 116) and Rohangia.

Similar manipulation has been done with many Scheduled Castes also. For example in the state of West Bengal, Bhangi has been listed as OBC (No. 26), with a rider "excluding those in the Scheduled Caste". On the other hand the SC list for West Bengal shows that Bhangi (at place no. 22 in the SC list) is an unconditional SC for the whole of the territory of the state. Halalkhor has also been listed as an OBC (No. 73) with a similar condition but this caste is also an unconditional SC (No. 21, spelled Halelkhor). A sub-caste of Dom (Maghaiya-Dom) has been listed as OBC at place No.

126. Dom as a whole has been a Scheduled Caste (No.17 in West Bengal SC list) for ages.

Bahelia (SC No. 2) has been listed by its synonym Chirimar (OBC 45). Bagal (OBC 11) is already there in the SC list at place number 1, with a spelling Bagll. Although Nat is an SC (No. 47), its sub-caste Karwal-Nat has been made an OBC (OBC 97). Jaliya Kaivartta (SC 23) is just the Sanskritized name of Machua listed as OBC (OBC 125). All the Nav-Buddhists (Neo-Buddhist) have been include in the OBC list, which is again an anomaly, because the Nav-Buddhists enjoy their SC status.

Not only synonyms or alternative spellings of the SCs and STs have been recorded as OBC, but also there are other types of manipulations like same OBC caste has been listed twice or sometimes thrice in the list of the same state. An example of this type of manipulation is Kahar in Bihar list (No. 23 as well as No. 70), Kewat (at no. 115 as well as 84.) At any rate the list is vitiated by such inclusions.

The Kuki tribes (ST) actually live in Nagaland, Meghalaya, Mizoram and Tripura, none of which are neighbouring to West Bengal. Even if any member of the tribe migrates to West Bengal or anywhere else in India, either it retains its ST status of the mother state or becomes General population. It is difficult to believe that some Kuki tribes live in West Bengal as OBC. Lushai tribe (ST) live mainly in Mizoram and are the principal Mizo tribe.

They are also found in Manipur as ST. Koli (ST) are found in a widespread area ranging from Orissa to Rajasthan up to Karnatak. Rohangia ((OBC 158) are actually a distant tribe which mainly live in Myanmar but are also found in Bangla Desh-Myanmar-Tripura border areas). Introduction of such castes to the West Bengal OBC list seems to be an act of fertile brain and raises doubt whether any actual survey was done at all. At any rate a small number of these tribes could be present in the former East Bengal (now Bangla Desh) in areas adjoining former state of Assam and Myanmar before partition. Some OBC caste names given in the list are obsolete of forward castes. Tyagi is an upper caste, which lives in UP,

Haryana and Delhi. This caste was earlier called Taga. But with a general trend of all the North Indian castes to Sanskritize their names, Taga people adopted a new name Tyagi which was similar to Taga.

But still in the remote village especially by the illiterate people Tyagis are often called Taga. We find the name of Taga in Haryana Mandal list (OBC 74), Delhi (OBC 81) and Uttar Pradesh (OBC 109, as Taga-Bhat). The principles and norms set in the very beginning regarding the criterion for the Non-Hindu communities have been violated flagrantly, hence now the Roman Catholic is not a religion but a caste in the eyes of the Mandal Commission (Latin Catholic, OBC 106, Kerala). Anglo-Indians, who are the off-springs of the British rulers, have also been made an Other Backward Caste (OBC 6, Kerala). Although it has been decided at the outset that only occupational castes among the Muslims and Christians and the castes bearing the same name as a Hindu OBC or SC will be included as a Muslim or Christian OBC caste, the set rule was violated wherever political expediency dictated.

For example Kayastha (Muslim) has been made an OBC (OBC 93, Uttar Pradesh) which does not fulfill the criteria set for inclusion of non-Hindu castes. A last word about credibility of the Mandal survey.

Presence of obsolete and archaic caste names like Taga (for Tyagi in Haryana, Delhi and UP), Bhuihar (for Bhumihar in Bihar), Domb (for Dom in all the southern states), listing of Kuki, Lushai, Rohangia tribes in West Bengal which are not found in West Bengal today but actually some of each of them lived in East Bengal in undivided India neighbouring Tripura, Meghalaya etc, and many such factors cannot be explained unless it is assumed that the Mandal list is not result of a recent survey, but it has been compiled by editing the caste list of 1931 census. But the editing was most inefficient. These names could not have crept in unless the old united Bengla caste list of 1931 was just copied and some named SC and ST, as well as well known forward caste names were just deleted, to arrive at the current OBC list of Mandal. Every state's OBC list has the same story. The entire list seems to be manipulated, but most carelessly and inefficiently manipulated. Most famous scheduled castes like Dusadh (Dhari), Mochi, Domb (Dom) and Bhangi have been put as OBCs in many states. If the Government does not reject this whole Mandal list, all the SCs and STs listed as OBC will have to be deleted from the respective SC and ST lists.

Because the Mandal Commission was a constitutional body which had done a survey and this survey was done at a later date than the surveys for the SC and ST, which were done during the British period without the authority of our present Indian Constitution.

Indeed any act (or survey) done under the authority of Indian Constitution automatically supersedes any act (or survey) of the British administration if there is an overlap or confusion.

PROTEST

A decade after the commission gave its report, V.P. Singh, the Prime Minister at the time, tried to implement its recommendations in 1989. The criticism was sharp and colleges across the country held massive protests against it. Soon after, Rajiv Goswami, student of Delhi University, committed self-immolation in protest of the government's actions. His act further sparked a series of self-immolations by other college students and led to a formidable movement against job reservations for Backward Castes in India. First student to die due to self immolation was Surinder Singh Chauhan on Sep 24, 1990.

ARGUMENTS AGAINST RESERVATIONS

The opponents of the issue argue:

- Allocating quotas on the basis of caste is a form of racial discrimination, and contrary to the right to equality. Although the exact relation between caste and race is far from well established
- As a consequence of legislating to provide reservations for Christians and Muslim, religious minorities in all government education institutions will be introduced which is contrary to the ideas of

secularism, and is a form of anti-discrimination on the basis of religion.

- Most often, only economically sound people (and rather rich) from the so-called lower castes will make use of most of the reserved seats, thus counteracting the spirit of reservations. Political parties know reservations are no way to improve the lot of the poor and the backward. They support them because of self-interest of the "creamy layer", who use the reservations to further their own family interests, and as a political flag of 'achievement' during election campaigns. In fact, several studies show that the OBC class is quite comparable with the general caste in terms of annual per capita consumption expenditure, and the top strata of OBC is ahead in a host of consumption areas.
- The quality of these elite institutes may go down, because merit is severely being compromised by reserving seats for certain caste-based communities.
- There are no efforts made to give proper primary education to truly deprived classes, so there is no need to reserve seats for higher studies. The government schools in India have absolutely no comparison to the public schools in the developed countries, and only about 65% of the Indian population is literate,. The critics argue that "reservation" only in higher institutions and jobs, without improving primary and secondary education, cannot solve this problem.
- The government is dividing people on the basis of castes for political advantages.
- The caste system is kept alive through these measures. Instead of coming up with alternative innovative ideas which make sure equal representation at the same time making the caste system irrelevant, the decision is only fortifying the caste system.
- The autonomy of the educational institutes are lost.
- Not everyone from the so-called upper classes are rich, and not all from so called lower classes are poor.

- The reservation policy of the Indian Congress will create a huge unrest in the Indian society. Providing quotas on the basis of caste and not on the basis of merit will deter the determination of many educated and deserving students of India.
- Multinational companies will be deterred by this action of the government, and foreign investment in India may dry down, hurting the growth of the Indian economy. Doubtless, urgent actions to improve the lot of the majority, which has not benefited from development—not achieved after 55 years of reservations for scheduled castes—are essential. But this must not hazard improving the economy's competitiveness in a very competitive world.
- There are already talks of reservations in the private sector. If even after providing so many facilities to reserved categories during education, if there is no adequate representation of those people in the work force, there must be some problems with the education system.

Critics of the Mandal Commission argue that it is unfair to accord people special privileges on the basis of caste, even in order to redress traditional caste discrimination. They argue that those that deserve the seat through merit will be at a disadvantage. They reflect on the repercussions of unqualified candidates assuming critical positions in society (doctors, engineers, etc.). As the debate on OBC reservations spreads, a few interesting facts which raise pertinent question are already apparent. To begin with, do we have a clear idea what proportion of our population is OBC? The Mandal Commission (1980) it is 52 per cent. In 2001 Indian Census, out of India's population of 1,028,737,436 the Scheduled Caste comprise 166,635,700 and Scheduled Tribes 84,326,240, that is 16.2% and 8.2% respectively.

There is no data on OBCs in the census. However, just as to National Sample Survey's 1999-2000 round around 36 per cent of the country's population is defined as belonging to the Other Backward Classes (OBC). The proportion falls to 32 per cent on excluding Muslim OBCs.

A survey conducted in 1998 by National Family Health Statistics (NFHS) puts the proportion of non-Muslim OBCs as 29.8 per cent. The NSSO data also shows that already 23.5 per cent of college seats are occupied by OBCs. That's just 8.6 per cent short of their share of population just as to the same survey. Other arguments include that entrenching the separate legal status of OBCs and SC/STs will perpetuate caste differentiation and encourage competition among communities at the expense of national unity. They believe that only a small new elite of educated Dalits, Adivasis, and OBCs benefit from reservations, and that such measures do nothing to lift the mass of people out of backwardness and poverty.

ARGUMENTS IN SUPPORT OF RESERVATIONS

- Affirmative Action has helped many-if not everyone from underprivileged and/or under-represented communities to grow and occupy top positions in the world's leading industries. Reservation in education is not the final solution, it is just one of the many solutions. Reservations is a means to increase representation of hitherto under-represented caste groups and thereby improve diversity on campus.
- Although Reservation schemes do undermine the quality of education but still affirmative Action schemes are in place in many countries including USA, South Africa, Malaysia, Brazil etc. It was researched in Harvard University that Affirmative Action programmes are beneficial to the underprivileged. The studies said that Blacks who enter elite institutions with lower test scores and grades than those of whites achieve notable success after graduation. They earn advanced degrees at rates identical to those of their white classmates. They are even slightly more likely than whites from the same

institutions to obtain professional degrees in law, business and medicine. They become more active than their white classmates in civic and community activities.

- Although Reservation schemes do undermine the quality of education but still they are needed to provide social justice to the most marginalized and underprivileged is our duty and their human right. Reservation will really help these marginalized people to lead successful lives, thus eliminating caste-based discrimination which is still widely prevalent in India especially in the rural areas. (over 60% of Indian population stays in Villages).
- But meritrocracy is meaningless without equality. First all people must be brought to the same level, whether it elevates a part or delevels another, regardless of merit. Only after that merit becomes meaningful. Privileged people have never known to go backward due to reservations or lack of "meritrocracy". Reservations have only slowed down the process of the 'forward' becoming richer and backward becoming poorer.
- In a perfectly functioning society the institutions and various walks of life must represent the many parts roughly in proportion to their share in population. In India it is clearly not the case and hence the need for reservations.
- India does not have the economic or institutional capacity for undertaking a grassroots based solution to the problem, so reservations remain the only practical solution for social anti-discrimination
- People who support reservations keenly invite all the anti-reservationists to lead the life of a backward class citizen and live within the means that they have for themselves. It is their contention that in a experimental set-up like this the differences in achievement/performance would disappear or reduce down to experimental errors/random error. Underlying idea being that everyone is born equal

but into an unequal circumstances. And when the circumstances have been a result of a social system then the system either needs to be abandoned or reformed.

- Reservations are a political necessity in India because vast influential parts of voting population. All governments have supported maintaining and/or increasing reservations. Reservations are legal and binding. As shown by Gujjar agitations (Rajasthan, 2007–2008), increasing reservations is also essential for peacekeeping in India.
- Reservations will go a long way in capacity building with rega. d to the human resource of the country. In the long run, it has tremendous economic benefits as it will raise the productivity of the majority of the potential workforce of the country
- The government of India, is bound and empowered by the constitution of the country to secure for all citizens equality in social, economic and political sphere.

NAMANTAR ANDOLAN

Namantar Andolan was started by Dalit Panthers. Namanter Andolan is a movement to change Marathwada University's name to Dr. B.R. Ambedkar University.

Marathwada is made up of five districts—Aurangabad, Parbhani, Beed, Nanded and Usmanabad—out of 28 districts that were part of the earlier Hyderabad state ruled by the Nizam of Hyderabad. The Marathwada part of the state was merged with Maharashtra after its trifurcation in 1956. As per the 1971 census, the population of this region was 8,058,347. This consisted of 80% Hindus; 9.52% belonged to Scheduled Castes; 11.8% Muslims, 7.2% Buddhists, and the rest were of other communities. Marathwada is an economically backward region of the state. 82% of the people are occupied in farming, as against the figure of 65% for the whole state. At that time (1971 census), industrial activity was almost nil, with only two persons out of 1,000 engaged in industry compared to 100 industrial workers out of every 1,000 in Mumbai.

Further, Dalits comprised about 17% (9.5% of Scheduled Castes and 7.2% of the population compared to about 12% for the whole of Maharashtra. About 75% of the Dalit population consisted of farm labourers, and 90% of the Dalit lived below the poverty line. The literacy rate among the Dalits in Marathwada was about 19% as compared to the general literacy rate of 35%. Among the Dalits, the Mahar community was supposed to be relatively better off and socially more conscious and with a higher rate of literacy. Unemployment was a severe problem in Marathwada. For example, on 23 March 1974, 2,000 youths who came to Parbhani town looking for jobs were told that only 40 posts were to be filled up. There was no scope for the youths in farming or in industry.

Thus education was the only field where there was a concentration of Dalit youths. After one united march with Panthers there was a split in the students' advisory committee, allegedly provoked by Panthers. The differences of opinion among the leaders of the committee were also caused by the meeting they had with Vasantrao Patil. Those opposing the renaming move organized themselves under the banner of 'Marathwada Vidyarthi Kriti Samiti'. This Samiti gave a call of colleges in Marathwada remained closed from 12 to 26 September 1977. The Samiti also organized a total Marathwada bandh on 19 September.

DALIT BUDDHIST MOVEMENT

The Dalit Buddhist movement (dubbed as Navayana by certain Ambedkerites) is arguably the most influential of a series of 19th and 20th century Buddhist revival movements in India. It received its most substantial impetus from B. R. Ambedkar's call for the conversion of Dalits to Buddhism in the context of a caste based society that considered them to be at the lowest end of the hierarchy.

ORIGINS

Buddhism was once dominant through much of India, it

had however begun to decline by the 12th century. The Buddhist revival began in India in 1891, when the Sri Lankan Buddhist leader Anagarika Dharmapala founded the Maha Bodhi Society The Maha Bodhi Society mainly attracted upper-caste people, most of whom did not identify themselves specifically as Buddhists, seeing no significant difference between Buddhism and Hinduism.

South India

In 1890, Pandit C. Ayodhya Dasa (1845-1914), better known as Iyothee Thass, founded the Sakya Buddhist Society (also known as the Indian Buddhist Association). The first president of the Indian Buddhist Association was the German born American Paul Carus, the author of The Gospel of Buddha (1894). Thass, a Tamil Siddha physician, was the pioneer of the Tamil Dalit movement. He argued that Tamil Dalits were originally Buddhists. He led a delegation of prominent Dalits to Henry Steel Olcott and asked for his help in the reestablishment of "Tamil Buddhism." Olcott helped Thass to visit Sri Lanka, where he received diksha from Bhikkhu Sumangala Nayake.

After returning to India, Thass established the Sakya Buddhist Society in Madras with branches in many places including Karnataka. Thass established a weekly magazine called Oru Paisa Tamizhan ("One Paisa Tamilian") in Chennai in 1907, which served as a newsletter linking all the new branches of the Sakya Buddhist Society. The magazine discussed traditions and practices of Tamil Buddhism, new developments in the Buddhist world, and the Indian subcontinent's history from the Buddhist point of view. Brahmananda Reddy, a Dalit leader of Andhra Pradesh, was also fascinated by Buddhism.

Uttar Pradesh

In the early 20th century, the Barua Buddhists of Bengal under the leadership of Kripasaran Mahasthavir (1865-1926), founder of the Bengal Buddhist Association in Calcutta (1892), established viharas in cities such as Lucknow, Hyderabad,

Shillong and Jamshedpur. In Lucknow, Bodhanand Mahastavir (1874-1952) advocated Buddhism for Dalits. Born Mukund Prakash in a Bengali Brahmin family, he was orphaned at a young age, and was then raised in Benaras by an aunt. He was initially attracted to Christianity, but became a Buddhist after a meeting with Buddhists monks from Ceylon at a Theosophical Conference in Benares.

He later lived in Lucknow where he came in contact with Barua Buddhists, many of whom were employed as cooks by the British. In 1914, Prakash was ordained Bodhanand Mahastavir in Calcutta in the presence of Kripasaran Mahasthvir. He began preaching Buddhism in Lucknow. He founded the Bharatiye Buddh Samiti in 1916, and set up a vihara in 1928.

In his book Mula Bharatavasi Aur Arya ("Original Inhabitants and Aryans"), Mahastavir stated that the shudras were the original inhabitants of India, who were enslaved by the Aryans. Bodhanand Mahastavir wrote another book on Buddhist rituals called Baudha Dvicharya. His associate, Chandrika Prasad Jigyasu, founded the Bahujan Kalyan Prakashan.

The two co-authored a book on the life and teaching of the Buddha. Acharya Ishvardatt Medharthi (1900-1971) of Kanpur also supported the cause of the Dalits. He had studied Pali at Gurukul Kangri and Buddhist scripture was well known to him. He was initiated into Buddhism by Gyan Keto and the Lokanatha in 1937. Gyan Keto (1906-1984), born Peter Schoenfeldt was a German who arrived to Ceylon in 1936 and became a Buddhist.

Although Medharthi heavily criticized the Indian caste system, he didn't criticize Hinduism. He claimed that the Dalits ("Adi Hindus") were the ancient rulers of India and had been trapped into slavery by the Aryan invaders. He also claimed that the sanatana dharma was the religion of "Adi Hindus", and tried to reconcile Buddhism with the Sant Mat. Another Bhikkhu of Kanpur, Bhikshu Uttam, was a strong supporter of the Arya Samaj and the Jat Pat Todak Mandal, the anti-caste wing of the Arya Samaj.

B. R. AMBEDKAR

At the Yeola conference in 1935, prominent Dalit leader B. R. Ambedkar declared that he would not die a Hindu, saying that it perpetuates caste injustices. Ambedkar was approached by various leaders of different denominations and faiths. Meetings were held to discuss the question of Dalit religion and the pros and cons of conversion. On May 22, 1936, an "All Religious Conference" was held at Lucknow. It was attended by prominent Dalit leaders including Jagjivan Ram, though Ambedkar could not attend it. At the conference, Muslim, Christian, Sikh, and Buddhist representatives presented the tenets of their respective religions in an effort to win over Dalits.

Buddhist monk Lokanatha visited Ambedkar's residence at Dadar on June 10, 1936 and tried to persuade him to embrace Buddhism. Later in an interview to the Press, Lokanatha said that Ambedkar was impressed with Buddhism and that his own ambition was to convert all Dalits to Buddhism. In 1937, Lokanatha published a pamphlet Buddhism Will Make You Free, dedicated to the Depressed Classes of India from his press in Ceylon. In early 1940s, Ambedkar visited Acharya Ishvardatt Medharthi's Buddhpuri school in Kanpur. Medharthi had earlier been initiated into Buddhism by Lokanatha, and by the mid-1940s, he had close contacts with Ambedkar. For a short while, Ambedkar also took Pali classes from Medharthi in Delhi. Bodhananda Mahastvir and B. R. Ambedkar first met in 1926, at the "Indian Non-Brahmin Conference" convened by Shahu IV of Kolhapur. They met on two more occasions and for a short while in the 1940s, where they discussed dhamma. Mahastavir objected to Dr Ambedkar's second marriage because his bride was a Brahmin. Later, his followers actively participated in Ambedkar's Republican Party of India.

Ambedkar's Conversion

After publishing a series of books and articles arguing that Buddhism was the only way for the Untouchables to gain equality, Ambedkar publicly converted on October 14, 1956 at

Deekshabhoomi, Nagpur. He took the three refuges and the Five Precepts from a Buddhist monk, Bhadant U Chandramani, in the traditional manner and then in his turn administered them to the 380,000 of his followers that were present.

The conversion ceremony was attended by Medharthi, his main disciple Bhoj Dev Mudit, and Mahastvir Bodhanand's Sri Lankan successor, Bhante Pragyanand. Ambedkar would die less than two months later, just after finishing his definitive work on Buddhism. Many Dalits employ the term "Ambedkar(ite) Buddhism" to designate the Buddhist movement, which started with Ambedkar's conversion and many converted people called themselves as "Nava-Bauddha" *i.e.* New Buddhists.

22 Vows of Ambedkar

After receiving ordination, Ambedkar gave dhamma diksha to his followers. The ceremony included 22 vows given to all new converts after Three Jewels and Five Precepts. On 16 October 1956, Ambedkar performed another mass religious conversion ceremony at Chanda.

He prescribed 22 vows to his followers:

1. I shall have no faith in Brahma, Vishnu and Maheshwara nor shall I worship them.
2. I shall have no faith in Rama and Krishna who are believed to be incarnation of God nor shall I worship them.
3. I shall have no faith in Gauri, Ganapati and other gods and goddesses of Hindus nor shall I worship them.
4. I do not believe in the incarnation of God.
5. I do not and shall not believe that Lord Buddha was the incarnation of Vishnu. I believe this to be sheer madness and false propaganda.
6. I shall not perform Shraddha nor shall I give pinddan.
7. I shall not act in a manner violating the principles and teachings of the Buddha.
8. I shall not allow any ceremonies to be performed by Brahmins.
9. I shall believe in the equality of man.

10. I shall endeavor to establish equality.
11. I shall follow the noble eightfold path of the Buddha.
12. I shall follow the ten paramitas prescribed by the Buddha.
13. I shall have compassion and loving kindness for all living beings and protect them.
14. I shall not steal.
15. I shall not tell lies.
16. I shall not commit carnal sins.
17. I shall not take intoxicants like liquor, drugs etc.
18. I shall endeavor to follow the noble eightfold path and practice compassion and loving kindness in every day life.
19. I renounce Hinduism, which is harmful for humanity and impedes the advancement and development of humanity because it is based on inequality, and adopt Buddhism as my religion.
20. I firmly believe the Dhamma of the Buddha is the only true religion.
21. I believe that I am having a rebirth.
22. I solemnly declare and affirm that I shall hereafter lead my life just as to the principles and teachings of the Buddha and his Dhamma.

Nowadays many Ambedkarite Organisations are working for these 22 vows (*i.e.* 22 Pratigya). They believe that these vows only are responsible for the existence and rapid growth of present Buddhism in India. The umbrella organization known as the 22 Pledges Practice and Propagation Movement (*i.e.* in Hindi- 22 Pratigya Aacharan aur Prachaar Abhiyan) is fully devoted for this purpose. This totally non-political movement is the brain-child of Arvind Sontakke, and comprises around 5,000,000 volunteers (Pracharaks) including many regional and local groups throughout India.

DALIT BUDDHISM MOVEMENT AFTER AMBEDKAR'S DEATH

The Buddhist movement was somewhat hindered by Dr. Ambedkar's death so shortly after his conversion. It did not receive the immediate mass support from the Untouchable population that Ambedkar had hoped for.

Division and lack of direction among the leaders of the Ambedkarite movement have been an additional impediment. The 2001 census, there are currently 7.95 million Buddhists in India, at least 5.83 million of whom are Buddhists in Maharashtra. This makes Buddhism the fifth-largest religion in India and 6% of the population of Maharashtra, but less than 1% of the overall population of India. The Buddhist revival remains concentrated in two states: Ambedkar's native Maharashtra, and Uttar Pradesh—the land of Bodhanand Mahastavir, Acharya Medharthi and their associates.

Developments in Uttar Pradesh

Acharya Medharthi retired from his Buddhapuri school in 1960, and shifted to an ashram in Haridwar. He turned to the Arya Samaj and conducted vedic yajnas all over India. After his death, he was cremated just as to Arya Samaj rites. His Buddhpuri school became embroiled in property disputes. His follower, Bhoj Dev Mudit, converted to Buddhism in 1968 and set up a school of his own. Rajendranath Aherwar appeared as an important Dalit leader in Kanpur. He joined the Republican Party of India and converted to Buddhism along with his whole family in 1961. In 1967, he founded the Kanpur branch of "Bharatiya Buddh Mahasabha". He held regular meetings where he preached Buddhism, officiated at Buddhist weddings and life cycle ceremonies, and organized festivals on Dr. Ambedkar's Jayanti (birth day), Buddha Jayanti, Diksha Divas (the day Ambedkar converted), and Dr Ambedkar Paranirvan Divas (the day Ambedkar died).

The Dalit Buddhist movement in Kanpur gained impetus with the arrival of Dipankar, a Chamar bhikkhu, in 1980. Dipankar had come to Kanpur on a Buddhist mission and his first public appearance was scheduled at a mass conversion drive in 1981. The event was organized by Rahulan Ambawadekar, an RPI Dalit leader. In April 1981, Ambawadekar founded the Dalit Panthers (U.P. Branch) inspired by the Maharashtrian Dalit Panthers. The event met with severe criticism and opposition from Vishwa Hindu Parishad and was banned.

In 2002, Kanshi Ram, a popular out-caste political leader from a Sikh religious background, announced his intention to convert to Buddhism on October 14, 2006, the fiftieth anniversary of Ambedkar's conversion. He intended for 20,000,000 of his supporters to convert at the same time. Part of the significance of this plan was that Ram's followers include not only Untouchables, but persons from a variety of castes, who could significantly broaden Buddhism's support. However, he died October 9, 2006 after a lengthy illness; he was cremated as per Buddhist rituals. Another popular Dalit leader, Bahujan Samaj Party chief Mayawati, has said that she and her followers will embrace Buddhism after the BSP gains control of the government.

Maharashtra

Japanese-born Bhadant Nagarjun Surai Sasai is an important Buddhist leader in India. Sasai came to India in 1966 and met Nichidatsu Fuji, whom he helped with the Peace Pagoda at Rajgir. He fell out with Fuji, however, and started home, but, by his own account, was stopped by a dream in which a figure resembling Nagarjuna appeared and said, "Go to Nagpur". In Nagpur, he met Wamanrao Godbole, the person who had organized the conversion ceremony for Dr. Ambedkar in 1956. Sasai claims that when he saw a photograph of Dr. Ambedkar at Godbole's home, he realised that it was Ambedkar who had appeared in his dream.

At first, Nagpur folk considered Surai Sasai very strange. Then he began to greet them with "Jai Bhim" (victory to Ambedkar) and to build viharas. In 1987 a court case to deport him on the grounds that he had overstayed his visa was dismissed, and he was granted Indian citizenship. Sasai is one of the main leaders of the campaign to free the Mahabodhi Temple at Bodh Gaya from Hindu control.

Organized Mass Conversions

Since Ambedkar's conversion, several thousand people

from different castes have converted to Buddhism in ceremonies including the twenty-two vows. The Tamil Nadu and Gujarat governments passed new laws in 2003 to ban "forced" religious conversions.

These laws were later withdrawn due to heavy opposition:

- 1957: In 1957, Mahastvir Bodhanand's Sri Lankan successor, Bhante Pragyanand, held a mass conversion drive for 15,000 people in Lucknow.
- 2001: A prominent Indian Dalit Buddhist leader and political activist, Udit Raj, organized a large mass conversion on November 4, 2001 where he gave the 22 vows, but the event met with active opposition from the government.
- 2006, Hyderabad: A report from the UK daily The Guardian said that some Hindus have converted to Buddhism. Buddhist monks from the UK and the U.S. attended the conversion ceremonies in India. In response, Hindu nationalists asserted that Dalits should concentrate on illiteracy and poverty rather than looking for new religions.
- 2006, Gulbarga: On October 14, 2006 hundreds of people converted from Hinduism to Buddhism in Gulburga (Karnataka).
- 2006: A Buddhist source claimed that "300,000 Dalits are estimated" to have converted to Buddhism as part of 50th year celebrations of Ambedkar's deeksha in 2006. Non-Partisan sources put the number of attendees (not converts) at 30,000. The move was criticized by Hindu groups as "unhelpful" and has been criticized as a "political stunt."
- 2007, Mumbai: On May 27, 2007 tens of thousands of Dalits from Maharashtra gathered at the Mahalakshmi racecourse in Mumbai to mark the 50th anniversary of the conversion of Ambedkar. The number of people who actually converted, however, versus the number of people in attendance was not clear. The event was organized by the Republican Party of India leader Ramdas Athvale.

Criticism of Conversions

Hindu critics have argued that efforts to convert Hindus to Ambedkarite Buddhism are political stunts rather than sincere commitments to social reform. In addition, several Dalit leaders have stated that they are not against the upper castes *per se*. Leaders of the Dalit Bahujan Samaj Party have said that they are being branded as "anti-Hindu" because of the publicity associated with the conversions is largely the work of "manuvadi vested interests, including political parties and parts of the media" and that they are only interested in peaceful dialogue with the Brahmins.

DISTINCTIVE INTERPRETATION

Dr. Gail Omvedt, an American-born and naturalized Indian sociologist and human rights activist:

- Ambedkar's Buddhism seemingly differs from that of those who accepted by faith, who 'go for refuge' and accept the canon. This much is clear from its basis: it does not accept in totality the scriptures of the Theravada, the Mahayana, or the Vajrayana. The question that is then clearly put forth: is a fourth yana, a Navayana, a kind of modernistic enlightenment version of the Dhamma really possible within the framework of Buddhism?

Most Dalit Indian Buddhists espouse an eclectic version of Buddhism, primarily based on Theravada, but with additional influences from Mahayana and Vajrayana. On many subjects, they give Buddhism a distinctive interpretation. Of particular note is their emphasis on Shakyamuni Buddha as a political and social reformer, rather than merely as a spiritual leader.

They point out that the Buddha required his monastic followers to ignore caste distinctions, and that he was critical of the social inequality that existed in his own time. Ambedkar's followers do not believe that a person's unfortunate conditions at birth are the result of previous karma. Famous as the test bench for these reforms, the picture is strikingly dismal in terms of inequality. In Brazil, the ratio of income or consumption of the top and the lowest 20% people increased from 26.1% to 32.1% between 1983 and 1989. In Columbia, between 1988 and 1991, the same had gone up from 13.3 to 15.5%. In all these countries the consumption of the bottom 20% population as a share of total consumption ranged from paltry 2.1 to 8.7%. The gap between poor and rich of the world has increased by 30% over the last decade along with the spread of these kinds of Reforms.

During 1987 to 1994, the number of billionaires in the world showed a remarkable increase. In USA, it went up from 49 to 120; in the Asia Pacific region, from 40 to 86; in Europe, from 36 to 91 and in west Asia and Africa, it went up from 8 to 14. The brief life sketches of these billionaires given in the Forbes magazine of July 18, 1994 show how these Reforms have been instrumental in enriching them.

IMPACT OF THE REFORMS ON DALITS AS A DISADVANTAGED SOCIAL GROUP

The social disadvantage suffered by the dalits in India was taken note of in the Constitution of India, which was drafted under the chairmanship of Dr. Ambedkar-a person who had spearheaded the most momentous anti-caste movement of the depressed classes. It provided the dalits with many safeguards, *viz,*

- Social, educational, cultural and religious safeguards,
- Economic safeguards,
- Political safeguards,
- Safeguards for employment.

The free market ethos unleashed by the Reforms, conceptually can neither confirm to the democratic spirit of the Indian Constitution of 'one vote, one value', nor can it coexist with the system of positive discrimination embodied in these safeguards. For, the market grants moneyed person more value, and overtly believes in the jungle law of 'might is right'. To a large extent, the primary motivation behind these Constitutional provisions was liberal democratic aspirations that characterised the freedom movement. However, these aspirations and the initial ideological zeal of the founding fathers withered away in no time and what survived was its utilitarian dimension for the electoral politics. The sorry state of the executive compliance with these Constitutional provisions amply bears out the fangs of the intrinsically iniquitous Indian society.

The Reforms will bring a kind of legitimacy to this attitudinal resistance of the upper castes and classes to the movements for change by the downtrodden. These safeguards will stand eroded as the Reforms gain in momentum. Influence of the Reforms is bound to be all pervasive. However, only a few issues of importance to the dalit masses have been picked up for discussion here.

RESERVATION AND FINANCIAL ASSISTANCE IN EDUCATION INSTITUTIONS

Reservation in the educational institutions and the financial assistance in the form of scholarships and freeships constitute perhaps the most important factor in the development scheme for dalits. For, it is primarily responsible to make the basic input of education available and affordable to them.

Without education, all the constitutional safeguards including the reservation in services would be infructuous. Under this scheme the dalit students whose parental income is below a specified level, get freeship, reservation in admissions to all the colleges getting grants-in-aid from the government, and scholarships.

Without this assistance, even today, it would be difficult even for the second-generation educated dalits to send their children to school. The Reforms have already resulted in freezing the grants to many institutions and in stagnating, if not lowering, the expenditure on education. The free market has entered the educational sphere in a big way. Commercialisation of education is no more a mere rhetoric; it is now the established fact. Commercial institutions offering specialised education that signify essential input from utilitarian viewpoint, have come up in a big way from cities to small towns.

Their product-prices are not only based on the demand-supply consideration in their market segment but also are manipulated by their promotional strategies. In a true spirit of globalisation, many foreign universities are invading the educational spheres through hitherto unfamiliar strategic alliances with non-descript commercial agencies, of course at hefty dollar equivalent prices.

Many elite institutions like IIMs and IITs, suddenly facing fund crunch had to resort to raising their fee structure and other prices many fold. They were already beyond the reach of the dalits. When they eventually turn self-financing, their prices would be benchmarked against their international counterparts, which any way would be affordable to the same top market segment that constitutes the focus of all the Reform-talk. As the job markets become acutely competitive, owing to a sharp decline in job opportunities, the polarisation between the elite and commoner would also sharpen.

Various kinds of price barriers would be erected to thwart the entry of downtrodden to the portals of development. Even the sphere of primary education the coverage of which has been so miserably inadequate as to leave out multitude of children in villages as illiterate, could not remain unaffected, notwithstanding its already existing divide between the vernacular and English schools.

Corporatisation has entered this arena, transforming the education into an enterprise for profits. The quality of input these expensive schools will provide will benchmark the products in the contracting job markets. Even today, because of preponderance of the English language in business circles, the divide between village and towns is almost complete in the field of education. It is so difficult for a village student, educated in vernacular medium to compete with his convent educated (now an understatement!) counterpart in cities and towns. If this is the situation of general village population, the plight of the dalits who besides being the poorest of the village population carry additional burden of social discrimination, is indeed a worrisome matter. Despite several kinds of State assistance, the dalits are plagued with alarming rate of school dropouts. This may be explained out as much by the need for dalit children to supplement their meagre family incomes for making the two ends meet as also by the erosion of their faith that education could be the instrument to change the pathetic course of their lives. This sense of alienation is going to grow with the progress of the Reforms, giving rise to increasing lumpenisation and criminalisation of the dalit youth.

RESERVATIONS IN SERVICES

Whatever may be the other costs, the government policy of reservations in employment sphere has undoubtedly played an important role in the process of advancement of the dalits. The policy broadly envisages representation of the dalits in proportion to their population in all the public services, which includes the government, the public sector, autonomous bodies and other institutions that receive grant-in-aid from the government. This representation is enough to get a pathetic state of implementation of this policy. Howsoever, unsatisfactory the results of implementation may be, the importance of reservations from the dalit viewpoint cannot be over emphasised. As could be evidenced by the organised private sector, where it would be difficult to find a dalit employee (save of course in scavenging and lowliest of the similar jobs), without reservations the dalits would have been totally doomed.

The importance of reservations thus could only be assessed in relation to situations where they do not exist. Whatever be their defects and deficiencies, they have given certain economic means of livelihood and some social prestige to the sons and daughters of over 1.5 million landless labourers. Whether they get real power or not, over 50,000 dalits could enter the sphere of bureaucratic authority with the help of reservations. More importantly these tangible benefits to few have instilled a hope in entire dalit people to strive for their betterment. This hope predominantly manifests in the form of spread of education among them. Their emotional bond with the nation and its Constitution despite heaps of injustice and ignominy they bear every moment of their life may also be significantly attributable to the Reservation Policy. The winds of privatisation under the Economic Reforms have already shaken the very foundations of Reservations.

Wherever the Reforms patterned on the Structural Adjustment Programme of the World Bank were carried out, denationalisation and privatisation of the public sector have come in a big way. Being a late starter, India has not reached the scales achieved by others, say, the Latin American countries. However, the start has not been any less impressive. Within a short time, almost all the sectors of economy stand opened up for private investment. The disinvestment in existing public sector companies has already been allowed up to 49 per cent by the policy.

The public stake being more than 50 per cent, the 'public sector' as such is not yet dismantled in the policy. It continues to be the State as before, and hence attracts application of the reservation policy. However, the Reform package has already endangered, if not abolished, the reservations through numerous back doors. In the name of preparing the Public Sector Undertakings (PSUs) for global free market regime, the PSUs are being allowed/encouraged to have strategic alliances with private companies from India and abroad. As such, over the last five years, many profit making PSUs have formed the joint venture companies (JVC).

Most of the PSU investments continue to be channelled through the JV route despite repeated failures of the joint ventures. These JVCs are strategically structured so as not to fall in the PSU-framework. The typical equity stake for the PSU and private could be 49:51. There appears to be a great deal of receptivity for this scheme in the government circles. There are no policy barriers on the business to be pursued by these JVCs. Theoretically, an existing PSU can hive off its business divisions into private JVCs and transform itself into a financial holding company with a Board of Directors and skeleton staff. Even if such an entity technically remains a PSU and follows the reservation policy sincerely, it would still have little or no scope to absorb the dalits in its staff. Whatever may be the strategic considerations, the fall out of this process practically amounted to shutting the doors of these new age companies to the dalits and to potential neutralisation of the reservation policy.

The policy of limited disinvestment of the PSUs not being in conformity with the spirit of the Reforms, is bound to be relaxed in favour of privatisation any time. But still, all the PSUs may not get privatised at once. The better ones would be gobbled up by the bigger sharks. The worst ones may be closed down or distress-sold. And the middle ones may for quite some time, continue to be the relic of their past. Whatever the scenario, the residual structures of the 'reformed' PSUs are never going tc ''e the same, as far as the dalits are concerned.

The privatisation and the excuse of global competition, superimposed on the traditional caste prejudice, will never allow reservations to happen, any more. Other public services are also bound to slip out of the reservation policy. Most of the sectors, which were the traditional domain of the government investment, have already been released for the private investment.

ATROCITIES

The caste atrocities are an integral feature of the dalit life. The government machinery keeps on collecting their statistics year after year and issues it in a report of its Commissioner for the SCs and the STs (now the National Commission for the SCs and the STs). There are at least three Articles (15,17 and 23) in the Constitution of India, which seek to mitigate the evil.

To give effect to these Constitutional provisions the following acts also have been in operation:

- The Untouchability (Offences) Act, 1955, later amended and retitled as the Protection of Civil Rights Act, 1955
- The Scheduled Castes and Scheduled Tribes (Prevention of Atrocities Act) 1989 and The Bonded Labour System (Abolition) Act, 1976

Despite this, the statistics of the registered atrocities read like a balance sheet of a blue chip company with consistent rise every successive year. It is pertinent to remember that owing to the dependency relationship of the dalits with the perpetrators of atrocities, not every occurrence of the atrocity gets registered. Rather, it can be safely assumed that behind each registered atrocity over ten atrocity cases go unreported. As per the latest statistics, every day nearly 50 cases of atrocities are registered all over the country. Over three dalit women are raped and six are disabled on each day round the year. The National Commission analysed the causes of each of the atrocities in a sample of 45 cases.

The analysis shows that out of 45 cases 13 are clearly attributable to the economic reasons. The balance can also be explained out by some kind of weakness of the dalits. Coupled with the weakness of the dalits, their growing assertiveness and the refusal to submit to the casteist dictates of the village lords, rebellion assimilated through the Ambedkarian struggle and the process of general awareness, also cause atrocities to increase. Atrocities are basically a rude reassertion of power over the powerless by the powerful in the wake of threat.

It is thus an expression of insecurity by the powerful who perceive power slipping their hand. In the pre-colonial closed loop production system of a typical village since everyone followed his or her calling under the divine authority of religion, there were no atrocities of the kind we experience in the saner age of globalisation today. If any one questioned or defied this system, the religious code provided for the punishment. In this scheme, it was more important to fortify the religious control on populace than physically taming them to comply. Although the emphasis was on enslavement of mind, physical punishment did exist as a contingency measure. Atrocities on the dalits today are in essence a physical punishment for their act of forsaking the bondage. The physical punishments or atrocities presuppose material power in the hands of perpetrators of atrocities.

Not only that the dalits lit the fire of anger in materially powerful upper castes by defying their notion of caste authority but also they added fuel to it by coming in competition for partaking scarce resources. The emergence of the land owning middle castes during the post-independence development process who at the one end replaced the traditional upper castes and wore their mantle of superiority but who at the other end found itself in competition with the dalits for resources like education and employment moreover led to accentuation of atrocities.

These middle castes lacked the cunning and sophistication of the upper castes and enraged themselves into physical response on slightest provocation. They could not stomach the dalits who were utterly dependent on them in the village setting asserting their human rights or competing with them on equal platform for scarce resources and eventually winning them away in some cases with the help of reservations. This commonplace experience is amplified by the vested interests of the ruling classes to make out all the dalits as robbers of the share of these middle castes.

Thus, the essential ingredients for atrocities on the dalits can be identified as the existence of material power in the hands of perpetrators of atrocities, enduring sense of social superiority, increasing scarcity of resources, and growing popularization of the masses. The directional impact of the Reforms on the atrocities on the dalits therefore can be inferred from the effect it would have on the existing dependency relationship in the villages that the dalits are engaged in with the powerful middle castes; on the caste system itself; on the availability of certain critical resources like jobs; health care, education etc.; and on the income distribution to the people. Atrocities are seen to occur where the dependency relationships are more pronounced. Villages, where the dalits as landless labourers depend upon landlords or rich farmers for their livelihood and where the traditional caste equations have a potential to yield economic surplus to the latter, provide ideal setting for atrocities. What impact would the new regime have on the socio-economic setting of Indian villages?

In face of it, this relationship cannot be altered till the dalits get land. Can the new regime afford this economic empowerment of the dalits? Can it, for instance, grant them land? The answer to all these questions will be in negative. Instead of talking about land reforms, the new regime will promote depeasantisation of Indian agriculture and consolidation of their holdings to start corporate farming. The capital influx in the rural areas will have natural ally in the rich farmers who have hegemonic hold over their areas. These parts will be the main beneficiaries of the improved terms of trade and capitalist development in the rural areas. The form that the new system may take will have the corporate structure of management and beneath the local vendors to provide various inputs and services.

While the rich farmers may assume the roles in this organisation as big or petty capitalist, the erstwhile landless labourers, marginal and small farmers shall together constitute the vast army of jobseekers. Although in notional terms the dalits might get rid of the old relationships, in reality they will still be dependent on their upper caste employers and certainly far more vulnerable than before.

With regards to impact of the economic Reforms on the caste system, the optimists and protagonists rely upon an old rhetoric of contradiction between feudalism and capitalism. The problem of annihilation of castes subsumes the change in the economic structure of the society in favour of the dalits and simultaneously a massive cultural movement to cleanse the minds of people of the caste notions and implant in its place the attitude of scientificism and virtue of liberty, equality and fraternity. Having seen that far from striving for economic equality, the Reforms are going to accentuate the existing inequalities, we can just examine its attitude towards the caste system. Will the Reforms promote the cultural movement for social equality? Does it have the wherewithal or motivation to catalyse struggles against the caste system?

The answers to these questions will also have to be in negative. The old rhetoric that capitalism will completely displace feudalism evokes positive expectations in some people about the prowess of the Reforms to annihilate castes. They would argue that the unbridled capitalism inherent in the

Reforms is not compatible with any feudal structure and hence implementation of the latter should remove these last blots of the caste system.

This simplistic thumb rule does not seem to be entirely validated by the developmental experience in India. The capitalism in India did not have to sprout through the bedrock of contradictions of feudalism as in Western Europe. It was planted in the fertile soil of the Indian feudalism. It has grown here on its nutrients. The caste institution has defied the classical mould of feudalism by possessing many unique features, the most important being its resilience and adaptability.

What we experience in the mysterious growth of casteist politics today in India is precisely this ability of caste to adapt to changing times. The vast army of unemployed created by the developmental dynamics of the economic Reforms will need appropriate instruments for being controlled. The history bears ample testimony to the fact that whenever the people tended to come together with a common identity, the ruling classes have deftly used the time-tested weapon of castes to divide them.

Caste with its divisive potential will never be abandoned by any iniquitous regime. Its resilience may diffuse its contours but in its essence the caste would coexist with the Reforms. Privatisation and free market components of the Reforms are certainly impacting very adversely on the job situation. Many resources for public consumption shall also be scarce, as they would be produced in private enterprises for profits. They would be beyond the reach of common people. The impact of the Reforms in terms of increasing inequality has been established beyond doubt. Therefore, it can be inferred that the Reforms are potentially incapable to alleviate the pain of dalit masses. In sum, the atrocities on the dalits not only shall continue but may also be increased on account of the Reforms.

SOCIO-CULTURAL SUPPRESSION

Privatisation, which is the pivotal component of the Economic Reforms, will eliminate the very basis of the reservation policy in its present form. Since the Reforms envisage minimalist role for the State, the space for the public domain and therefore for the reservations shall be greatly constricted. Reservation policy that represented the strategic response of liberal bourgeoisie to the aspirations of the dalit movement not quite unlike that of the colonial State at the time of its inception, was never swallowed by the civil society as rightful share of the dalits.

Its response initially reflected feudal magnanimity but once the first generation of the dalits started pouring out of the university portals into the job markets and claimed their share of pie, the reaction reflected feudal ferocity. The cunning of upper caste dominated State apparatus was evident in full measure in the manner the circulars proclaiming this policy were issued. Their convoluted language facilitated the unwilling bureaucracy to thwart it to the possible extent and judiciary to be labour over several years on what should have been so evident. The broad statistic on the implementation of this policy is enough to reveal the extent of prejudice of the State machinery as well as the civil society.

One of the provisions of the policy states that a dalit candidate qualifying without any concession should not be placed in the reserved seat, implying thereby that the percentage representation of the dalits in services or the educational institutions would be more than its prescribed value. But, over the five decades of implementation of the reservation policy it refuses to reach even the prescribed levels confirming the casteist notion still prevalent in society that the dalits are intrinsically an inferior specie. Despite this vile attitude of the establishment the reservations by far has been the sole contributor to advancement of the dalits. Privatisation is meant to directly hit it.

The benefits of the reservation policy to the dalit community have been more indirect than direct. Directly it benefited a few but indirectly it has created hope for advancement in the entire dalit population. This hope is already faded even when not much of privatisation has happened so far.

Their ideological amount is proving insufficient to resist it. There is a visible alienation, hopelessness and dejection setting in among them, which is getting manifested in increasing lumpenisation and criminalisation of dalit youth. This trend portends doom not only for the dalits but also for the entire oppressed people thirsting for some radical change. For, no radical change is possible in this country without dalit participation. The dalit consciousness formed over centuries of struggle is getting obliterated by the contemporary compulsions created by the Reforms.

This phenomenon will catapult dalit masses back onto the vicious spiral of backwardness and fortify reactionary regimes in the similar proportion. This irrevocable loss would prove dearest to the dalits. While privatisation might set in slowly, the free market that it engenders much before could hit the dalits really harder through the legitimacy it grants to the base instincts against any emancipation project. For, the likely victims of the privatisation is still a miniscule part of the dalit population but the impact of these social would engulf entire dalit population.

Howsoever base the individual conviction might have been, the yesteryears had nearly forbidden them from surfacing openly. But, now the emergent free market is not only permitting but also promoting the vilest and venomous discourse against the dalits and the minorities. The vehemence with which the reservations or any kind of subsidy or any positive discrimination are derided today has a qualitatively distinctive edge. It is interesting to note that there is not yet a dalit voice raised against this fascist hegemony. It would indeed be difficult for the dalits to resist this onslaught. The emergence of right wing politics to national prominence is merely a corollary or consequence of this transformation. Social consequences of the economic miseries associated with these Reforms are indeed ominous for the dalits.

On one side they shall be subject to increasing popularization and on the other stand in competition with the multitude of masses in the job market. Increasing tendency of businesses to downsize, virtual abolition of the reservation system through privatisation, the strategies of flexibilisation and informalisation of labour; corporatisation and depeasantisation of farming etc. will release vast numbers of people to the job market. The resident caste prejudices in such situations will certainly get activated to the detriment of the dalits.

CONCLUSION

The economic reforms in the mould of macro-economic stabilisation and structural adjustment programme of IMF and World Bank have essentially a pro-rich bias. Wherever they were implemented, they have worsened the situation of the masses of poor people in absolute as well as relative terms. Some contrary data to this general observation are rather attributed to the departures from the standard blueprint given by the Bretton Wood institutions.

The dalits in India, being the poorest of the poor have been hit the hardest. Their social disabilities, largely reinforced by and sustained on the economic deprivations, are bound to get accentuated with these policies. The Indian reforms were essentially 'crisis driven' and not 'strategy driven' when they were adopted. There have since been changes in the formation and key persona.

The new government for instance has imparted them a form of 'strategy' through their Common Minimum Programme. However, there has not yet been any evidence of this strategy being any different from the course followed by the previous government. The complete discourse of the Reforms appears to be either grossly off the mark of Indian reality or to assume out its momentous features. The broad Indian reality is that India has too many poor. As per the Human Development Report, 1996, there are 229 million income poor but more than twice as many, 554 million are capability poor.

In terms of capability poverty, its 61.5% population is poor. Its rank just as to descending poverty among the 174 countries of the world is 135. Even today India is predominantly an agrarian economy, with over 70 per cent of its population living in villages. No statistics moreover can adequately capture the heinous socio-cultural inequality that is an abiding part of the Indian reality. It has acute inequalities not only in economic terms but also in the socio-cultural terms. The free market oriented reforms ought to take this grave Indian reality into consideration.

Unless there is a wide spread purchasing power in the economy the market can never be free and sustainable. The reform strategy thus should embody sustainable economic empowerment of the rural masses; investments to enhance their capability and effective measures for accelerated development of the disadvantaged parts like the dalits. The pre-requisite to reforms therefore could be the radical land reforms, massive investments in rural areas into agriculture-related infrastructural projects, universalisation of primary education, primary health care system and reinforcement of positive discrimination in favour of the dalits.

The devil of casteism could be tamed only by freeing general masses of the people from the anxieties and uncertainties about basic survival. The general condition of deprivation has rendered them vulnerable to be the preys to the frequent machinations of the vested interests that make them see the enemy within their own class. The relative equality thus can be the bedrock for launching the socio-cultural offensive in the form of mass-education programmes. But this all may still not be enough. The policy of positive discrimination in favour of the dalits will have to be reinforced much more vigourously in all the sectors of economy, than ever before. They need to be reframed and simplified for the effective implementation. Unlike the current provisions, this may be stopped once their representation in services comes on par with the general population. The specific reform package can be formulated in terms of the conditions existing then. There arises a question of capital.

Where will the capital for the investment in basic reforms come from? Not an easy question to answer, indeed. But some pointers may not be impertinent. It is acknowledged since number of years that India has a parallel economy in black money. The recent spate of scams is a mere corroboration of this hypothesis. The Reforms appear to have given them a boost. Whatever little has surfaced can be likened to a tip of iceberg.

Some five years ago, an unofficial estimate by the World Bank had put the unaccounted money of Indians kept in various tax havens at ₹ 100 billion. As per Finance India, the range of capital outflows was from ₹ 1065 million to ₹ 370 million just in one single year-1993. Much of the ₹ 10 billion money in the non-resident account is said to be belonging to the resident Indians.

The evidence of this kind abounds. As against this vast sum of our own money, what the government aims at out of the Reforms is the paltry sum of some four to five billion dollars of foreign direct investment a year to come in the country! The size of the money that rightfully belongs to the people of the country may be good enough for the task. But to unearth this treasure certainly requires a political will. India does not need capital as much as it does the political will to better its destiny.

Bibliography

Bandhu, P.: *Dalit Women's Cry for Liberation: My Rights are Rising Like the Sun, will you Deny this Sunrise?*, New Delhi: Long Life Publication, 2003.

Bhat, Chandrashekhar: *Emerging Ethnic Identity and Social Mobility Among the Waddars of South India*, New Delhi: Concept Publishing Company, 2003.

Clough, John E.: *The Story of a Man, A Mission and a Movement*, New York: The Macmillan Company, 2001.

Deliege, Robert: *Replication and Consensus: Untouchability, Caste and Ideology in India*, London: Cambridge University, 2003.

Fromm, E.: *Dalit Human Rights Report of the Proceedings of International Conference on Dalit Human Rights*, London: Kogan Page, 2000.

Kale, R.: *Kolhatyachre Por*, London: Cambridge Perseus Publishing, 2006.

Kumar, N.: *Dalit Policies, Politics and Parliament*, Banglore: Shipra Publication, 2004.

Mary, G.: *The Struggle of Dalit Women, Resource Sheet Paper Presented in Dalit Theology Seminar, Barmingham*, New York: Cambridge University Press, 2004.

Pandit, V.: *Handbook on Prevention of Atrocities (SC/ST)*, Maharashtra: Pune University, 2002.

Pillai, T.: *Ambedkar's Daughters: A Study of Mahar Women in Ahmednagar District of Maharashtra*, New Delhi, Vistar Publication, 2005.

Tirmare, P.: *Violation of Human Rights of Dalit Women: Issues and Facts*, Maharashtra: Pune University, 2000.

Index

U

V